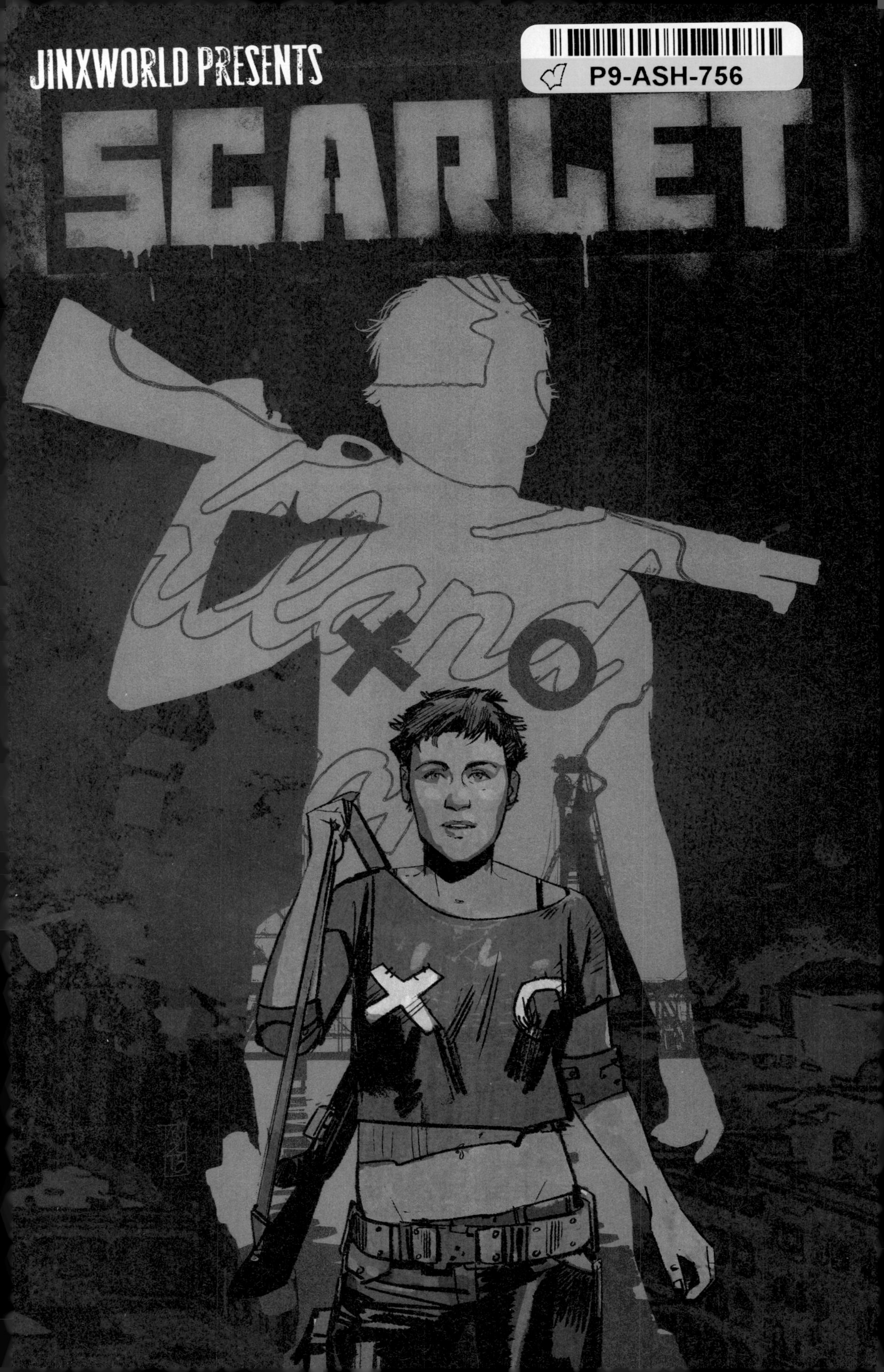
JINXWORLD PRESENTS
SCARLET

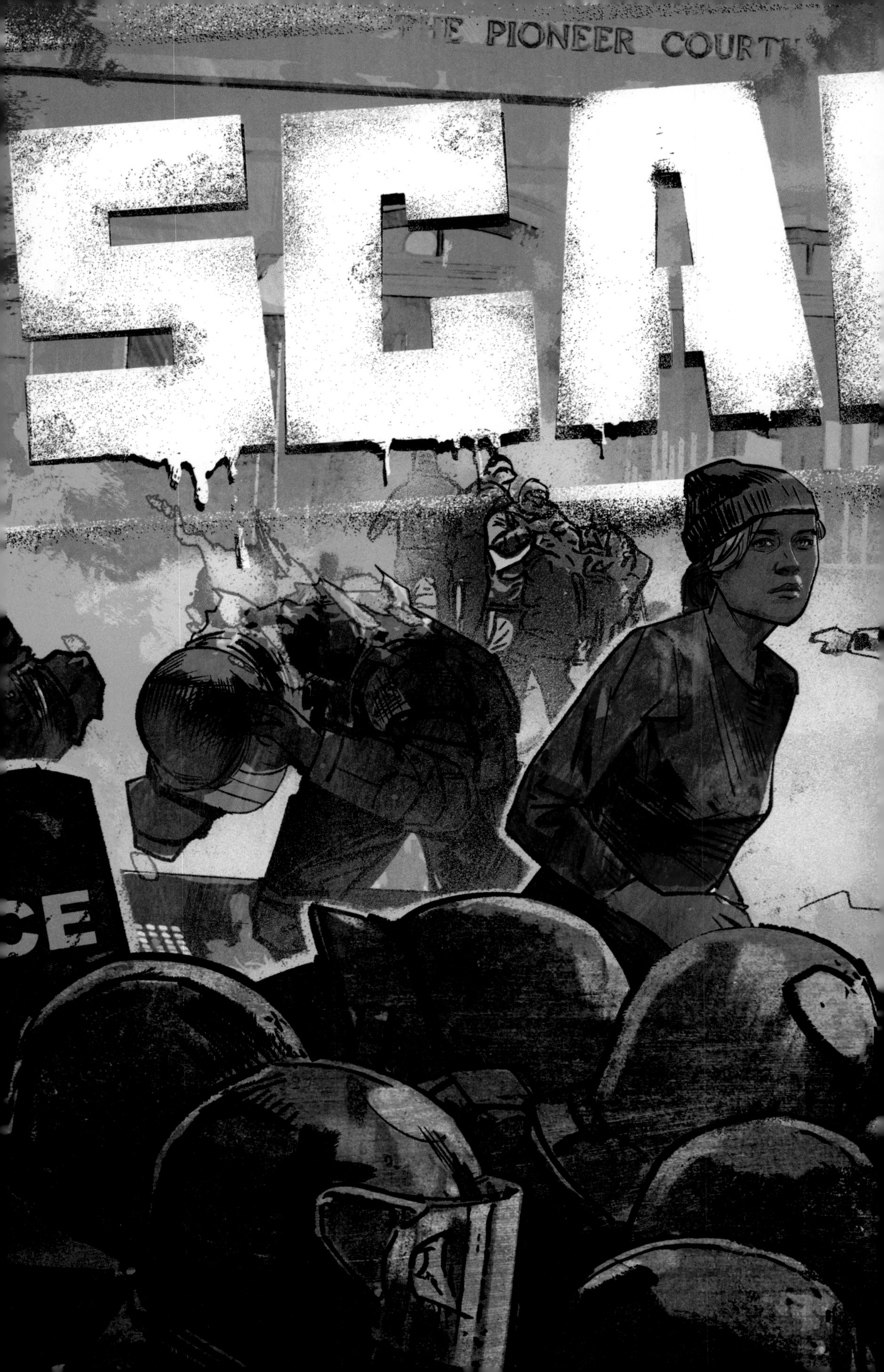
THE PIONEER COURTH
CE

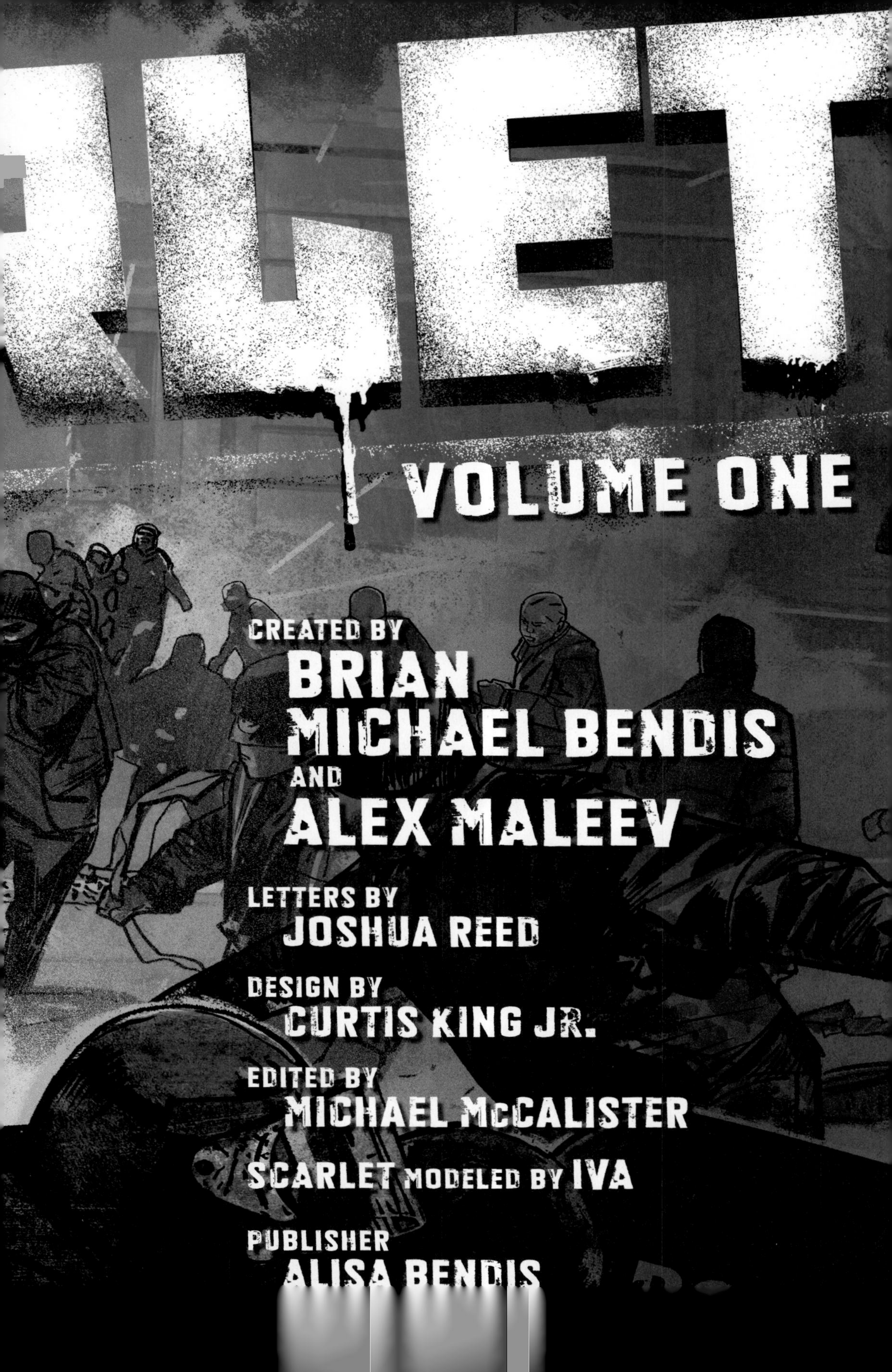

VOLUME ONE

CREATED BY
BRIAN MICHAEL BENDIS
AND
ALEX MALEEV

LETTERS BY
JOSHUA REED

DESIGN BY
CURTIS KING JR.

EDITED BY
MICHAEL McCALISTER

SCARLET MODELED BY **IVA**

PUBLISHER
ALISA BENDIS

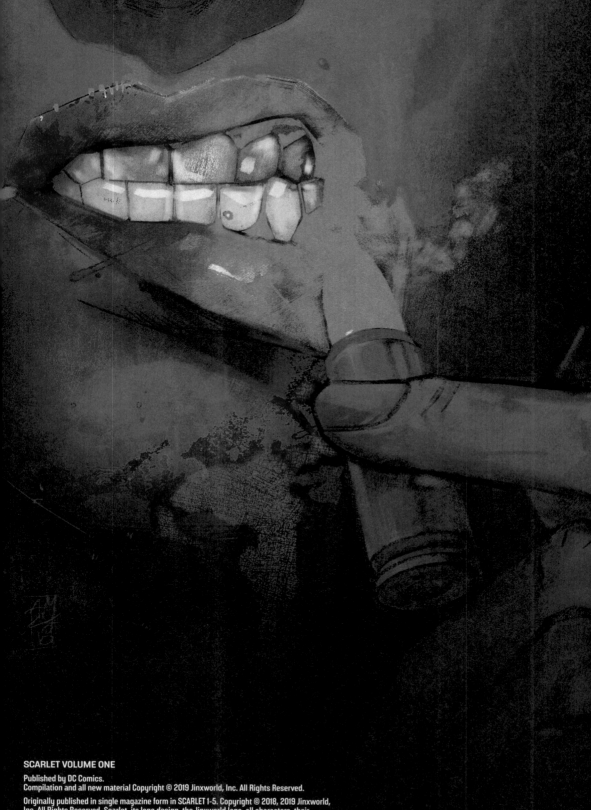

SCARLET VOLUME ONE

Published by DC Comics.
Compilation and all new material Copyright © 2019 Jinxworld, Inc. All Rights Reserved.

Originally published in single magazine form in SCARLET 1-5. Copyright © 2018, 2019 Jinxworld, Inc. All Rights Reserved. Scarlet, its logo design, the Jinxworld logo, all characters, their distinctive likenesses and related elements featured in this publication are trademarks of Jinxworld, Inc. The stories, characters and incidents featured in this publication are entirely fictional. DC Comics does not read or accept unsolicited submissions of ideas, stories or artwork.

DC Comics
2900 West Alameda Ave., Burbank, CA 91505

Printed by LSC Communications,
Owensville, MO, USA. 3/22/19. First Printing.

ISBN: 978-1-4012-9062-7

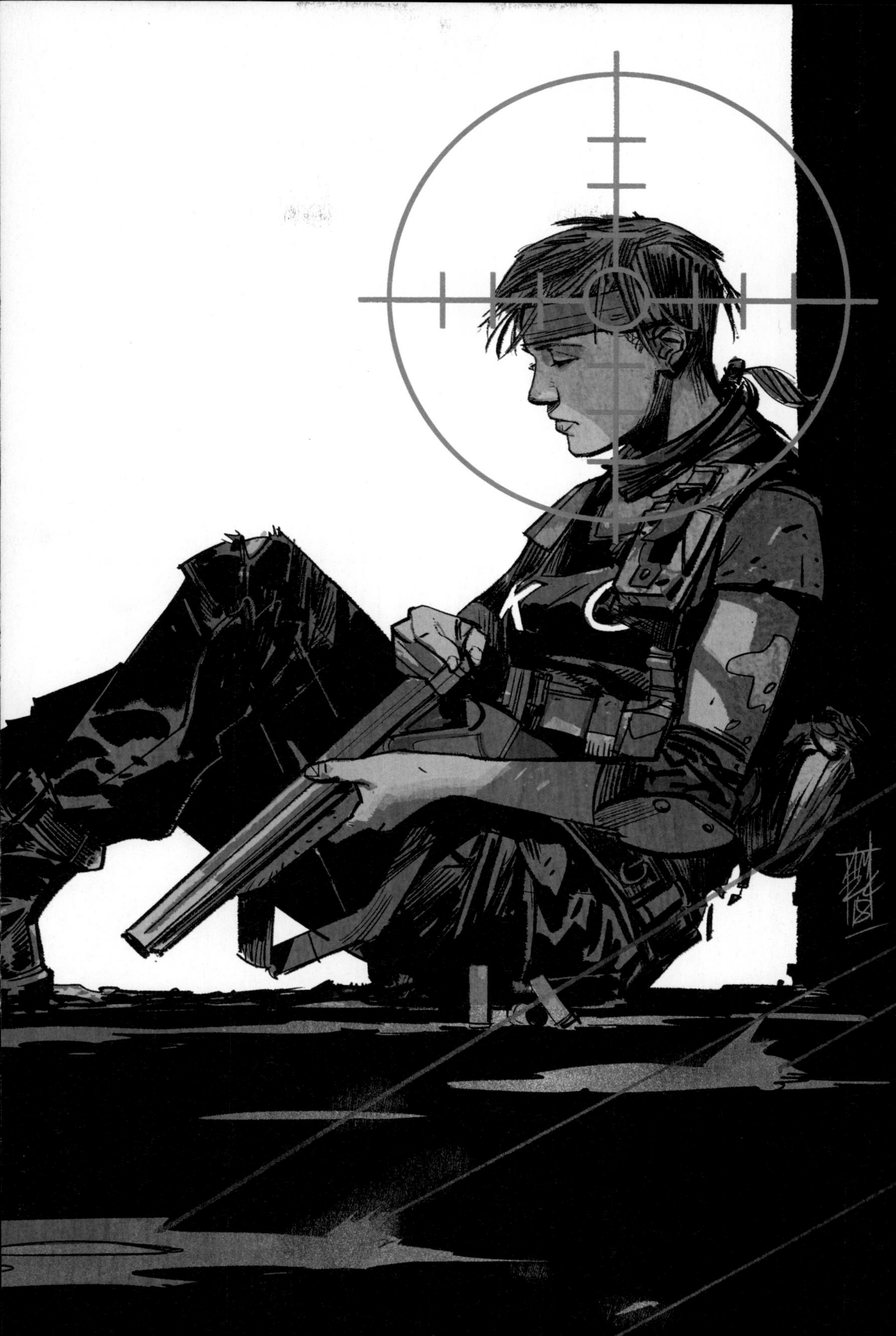

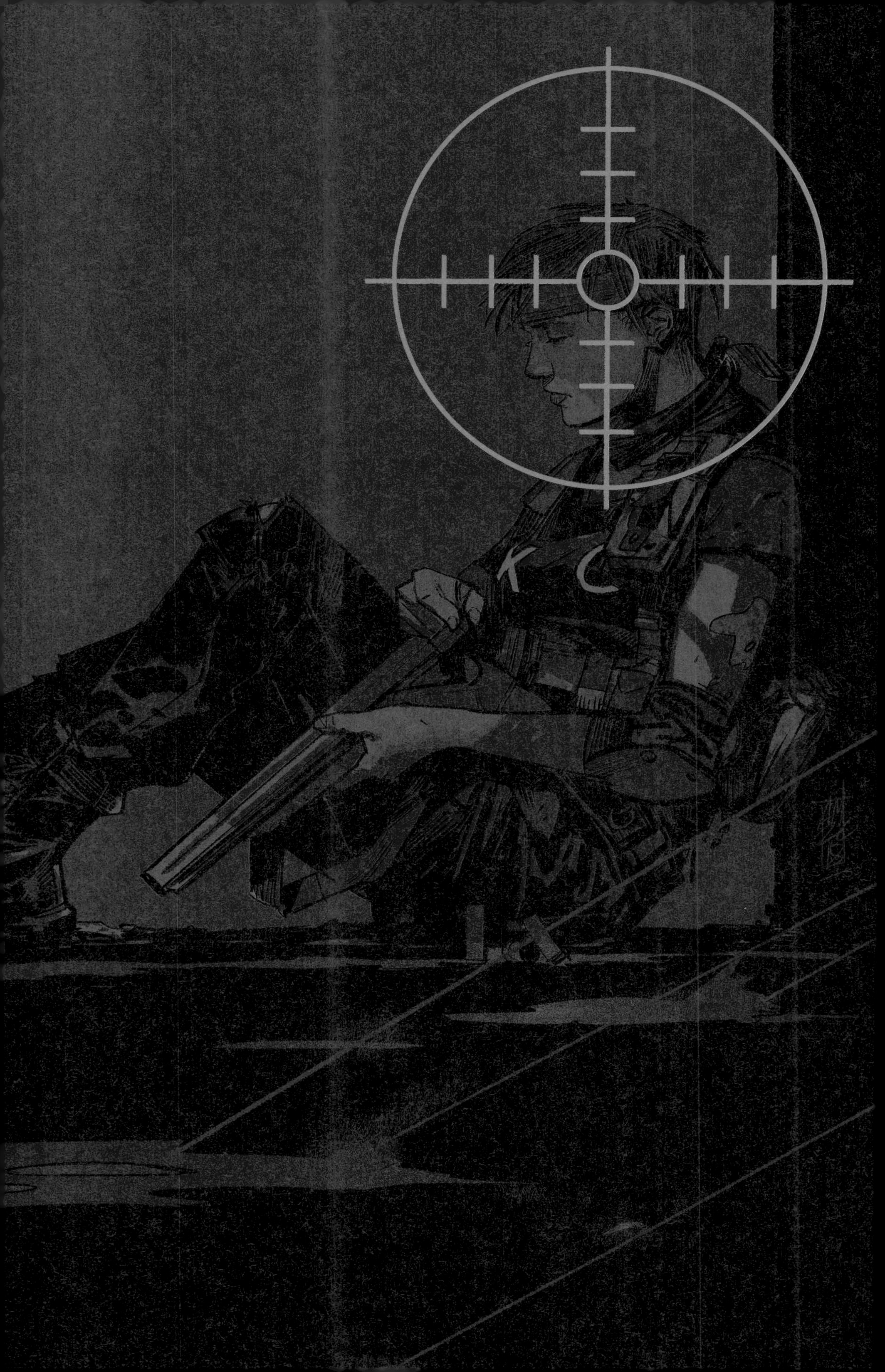
K C

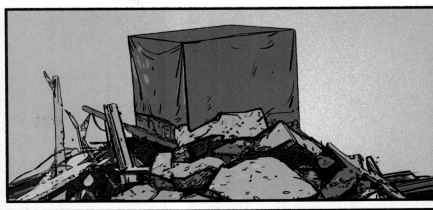

STAY DOWN.

AH-DOY.

WHAT ARE WE WAITING FOR?

A SIGN...

WHAT KIND OF SIGN? I'D LIKE TO LOOK FOR IT, TOO.

COME ON.

I WAS LIKE THIS BEFORE.

SO BOSSY NOW, ICE.

IT'S A TRAP.

I HOPE IT'S CANDY.

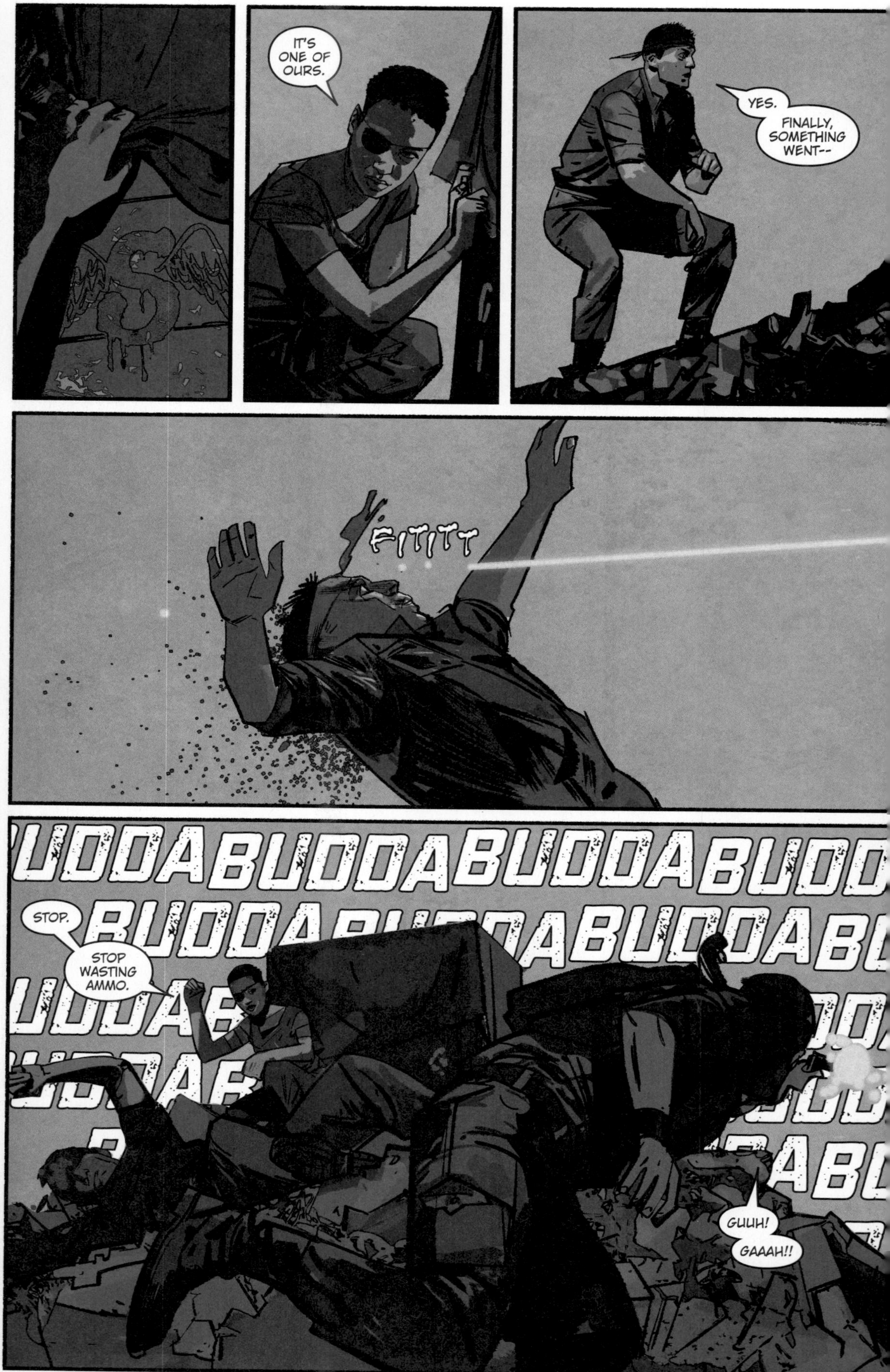
IT'S ONE OF OURS.
YES.
FINALLY, SOMETHING WENT--
FITITT
BUDDABUDDABUDDABUDD
STOP.
STOP WASTING AMMO.
GUUH!
GAAAH!!

SORRY.

IT HAPPENS.

I-I WAS A BIKE STORE MECHANIC BEFORE THIS.

I WORKED AT THE HUMANE SOCIETY.

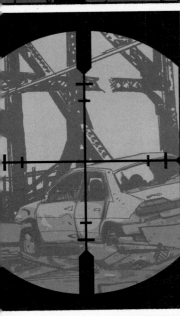

YOU'LL NEVER SEE THEM.

SHIT! I SEE THEM...

CAN YOU FIRE IT?

I WAS A BIKE MECHANIC.

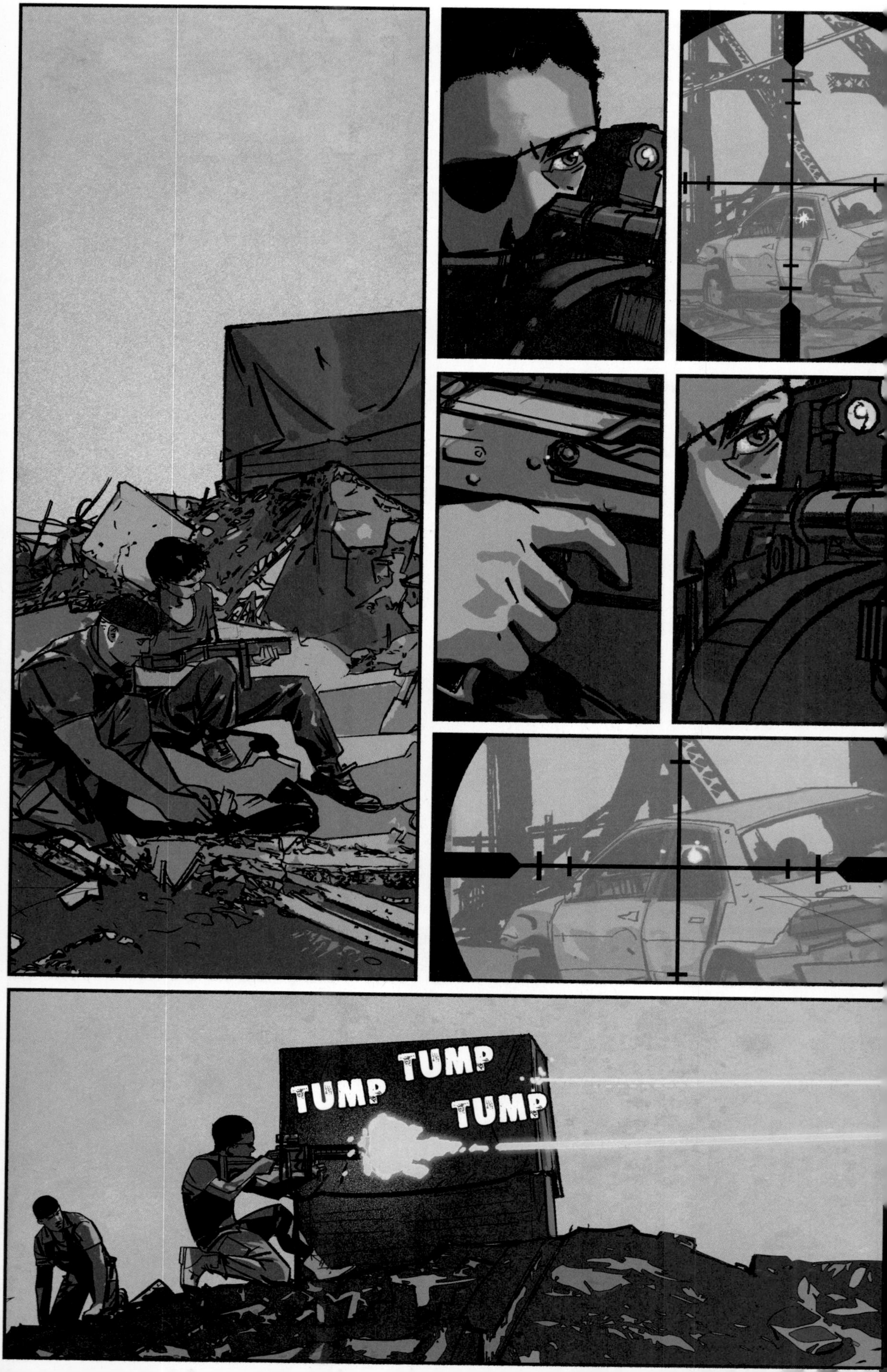
TUMP TUMP
TUMP
TUMP

KABOOM
BOOM BOOM

THE HUMANE SOCIETY?

GRAB A SIDE.

WHAT ABOUT GARY?

SHOULD WE, I DON'T KNOW, PUSH HIM INTO THE RIVER?

NO, NO. KEEP THE WATER CLEAN AS WE CAN. SCARLET'LL SEND SOMEONE TO GET HIM.

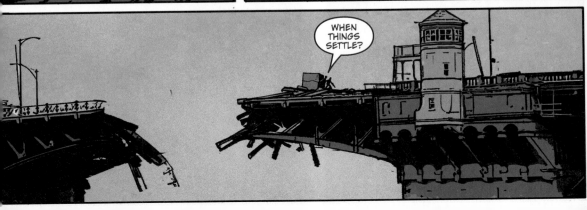

WHEN THINGS SETTLE?

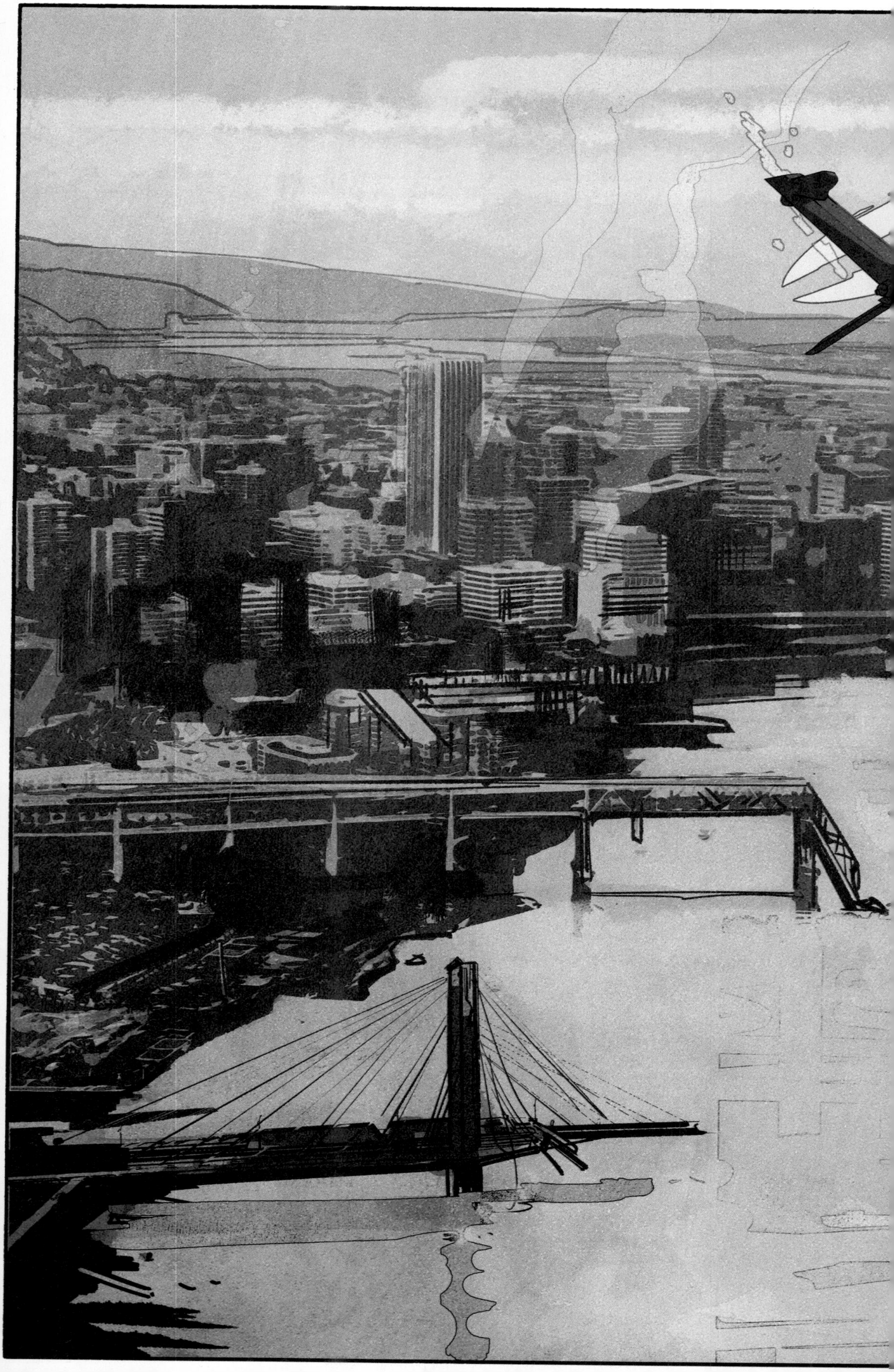

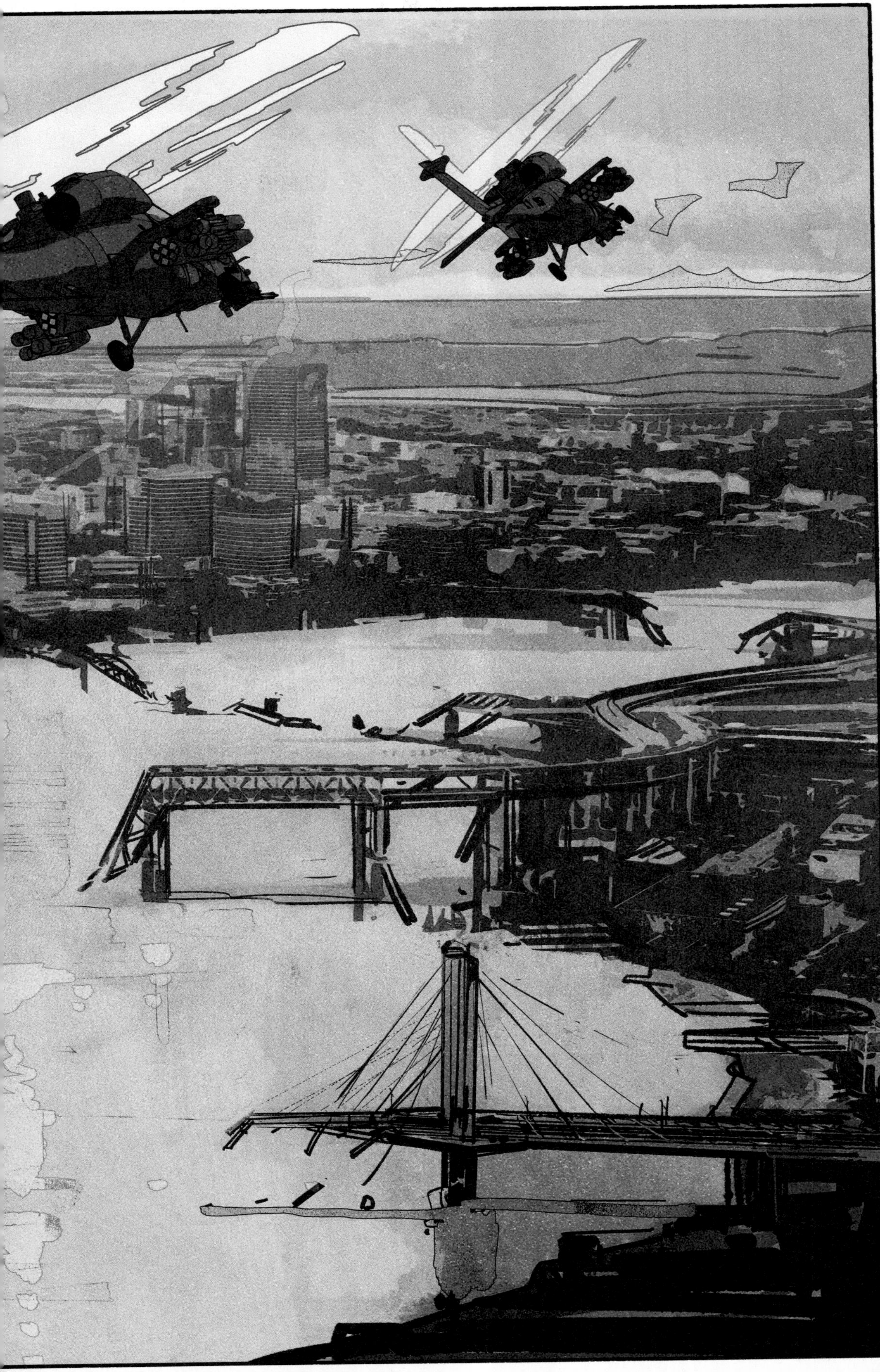

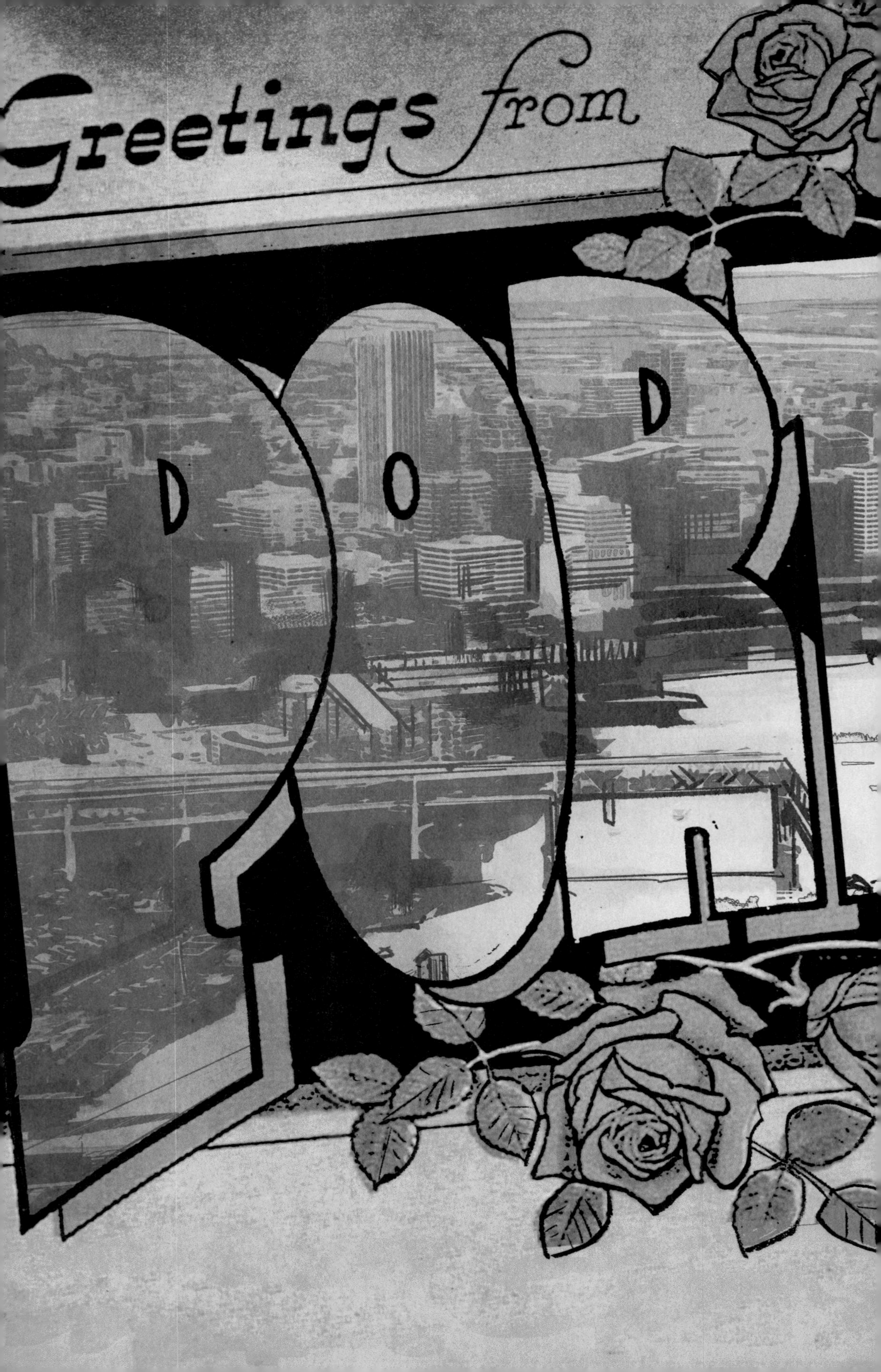
Greetings from

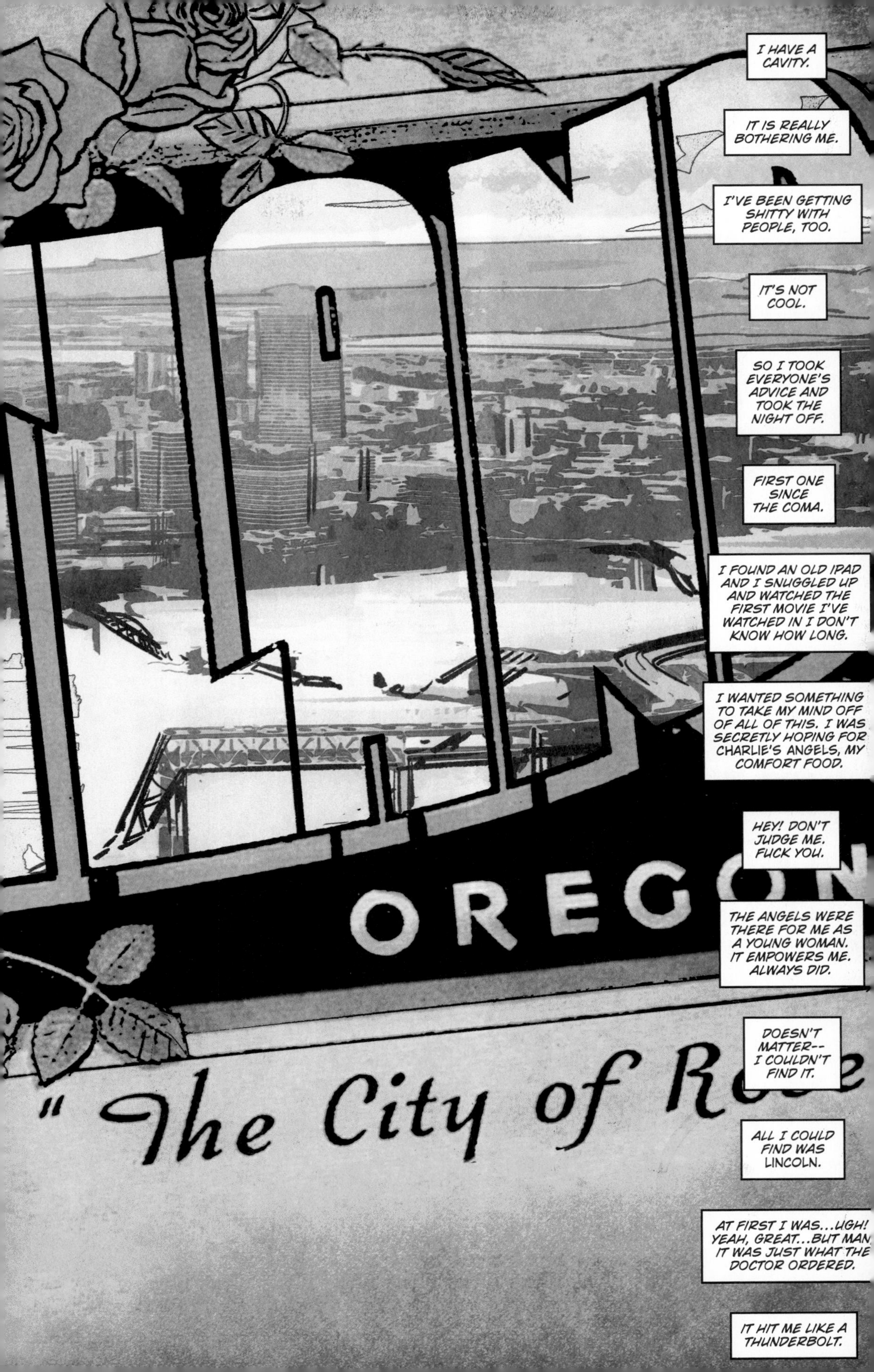
I HAVE A CAVITY.
IT IS REALLY BOTHERING ME.
I'VE BEEN GETTING SHITTY WITH PEOPLE, TOO.
IT'S NOT COOL.
SO I TOOK EVERYONE'S ADVICE AND TOOK THE NIGHT OFF.
FIRST ONE SINCE THE COMA.
I FOUND AN OLD IPAD AND I SNUGGLED UP AND WATCHED THE FIRST MOVIE I'VE WATCHED IN I DON'T KNOW HOW LONG.
I WANTED SOMETHING TO TAKE MY MIND OFF OF ALL OF THIS. I WAS SECRETLY HOPING FOR CHARLIE'S ANGELS, MY COMFORT FOOD.
HEY! DON'T JUDGE ME. FUCK YOU.
THE ANGELS WERE THERE FOR ME AS A YOUNG WOMAN. IT EMPOWERS ME. ALWAYS DID.
DOESN'T MATTER-- I COULDN'T FIND IT.
ALL I COULD FIND WAS LINCOLN.
AT FIRST I WAS...UGH! YEAH, GREAT...BUT MAN IT WAS JUST WHAT THE DOCTOR ORDERED.
IT HIT ME LIKE A THUNDERBOLT.
OREGON
"The City of Ro

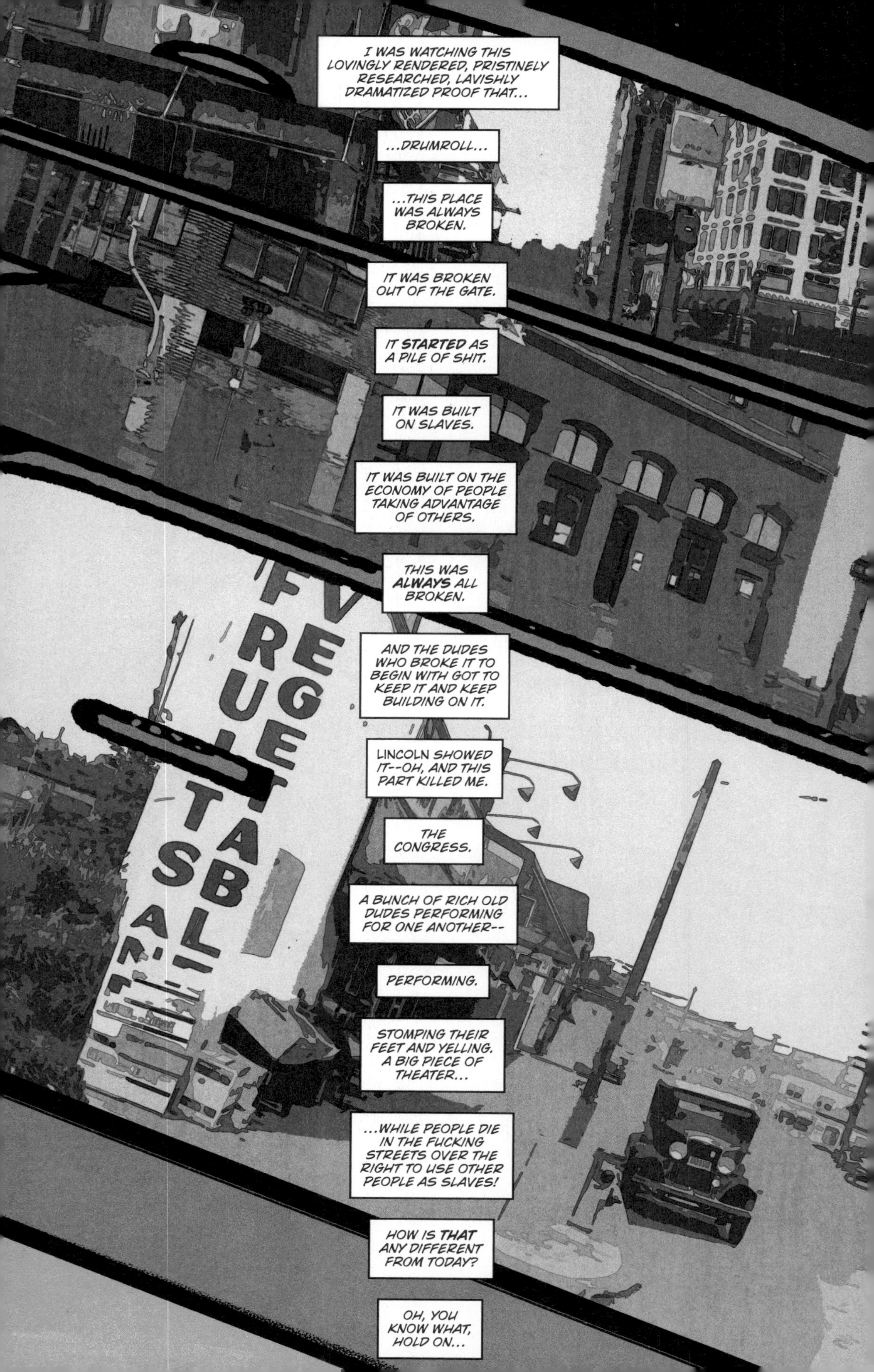
I WAS WATCHING THIS LOVINGLY RENDERED, PRISTINELY RESEARCHED, LAVISHLY DRAMATIZED PROOF THAT...
...DRUMROLL...
...THIS PLACE WAS ALWAYS BROKEN.
IT WAS BROKEN OUT OF THE GATE.
IT **STARTED** AS A PILE OF SHIT.
IT WAS BUILT ON SLAVES.
IT WAS BUILT ON THE ECONOMY OF PEOPLE TAKING ADVANTAGE OF OTHERS.
THIS WAS **ALWAYS** ALL BROKEN.
AND THE DUDES WHO BROKE IT TO BEGIN WITH GOT TO KEEP IT AND KEEP BUILDING ON IT.
LINCOLN SHOWED IT--OH, AND THIS PART KILLED ME.
THE CONGRESS.
A BUNCH OF RICH OLD DUDES PERFORMING FOR ONE ANOTHER--
PERFORMING.
STOMPING THEIR FEET AND YELLING. A BIG PIECE OF THEATER...
...WHILE PEOPLE DIE IN THE FUCKING STREETS OVER THE RIGHT TO USE OTHER PEOPLE AS SLAVES!
HOW IS **THAT** ANY DIFFERENT FROM TODAY?
OH, YOU KNOW WHAT, HOLD ON...

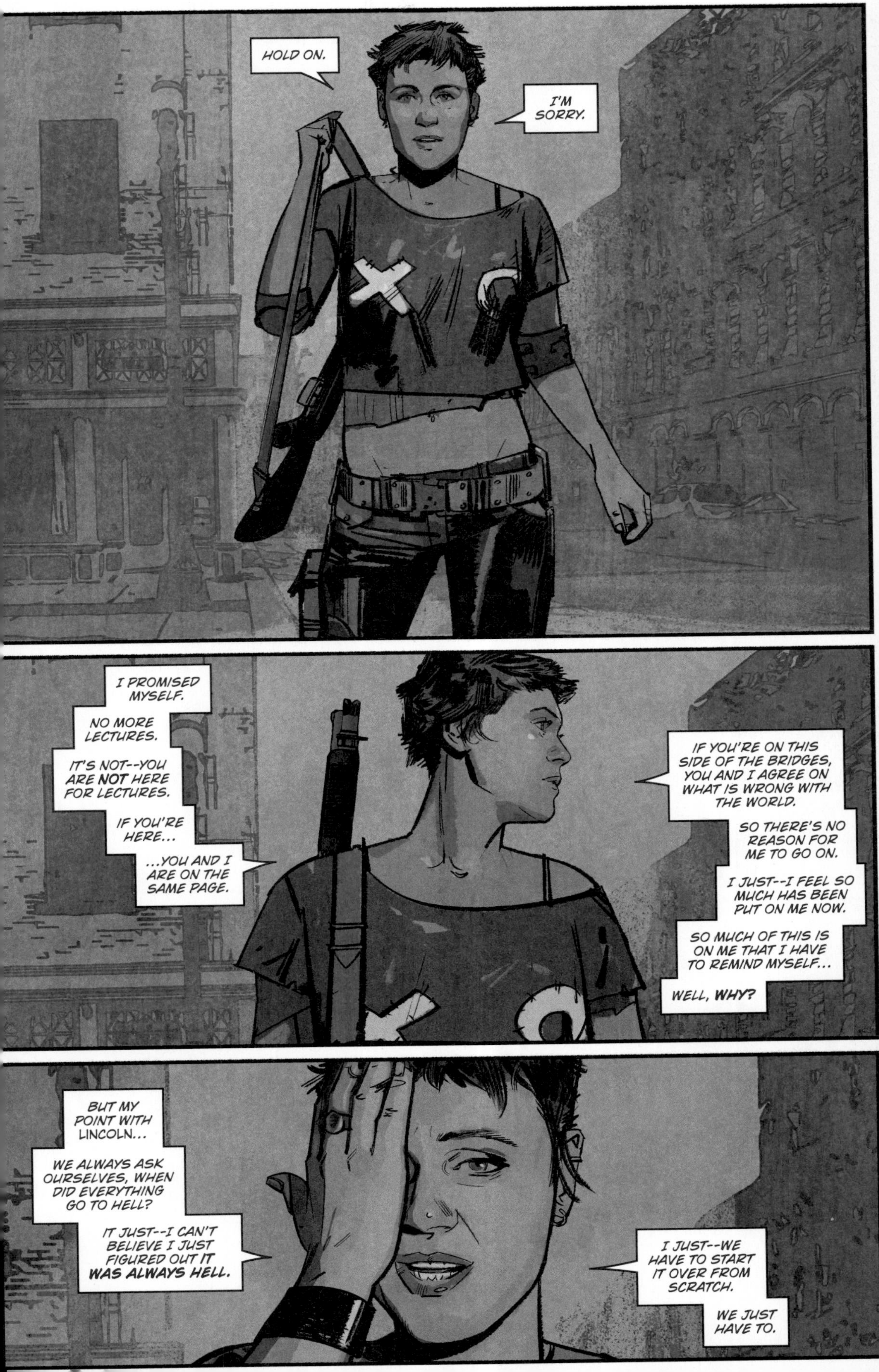
HOLD ON.
I'M SORRY.
I PROMISED MYSELF.
NO MORE LECTURES.
IT'S NOT--YOU ARE NOT HERE FOR LECTURES.
IF YOU'RE HERE...
...YOU AND I ARE ON THE SAME PAGE.
IF YOU'RE ON THIS SIDE OF THE BRIDGES, YOU AND I AGREE ON WHAT IS WRONG WITH THE WORLD.
SO THERE'S NO REASON FOR ME TO GO ON.
I JUST--I FEEL SO MUCH HAS BEEN PUT ON ME NOW.
SO MUCH OF THIS IS ON ME THAT I HAVE TO REMIND MYSELF...
WELL, WHY?
BUT MY POINT WITH LINCOLN...
WE ALWAYS ASK OURSELVES, WHEN DID EVERYTHING GO TO HELL?
IT JUST--I CAN'T BELIEVE I JUST FIGURED OUT IT WAS ALWAYS HELL.
I JUST--WE HAVE TO START IT OVER FROM SCRATCH.
WE JUST HAVE TO.

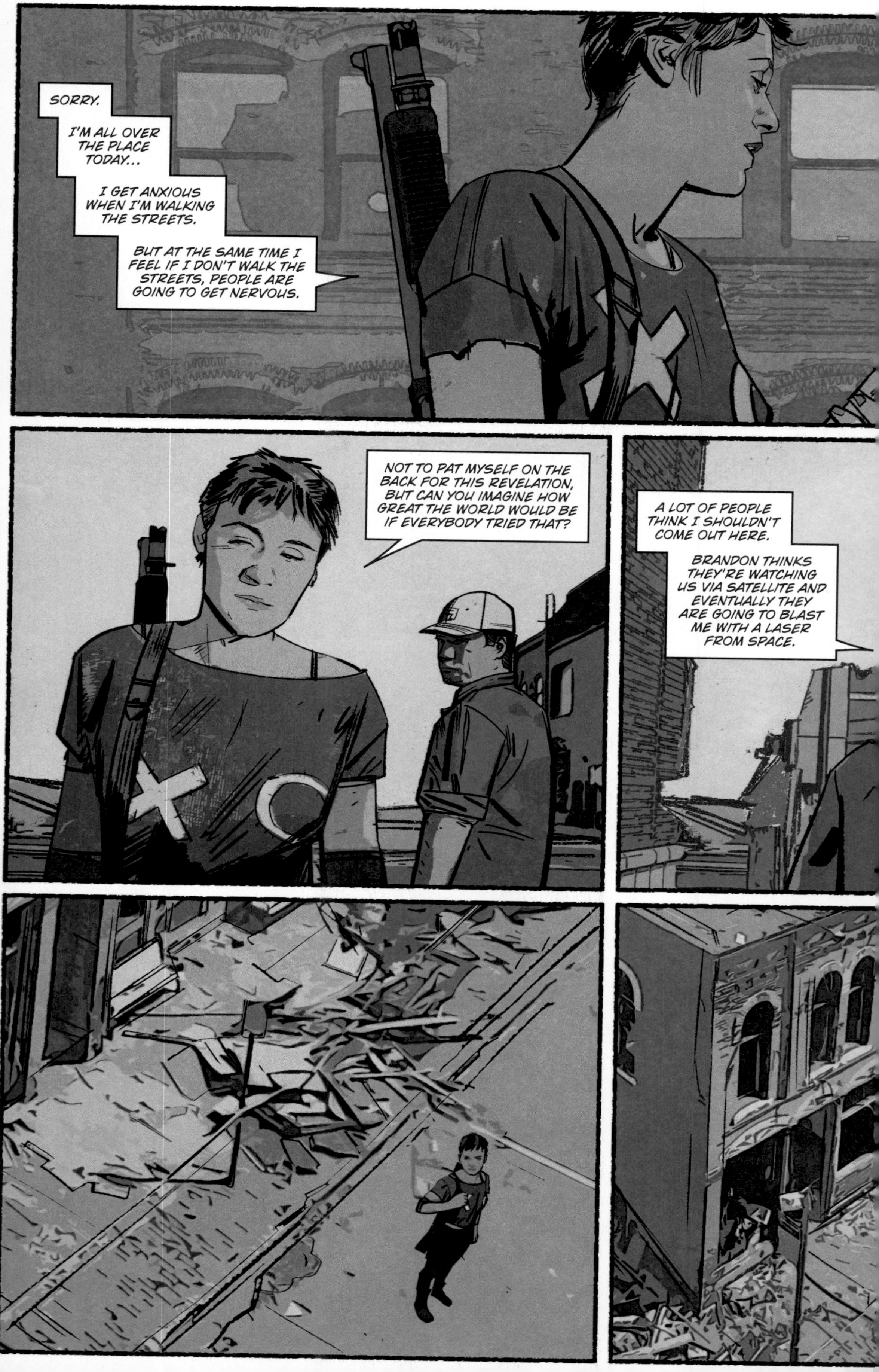
SORRY.
I'M ALL OVER THE PLACE TODAY...
I GET ANXIOUS WHEN I'M WALKING THE STREETS.
BUT AT THE SAME TIME I FEEL IF I DON'T WALK THE STREETS, PEOPLE ARE GOING TO GET NERVOUS.
NOT TO PAT MYSELF ON THE BACK FOR THIS REVELATION, BUT CAN YOU IMAGINE HOW GREAT THE WORLD WOULD BE IF EVERYBODY TRIED THAT?
A LOT OF PEOPLE THINK I SHOULDN'T COME OUT HERE.
BRANDON THINKS THEY'RE WATCHING US VIA SATELLITE AND EVENTUALLY THEY ARE GOING TO BLAST ME WITH A LASER FROM SPACE.

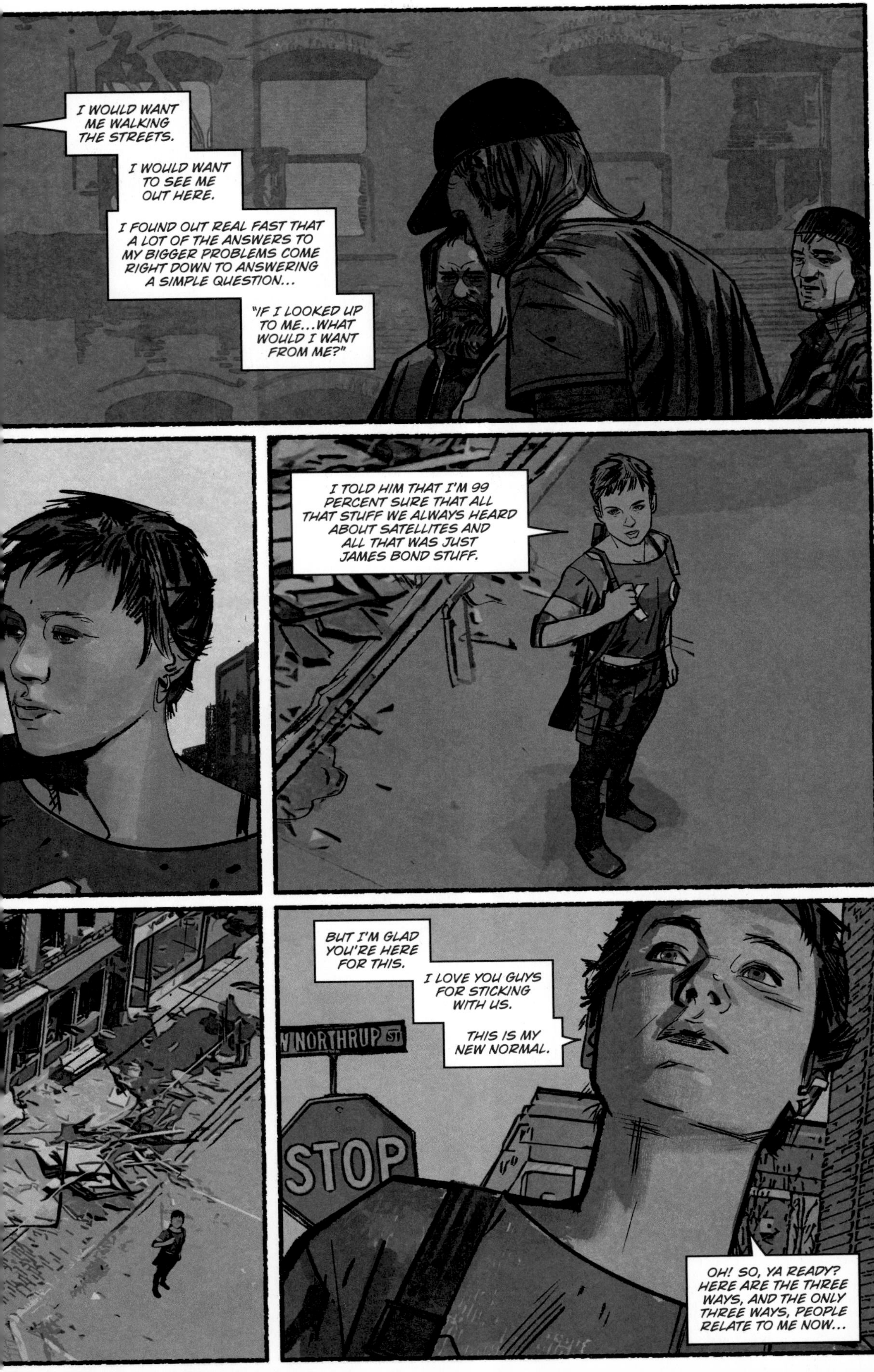
I WOULD WANT ME WALKING THE STREETS.
I WOULD WANT TO SEE ME OUT HERE.
I FOUND OUT REAL FAST THAT A LOT OF THE ANSWERS TO MY BIGGER PROBLEMS COME RIGHT DOWN TO ANSWERING A SIMPLE QUESTION...
"IF I LOOKED UP TO ME...WHAT WOULD I WANT FROM ME?"
I TOLD HIM THAT I'M 99 PERCENT SURE THAT ALL THAT STUFF WE ALWAYS HEARD ABOUT SATELLITES AND ALL THAT WAS JUST JAMES BOND STUFF.
BUT I'M GLAD YOU'RE HERE FOR THIS.
I LOVE YOU GUYS FOR STICKING WITH US.
THIS IS MY NEW NORMAL.
W NORTHRUP ST
STOP
OH! SO, YA READY? HERE ARE THE THREE WAYS, AND THE ONLY THREE WAYS, PEOPLE RELATE TO ME NOW...

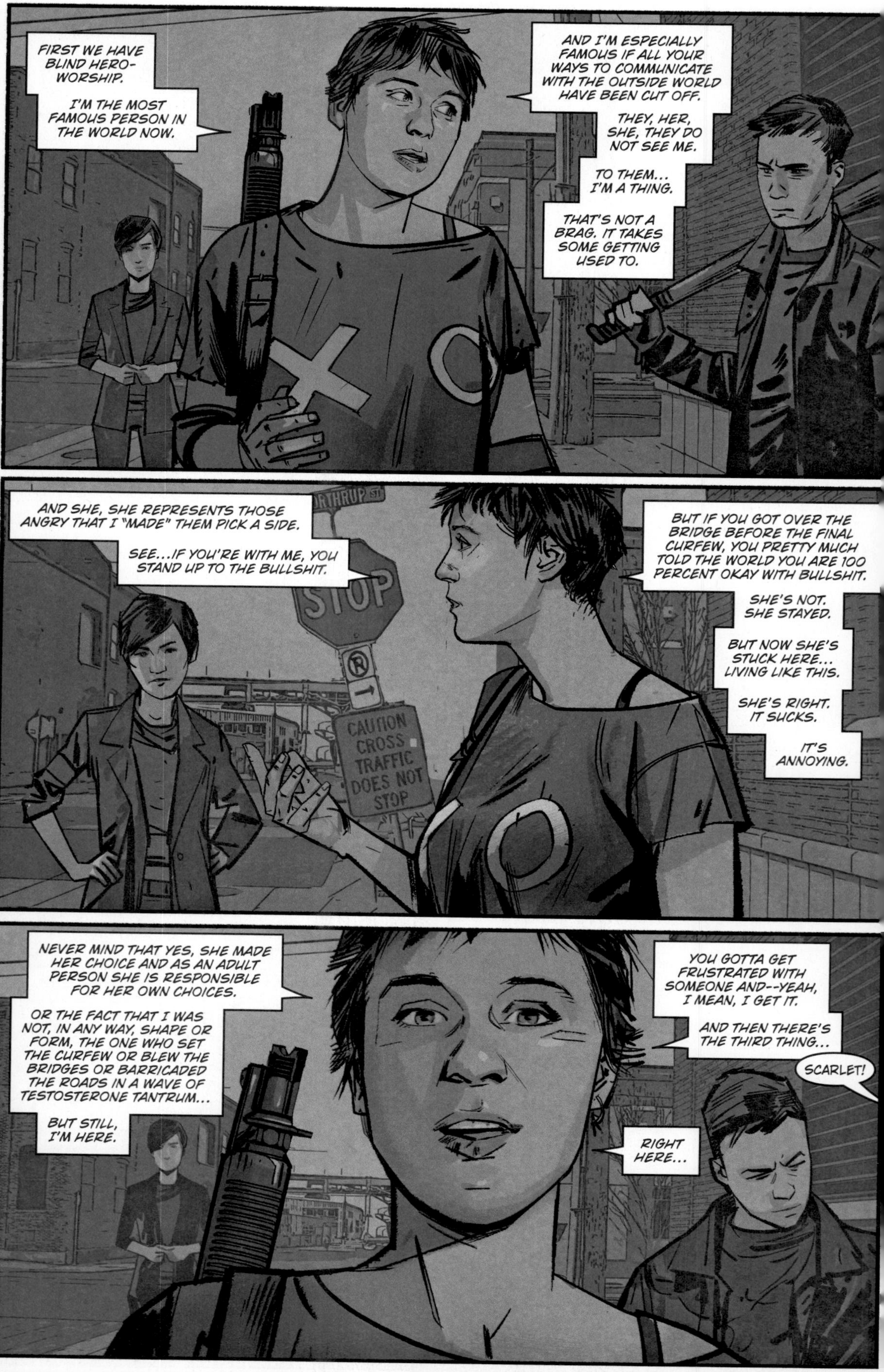
FIRST WE HAVE BLIND HERO-WORSHIP.
I'M THE MOST FAMOUS PERSON IN THE WORLD NOW.
AND I'M ESPECIALLY FAMOUS IF ALL YOUR WAYS TO COMMUNICATE WITH THE OUTSIDE WORLD HAVE BEEN CUT OFF.
THEY, HER, SHE, THEY DO NOT SEE ME.
TO THEM... I'M A THING.
THAT'S NOT A BRAG. IT TAKES SOME GETTING USED TO.
AND SHE, SHE REPRESENTS THOSE ANGRY THAT I "MADE" THEM PICK A SIDE.
SEE...IF YOU'RE WITH ME, YOU STAND UP TO THE BULLSHIT.
BUT IF YOU GOT OVER THE BRIDGE BEFORE THE FINAL CURFEW, YOU PRETTY MUCH TOLD THE WORLD YOU ARE 100 PERCENT OKAY WITH BULLSHIT.
SHE'S NOT. SHE STAYED.
BUT NOW SHE'S STUCK HERE... LIVING LIKE THIS.
SHE'S RIGHT. IT SUCKS.
IT'S ANNOYING.
STOP
CAUTION CROSS TRAFFIC DOES NOT STOP
NEVER MIND THAT YES, SHE MADE HER CHOICE AND AS AN ADULT PERSON SHE IS RESPONSIBLE FOR HER OWN CHOICES.
OR THE FACT THAT I WAS NOT, IN ANY WAY, SHAPE OR FORM, THE ONE WHO SET THE CURFEW OR BLEW THE BRIDGES OR BARRICADED THE ROADS IN A WAVE OF TESTOSTERONE TANTRUM...
BUT STILL, I'M HERE.
YOU GOTTA GET FRUSTRATED WITH SOMEONE AND--YEAH, I MEAN, I GET IT.
AND THEN THERE'S THE THIRD THING...
SCARLET!
RIGHT HERE...

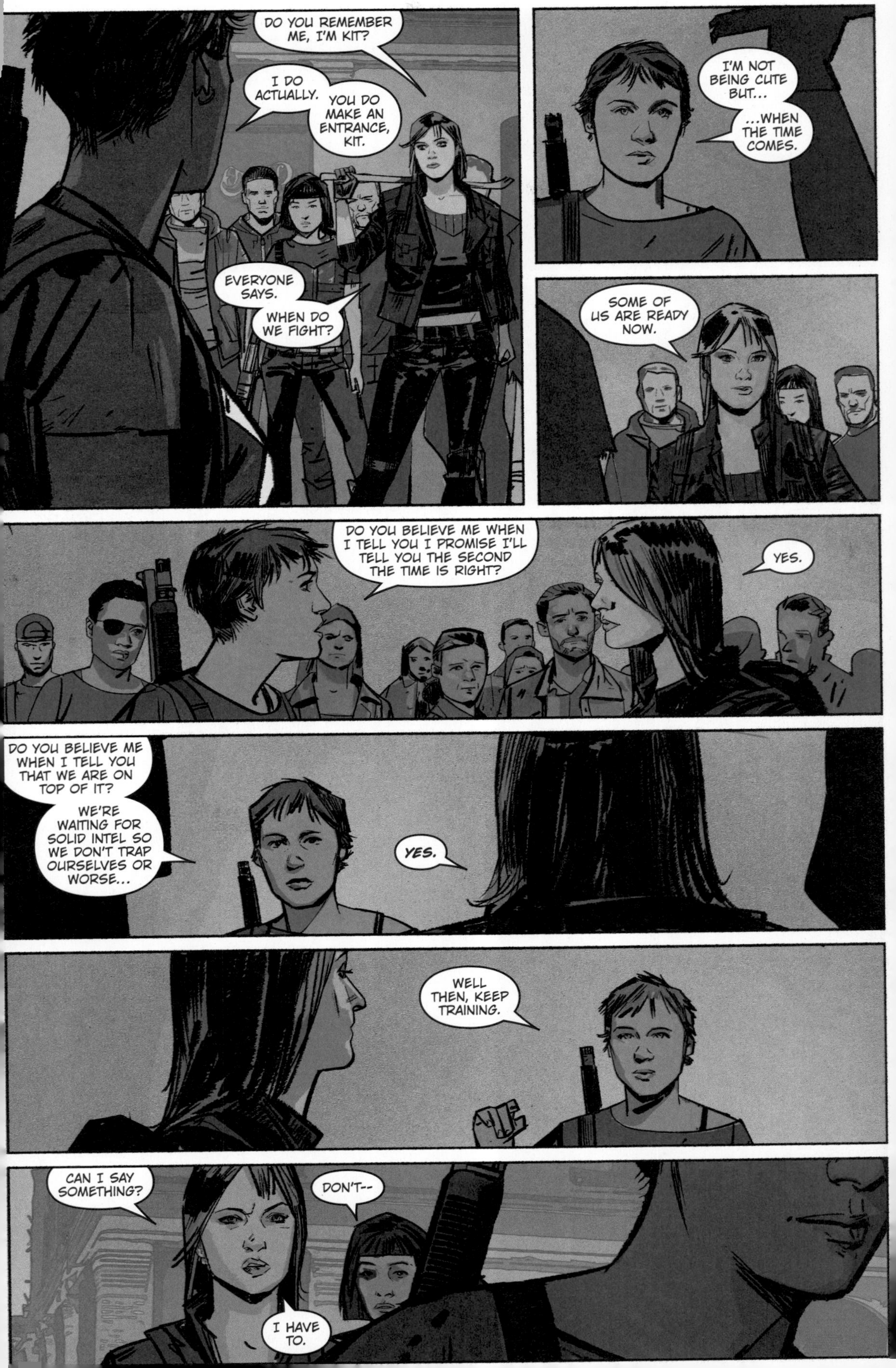
DO YOU REMEMBER ME, I'M KIT?
I DO ACTUALLY.
YOU DO MAKE AN ENTRANCE, KIT.
EVERYONE SAYS.
WHEN DO WE FIGHT?
I'M NOT BEING CUTE BUT...
...WHEN THE TIME COMES.
SOME OF US ARE READY NOW.
DO YOU BELIEVE ME WHEN I TELL YOU I PROMISE I'LL TELL YOU THE SECOND THE TIME IS RIGHT?
YES.
DO YOU BELIEVE ME WHEN I TELL YOU THAT WE ARE ON TOP OF IT?
WE'RE WAITING FOR SOLID INTEL SO WE DON'T TRAP OURSELVES OR WORSE...
YES.
WELL THEN, KEEP TRAINING.
CAN I SAY SOMETHING?
DON'T--
I HAVE TO.

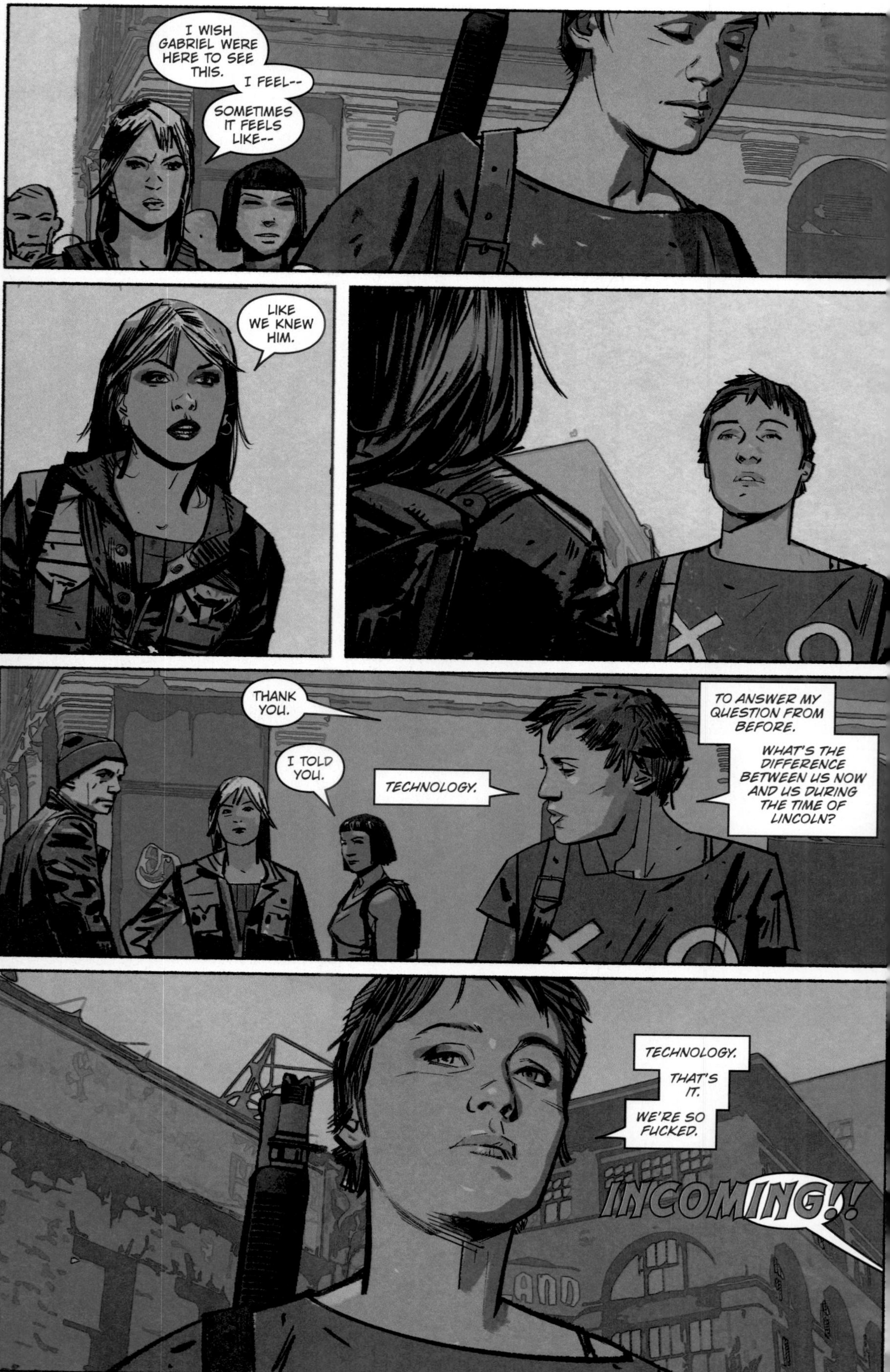
I WISH GABRIEL WERE HERE TO SEE THIS.
I FEEL--
SOMETIMES IT FEELS LIKE--
LIKE WE KNEW HIM.
THANK YOU.
I TOLD YOU.
TECHNOLOGY.
TO ANSWER MY QUESTION FROM BEFORE.
WHAT'S THE DIFFERENCE BETWEEN US NOW AND US DURING THE TIME OF LINCOLN?
TECHNOLOGY.
THAT'S IT.
WE'RE SO FUCKED.
INCOMING!!

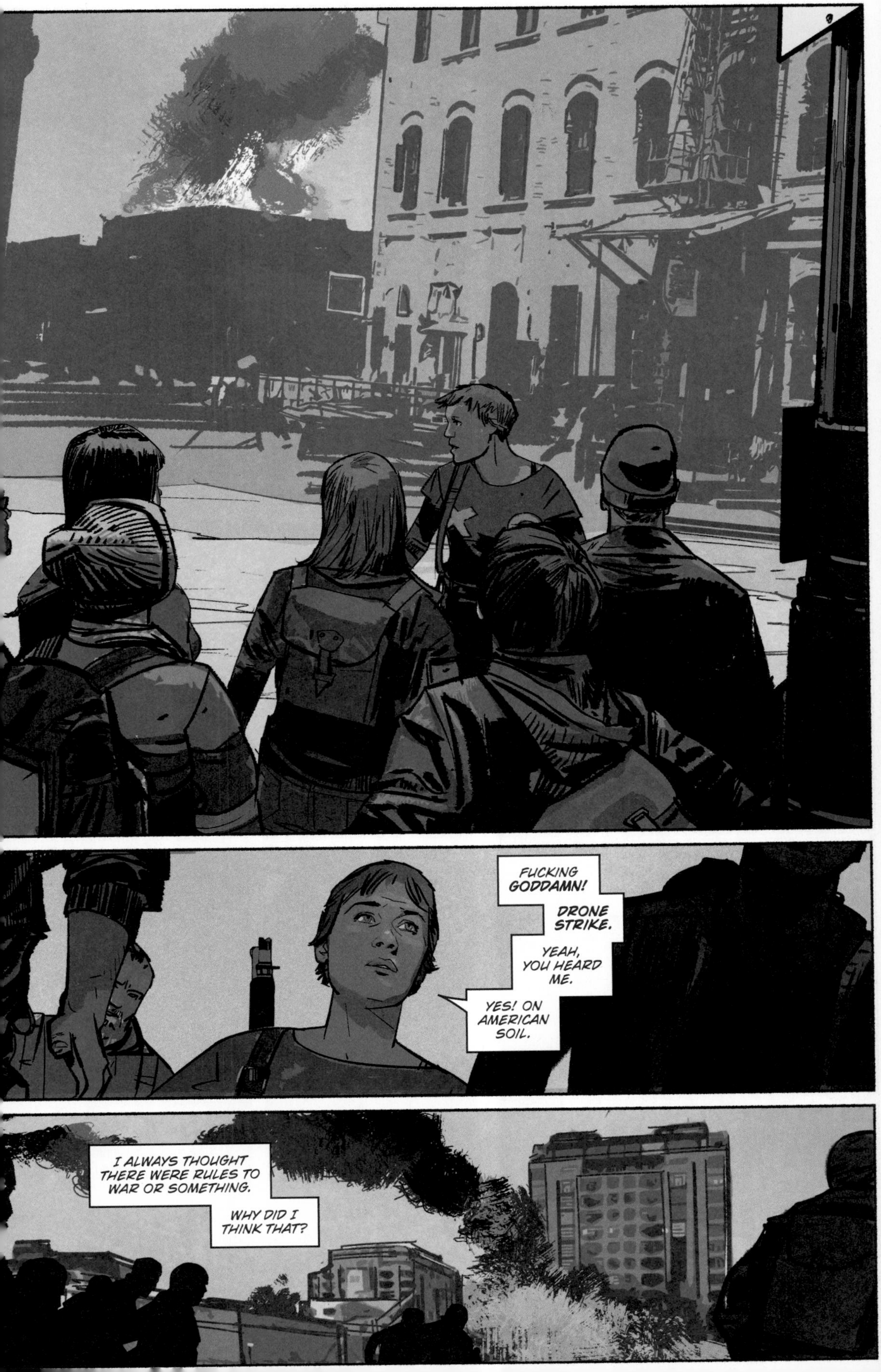
FUCKING GODDAMN!
DRONE STRIKE.
YEAH, YOU HEARD ME.
YES! ON AMERICAN SOIL.
I ALWAYS THOUGHT THERE WERE RULES TO WAR OR SOMETHING.
WHY DID I THINK THAT?

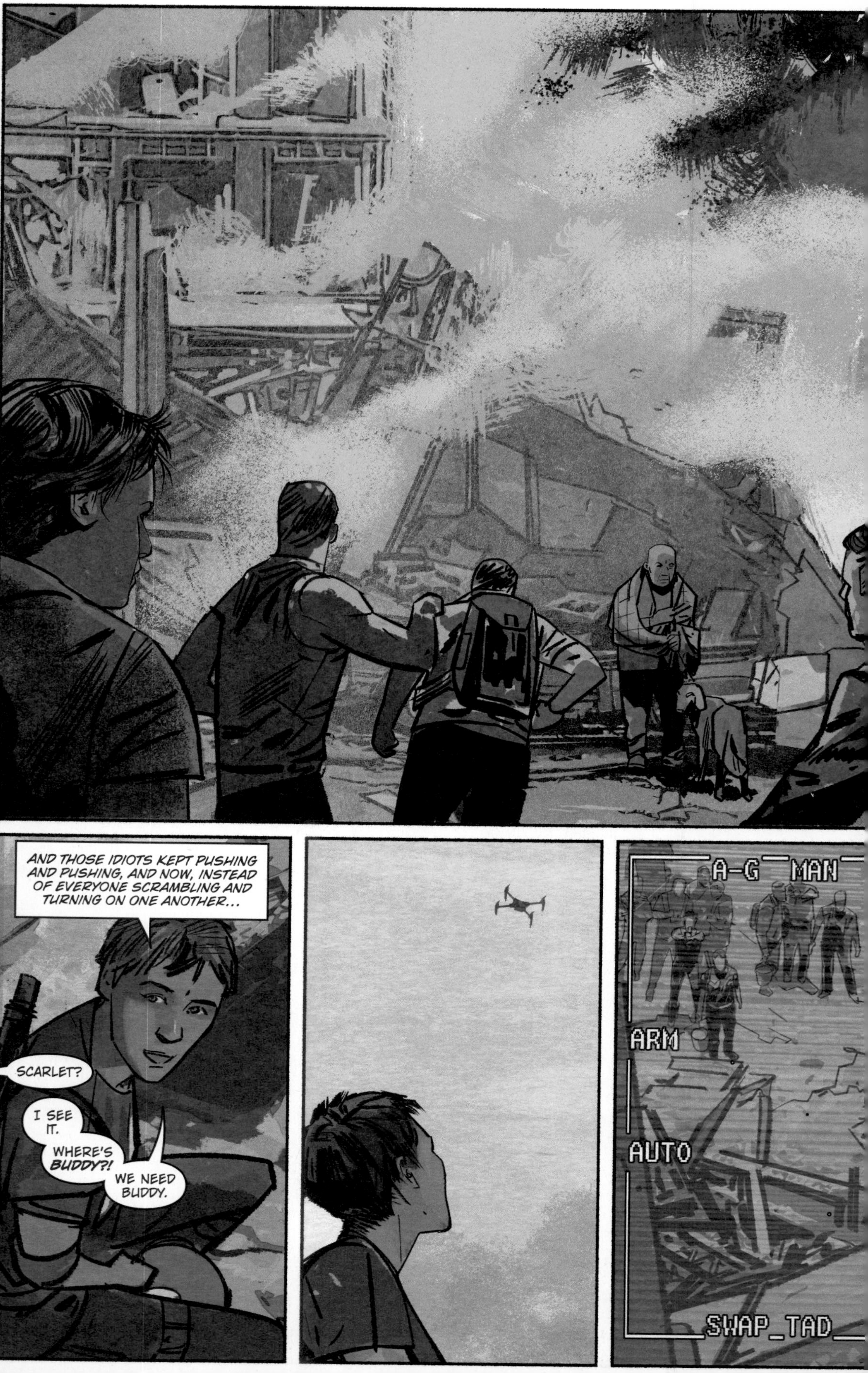
AND THOSE IDIOTS KEPT PUSHING AND PUSHING, AND NOW, INSTEAD OF EVERYONE SCRAMBLING AND TURNING ON ONE ANOTHER...
SCARLET?
I SEE IT.
WHERE'S BUDDY?!
WE NEED BUDDY.
A-G MAN
ARM
AUTO
SWAP_TAD

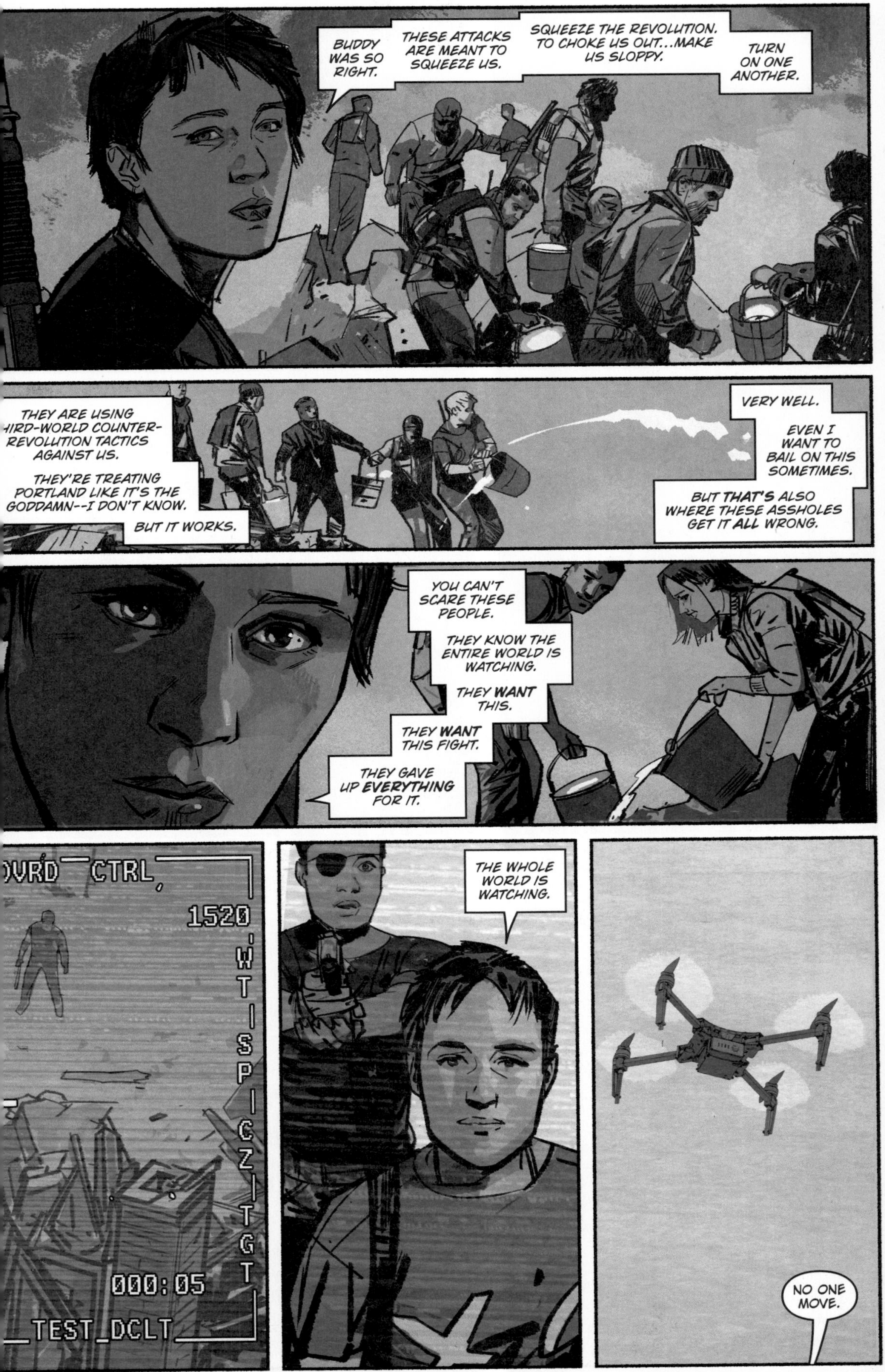
BUDDY WAS SO RIGHT.
THESE ATTACKS ARE MEANT TO SQUEEZE US.
SQUEEZE THE REVOLUTION. TO CHOKE US OUT...MAKE US SLOPPY.
TURN ON ONE ANOTHER.
THEY ARE USING HIRD-WORLD COUNTER-REVOLUTION TACTICS AGAINST US.
THEY'RE TREATING PORTLAND LIKE IT'S THE GODDAMN--I DON'T KNOW.
BUT IT WORKS.
VERY WELL.
EVEN I WANT TO BAIL ON THIS SOMETIMES.
BUT THAT'S ALSO WHERE THESE ASSHOLES GET IT ALL WRONG.
YOU CAN'T SCARE THESE PEOPLE.
THEY KNOW THE ENTIRE WORLD IS WATCHING.
THEY WANT THIS.
THEY WANT THIS FIGHT.
THEY GAVE UP EVERYTHING FOR IT.
OVRD CTRL,
1520
WT
SPIC
Z
TGT
000:05
_TEST_DCLT
THE WHOLE WORLD IS WATCHING.
NO ONE MOVE.

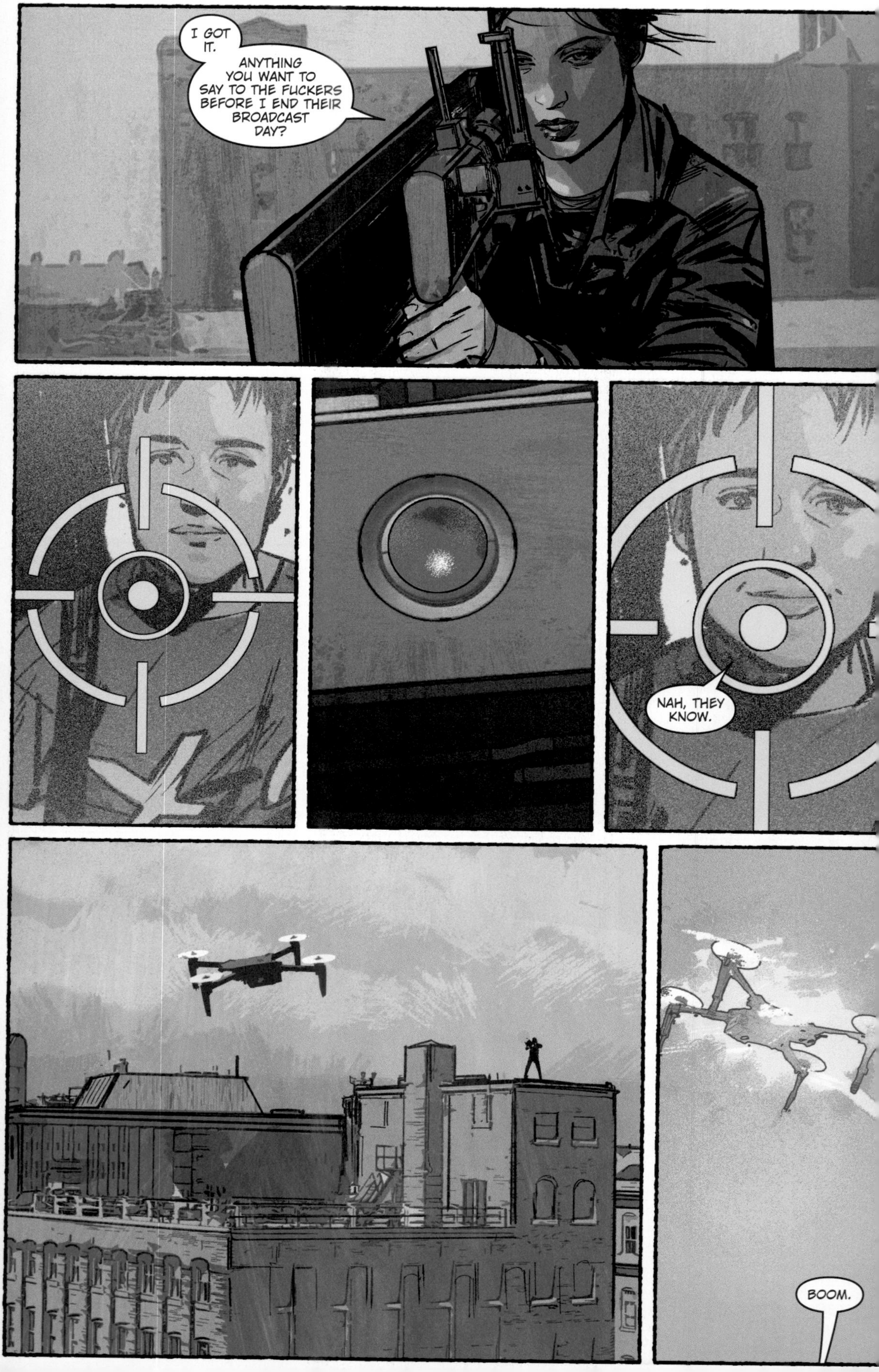
I GOT IT.
ANYTHING YOU WANT TO SAY TO THE FUCKERS BEFORE I END THEIR BROADCAST DAY?
NAH, THEY KNOW.
BOOM.

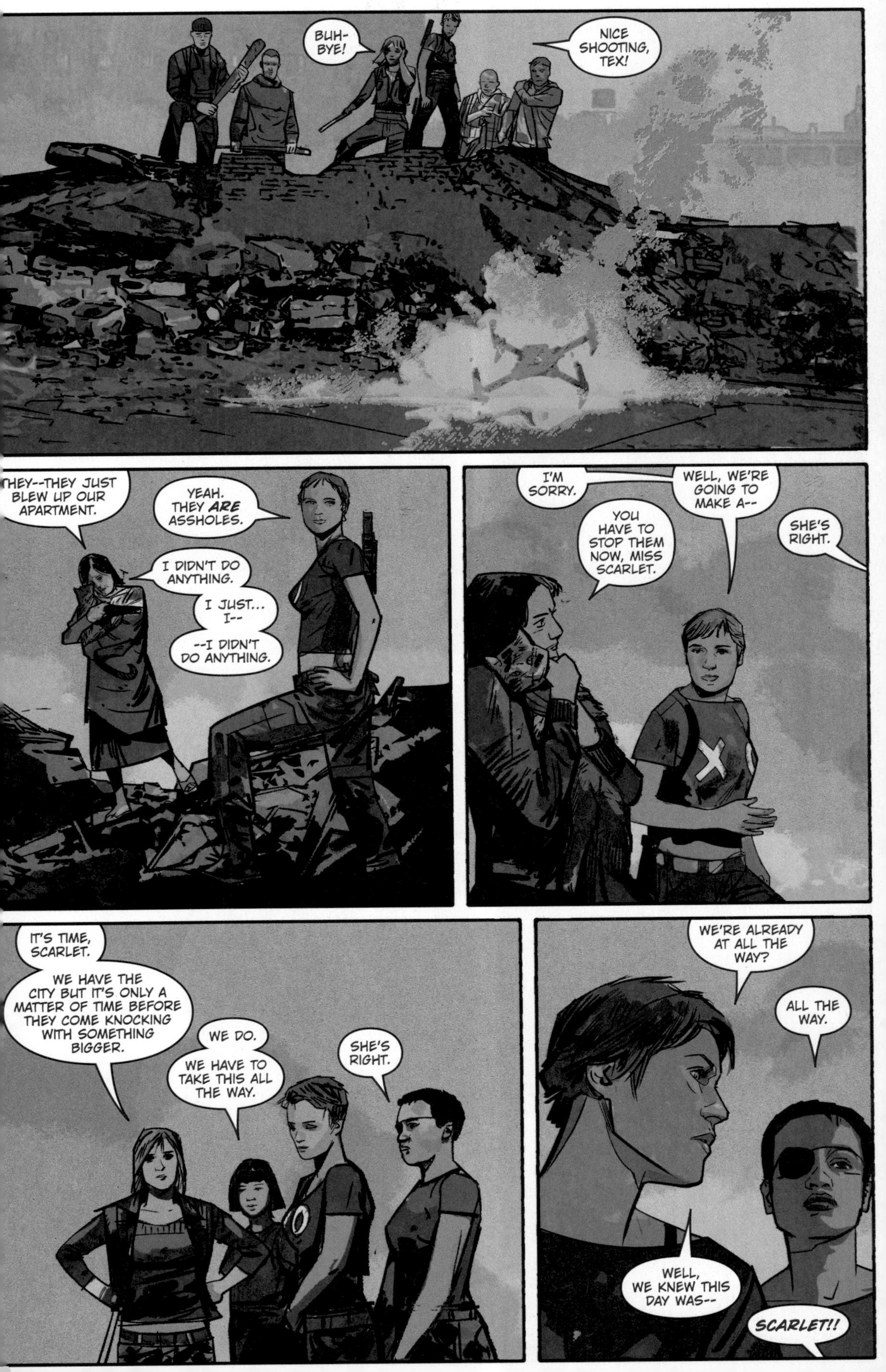
BUH-BYE!
NICE SHOOTING, TEX!
THEY--THEY JUST BLEW UP OUR APARTMENT.
YEAH. THEY *ARE* ASSHOLES.
I DIDN'T DO ANYTHING.
I JUST... I--
--I DIDN'T DO ANYTHING.
I'M SORRY.
WELL, WE'RE GOING TO MAKE A--
YOU HAVE TO STOP THEM NOW, MISS SCARLET.
SHE'S RIGHT.
IT'S TIME, SCARLET.
WE HAVE THE CITY BUT IT'S ONLY A MATTER OF TIME BEFORE THEY COME KNOCKING WITH SOMETHING BIGGER.
WE DO.
WE HAVE TO TAKE THIS ALL THE WAY.
SHE'S RIGHT.
WE'RE ALREADY AT ALL THE WAY?
ALL THE WAY.
WELL, WE KNEW THIS DAY WAS--
SCARLET!!

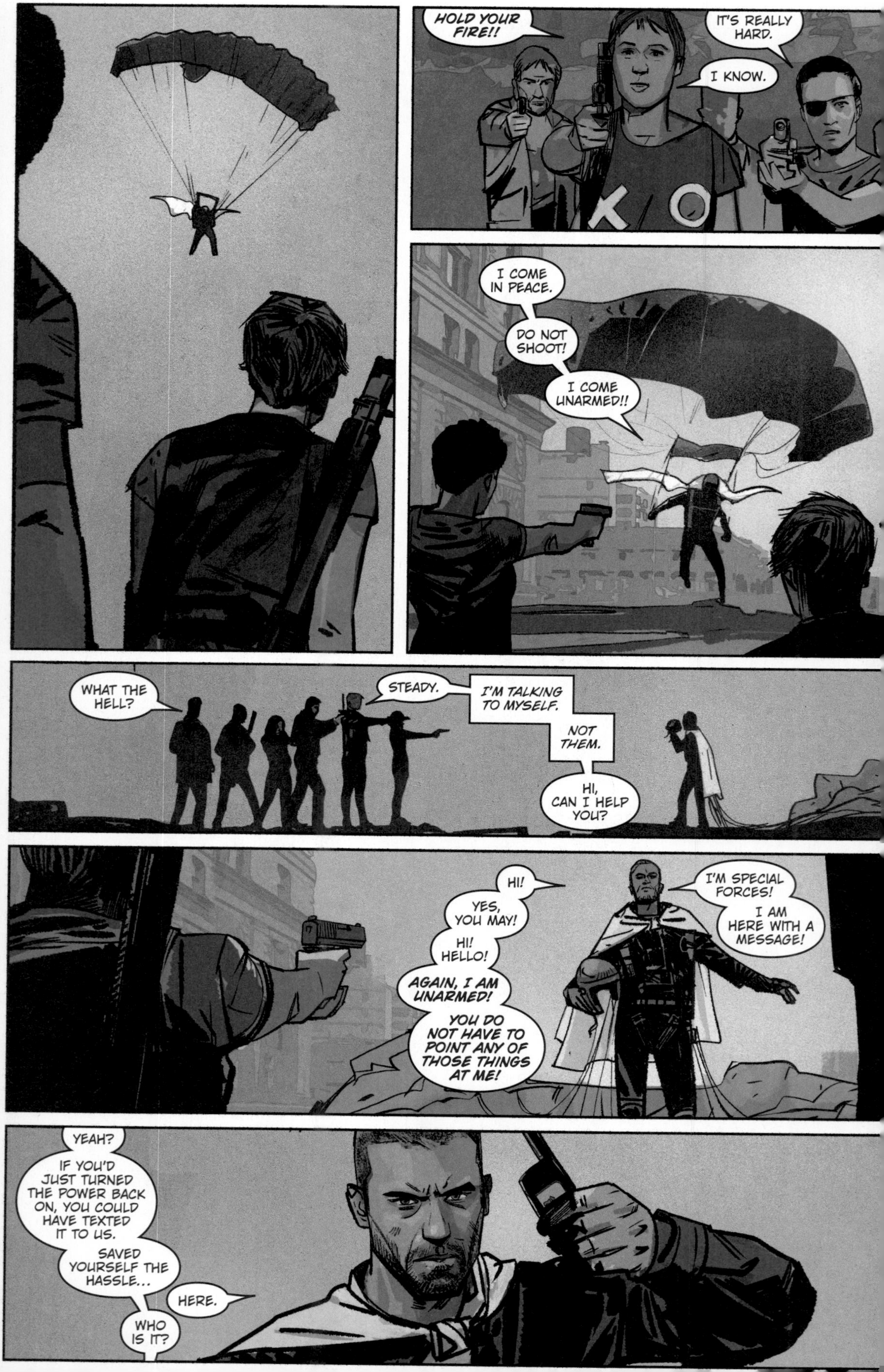
HOLD YOUR FIRE!!
IT'S REALLY HARD.
I KNOW.
I COME IN PEACE.
DO NOT SHOOT!
I COME UNARMED!!
WHAT THE HELL?
STEADY.
I'M TALKING TO MYSELF.
NOT THEM.
HI, CAN I HELP YOU?
HI!
YES, YOU MAY!
HI! HELLO!
AGAIN, I AM UNARMED!
YOU DO NOT HAVE TO POINT ANY OF THOSE THINGS AT ME!
I'M SPECIAL FORCES!
I AM HERE WITH A MESSAGE!
YEAH?
IF YOU'D JUST TURNED THE POWER BACK ON, YOU COULD HAVE TEXTED IT TO US.
SAVED YOURSELF THE HASSLE...
HERE.
WHO IS IT?

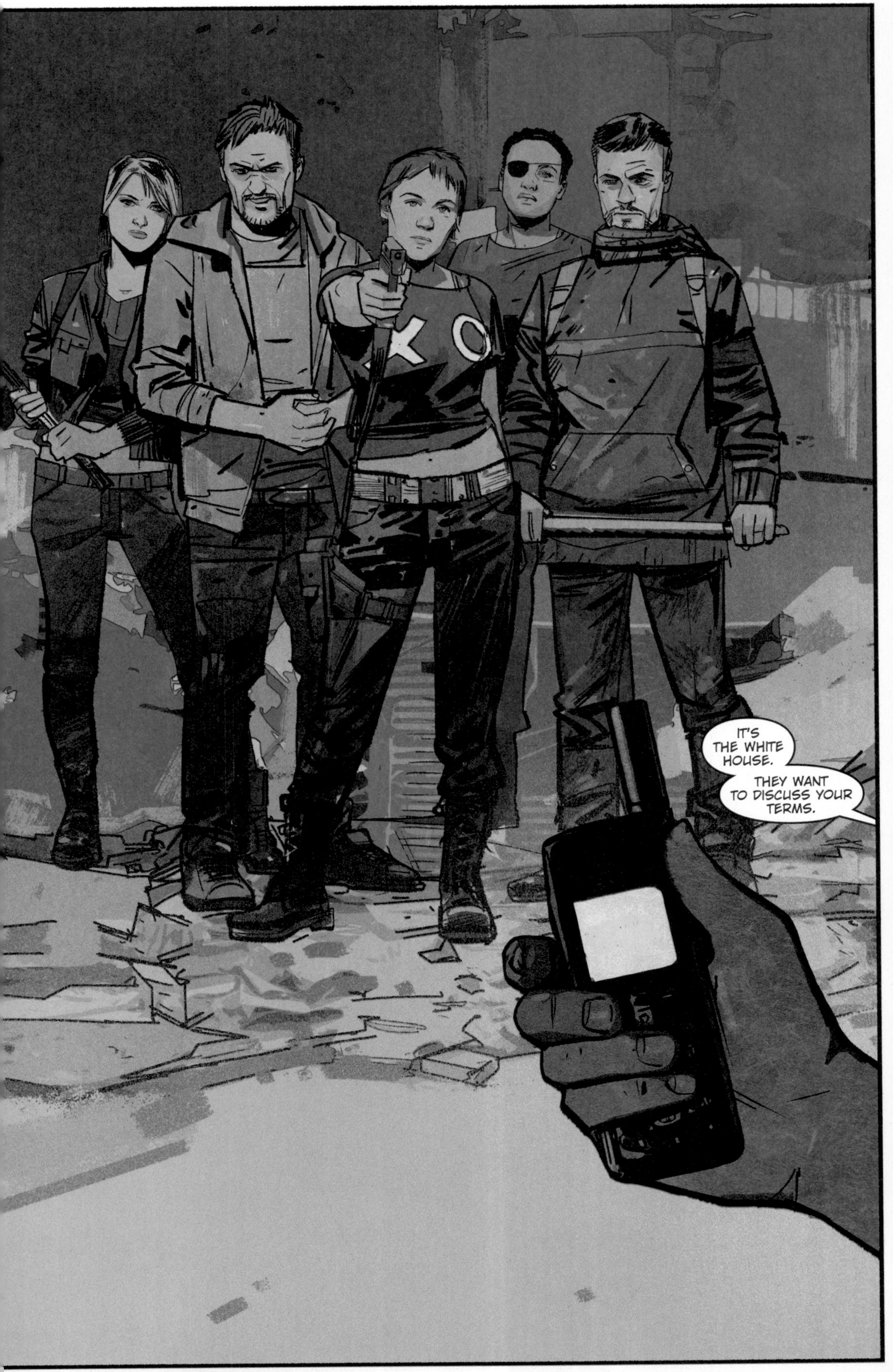
IT'S THE WHITE HOUSE.
THEY WANT TO DISCUSS YOUR TERMS.

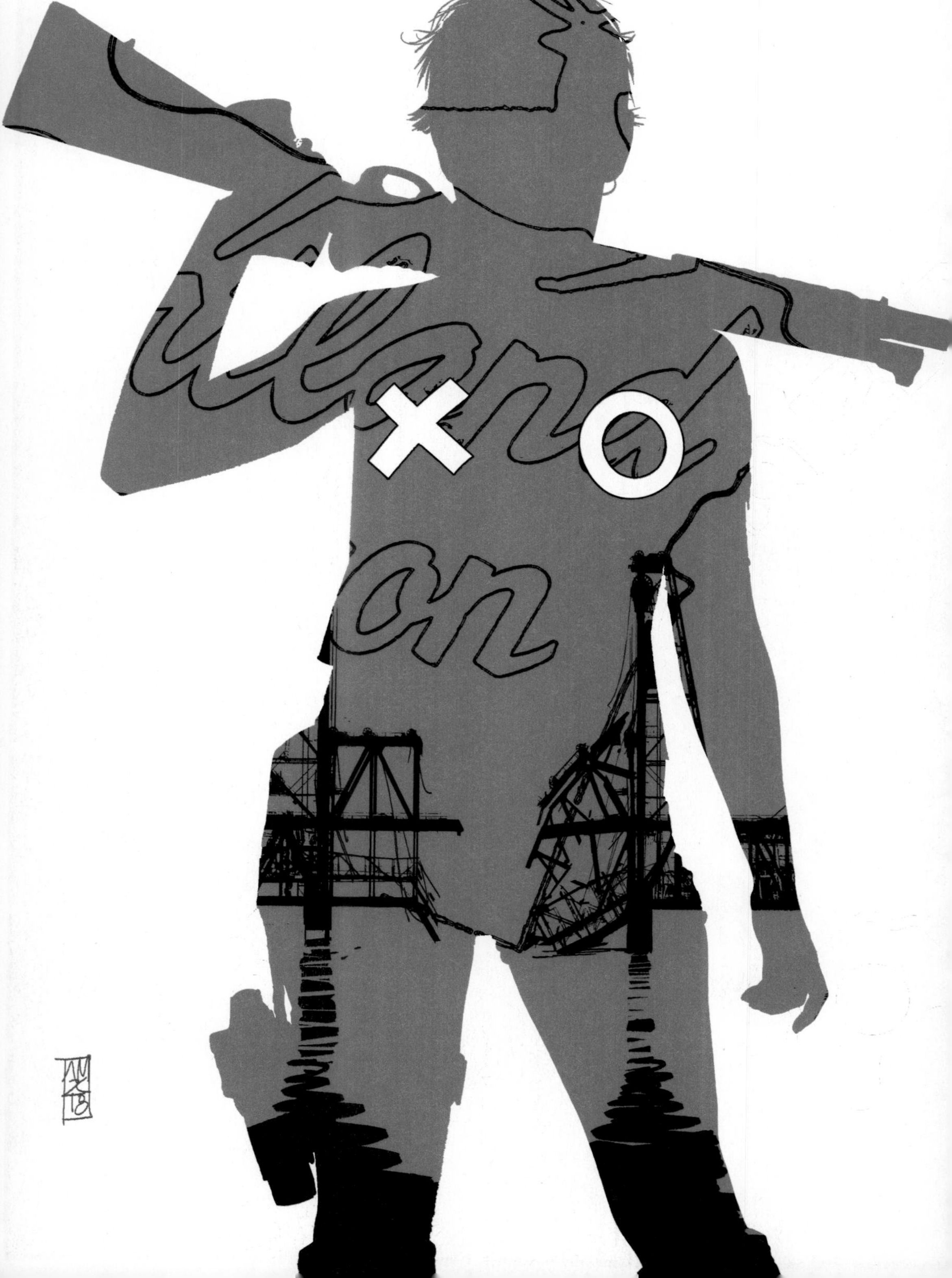

MY NAME IS SCARLET!!

THEY DECLARED WAR ON US!!

THEY DECLARED WAR ON OUR FREEDOM!!

THIS CITY IS OURS, NOT THEIRS!!

TODAY, WE TAKE IT BACK!!!

BUDDABUDDABUDDABUDDABUDDABUDDA

ABOUT THREE WEEKS AGO.

AAGGH!!

OH GOD!!!

AAAIEEEAA!

BUDDABUDDABUDDABUDDA

BUDDABUDDABUDDA

AAAGGH!!

HOLD!

SPASSHH

WE'RE UNDER SIEGE!!

OH GOD!!

SARGE?!

NOT STOPPING!!

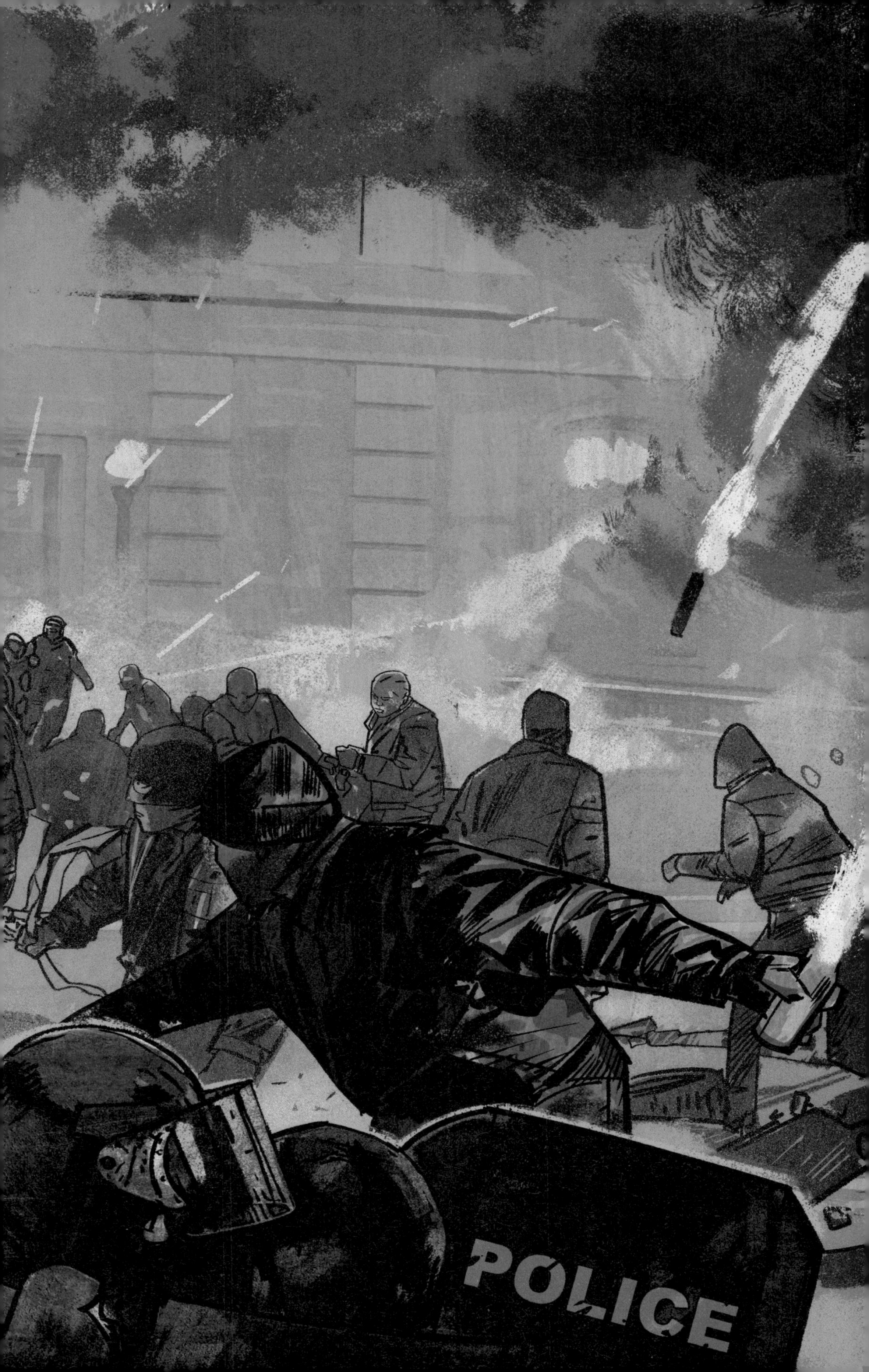
POLICE

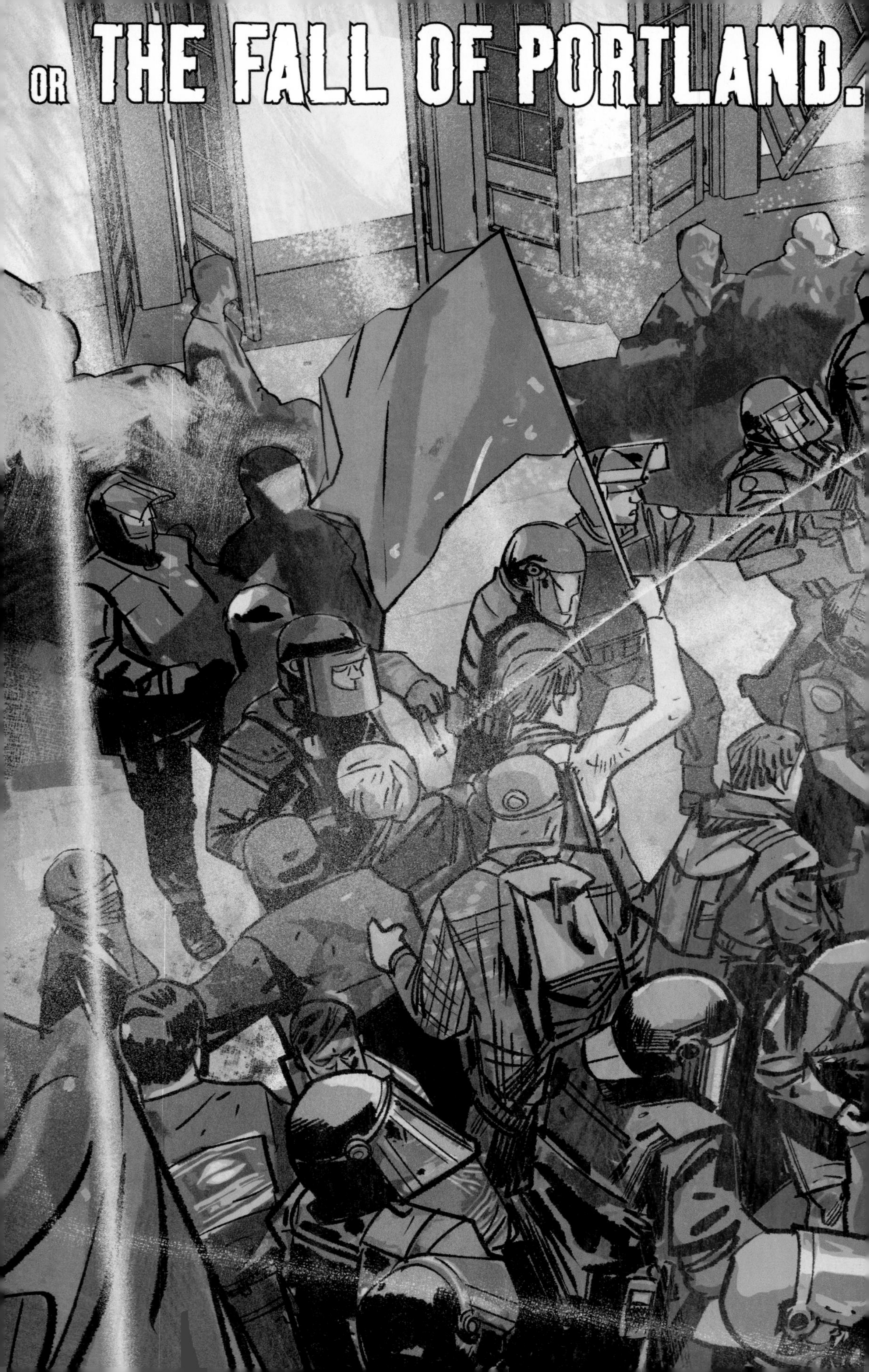
OR THE FALL OF PORTLAND.

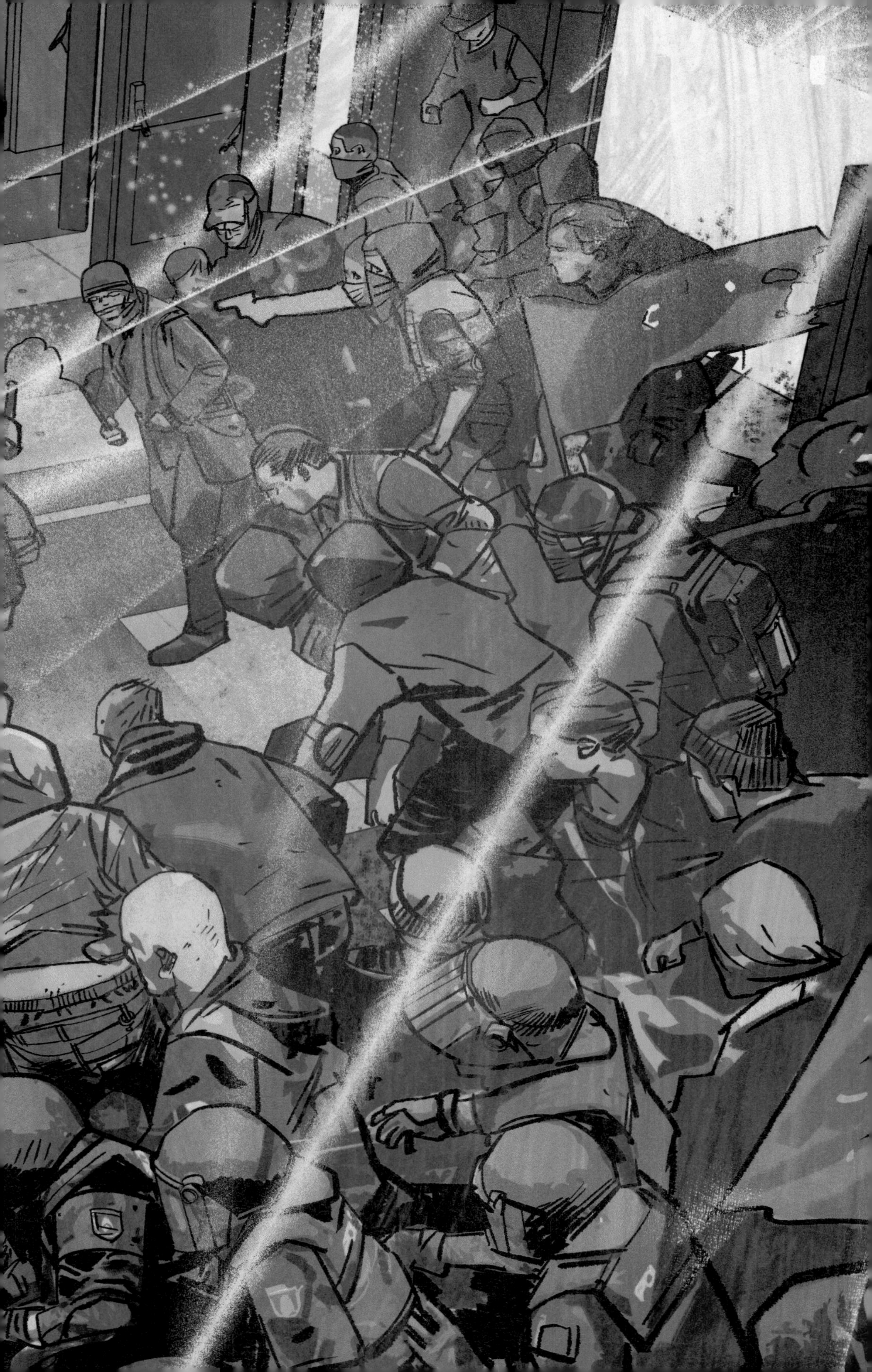

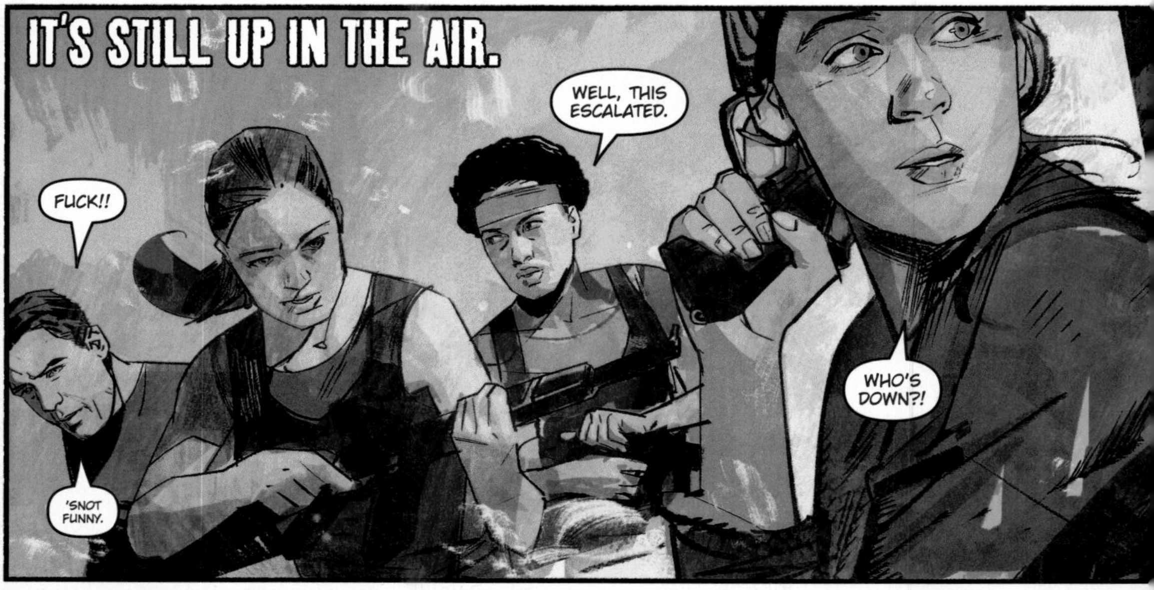
IT'S STILL UP IN THE AIR.
FUCK!!
WELL, THIS ESCALATED.
WHO'S DOWN?!
'SNOT FUNNY.

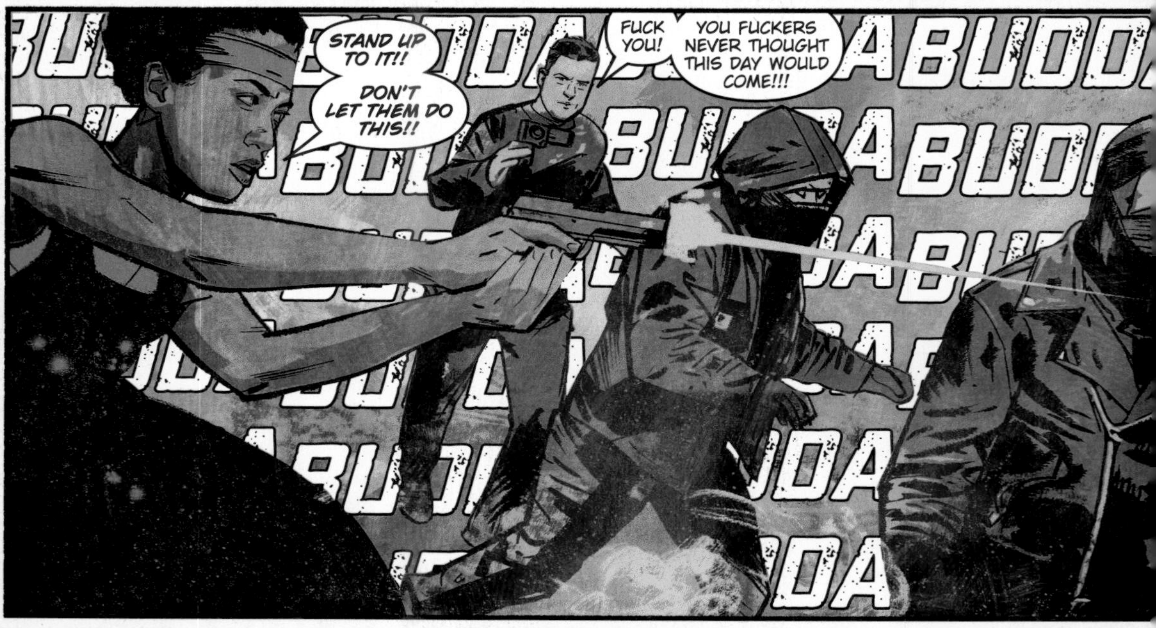
STAND UP TO IT!!
DON'T LET THEM DO THIS!!
FUCK YOU!
YOU FUCKERS NEVER THOUGHT THIS DAY WOULD COME!!!
BUDDA BUDDA BUDDA

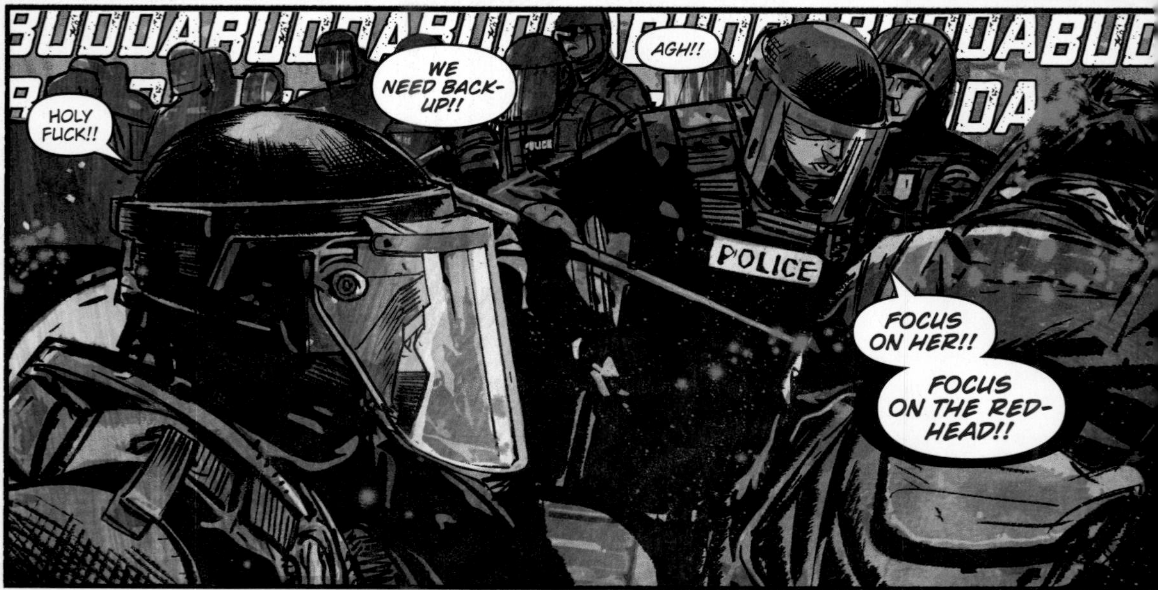
BUDDABUDDA BUDDA
HOLY FUCK!!
WE NEED BACK-UP!!
AGH!!
POLICE
FOCUS ON HER!!
FOCUS ON THE RED-HEAD!!

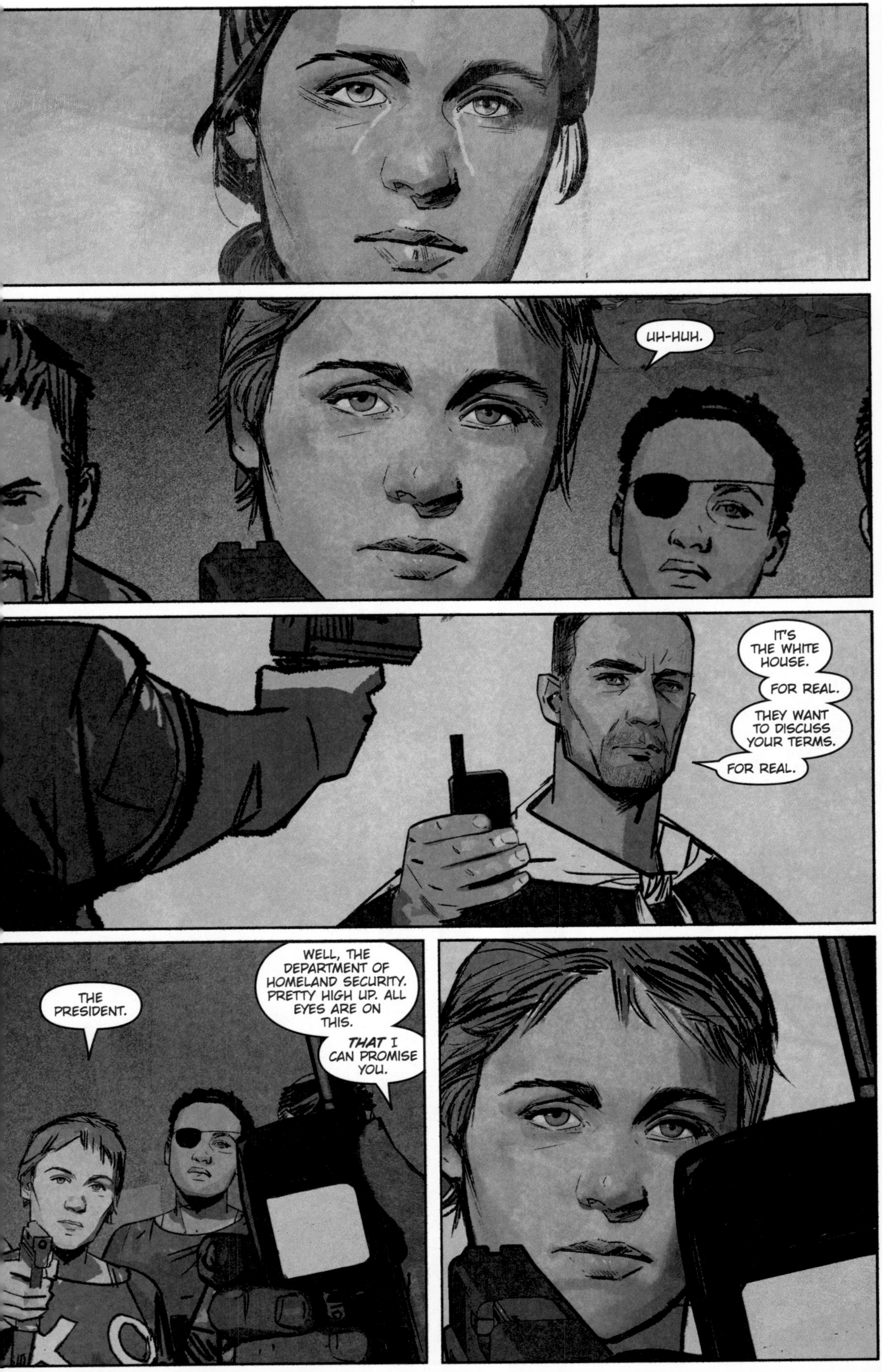
UH-HUH.
IT'S THE WHITE HOUSE.
FOR REAL.
THEY WANT TO DISCUSS YOUR TERMS.
FOR REAL.
THE PRESIDENT.
WELL, THE DEPARTMENT OF HOMELAND SECURITY. PRETTY HIGH UP. ALL EYES ARE ON THIS.
THAT I CAN PROMISE YOU.

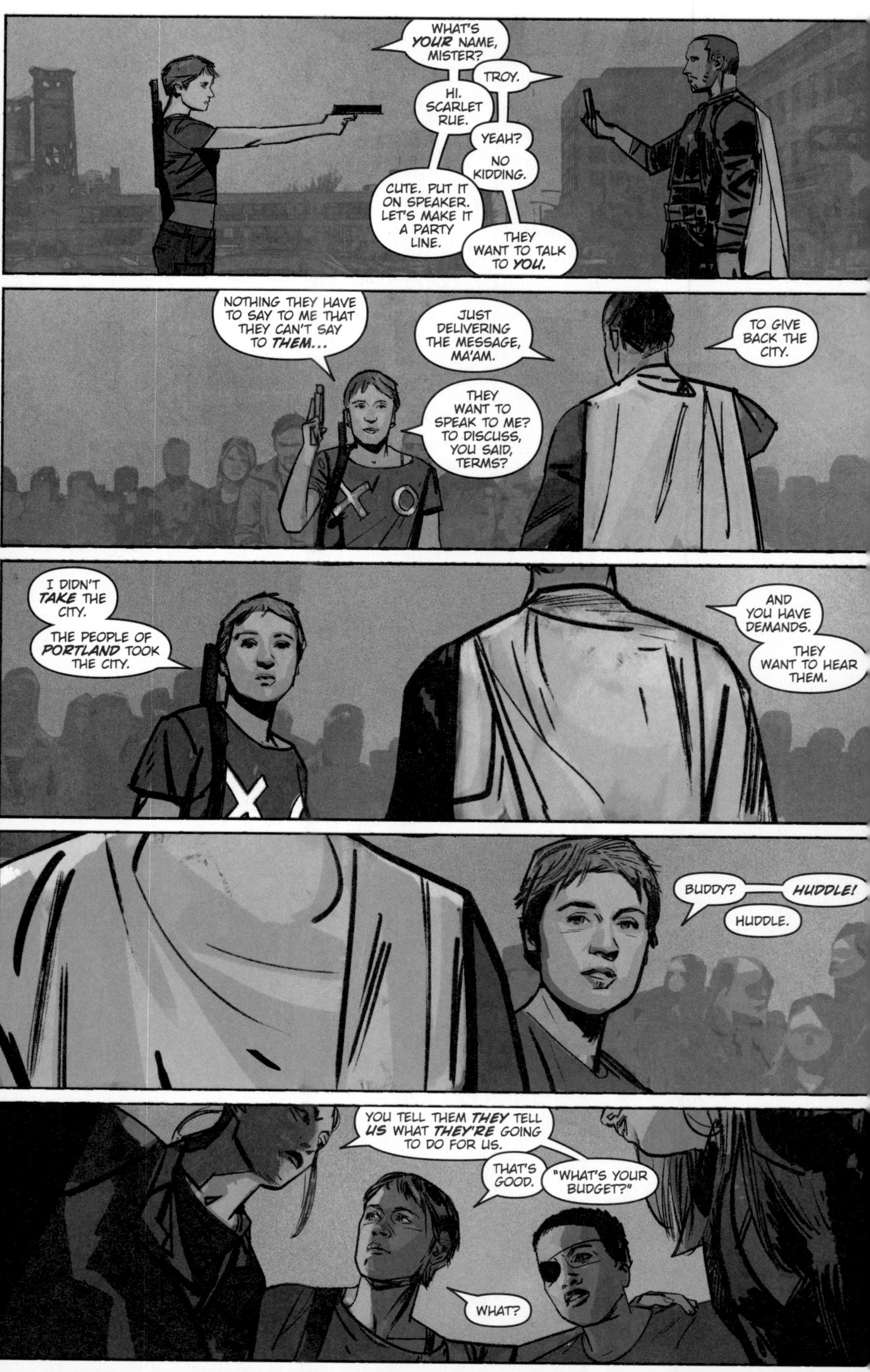
WHAT'S YOUR NAME, MISTER?
TROY.
HI. SCARLET RUE.
YEAH?
NO KIDDING.
CUTE. PUT IT ON SPEAKER. LET'S MAKE IT A PARTY LINE.
THEY WANT TO TALK TO YOU.
NOTHING THEY HAVE TO SAY TO ME THAT THEY CAN'T SAY TO THEM...
JUST DELIVERING THE MESSAGE, MA'AM.
TO GIVE BACK THE CITY.
THEY WANT TO SPEAK TO ME? TO DISCUSS, YOU SAID, TERMS?
I DIDN'T TAKE THE CITY.
THE PEOPLE OF PORTLAND TOOK THE CITY.
AND YOU HAVE DEMANDS.
THEY WANT TO HEAR THEM.
BUDDY?
HUDDLE!
HUDDLE.
YOU TELL THEM THEY TELL US WHAT THEY'RE GOING TO DO FOR US.
THAT'S GOOD.
"WHAT'S YOUR BUDGET?"
WHAT?

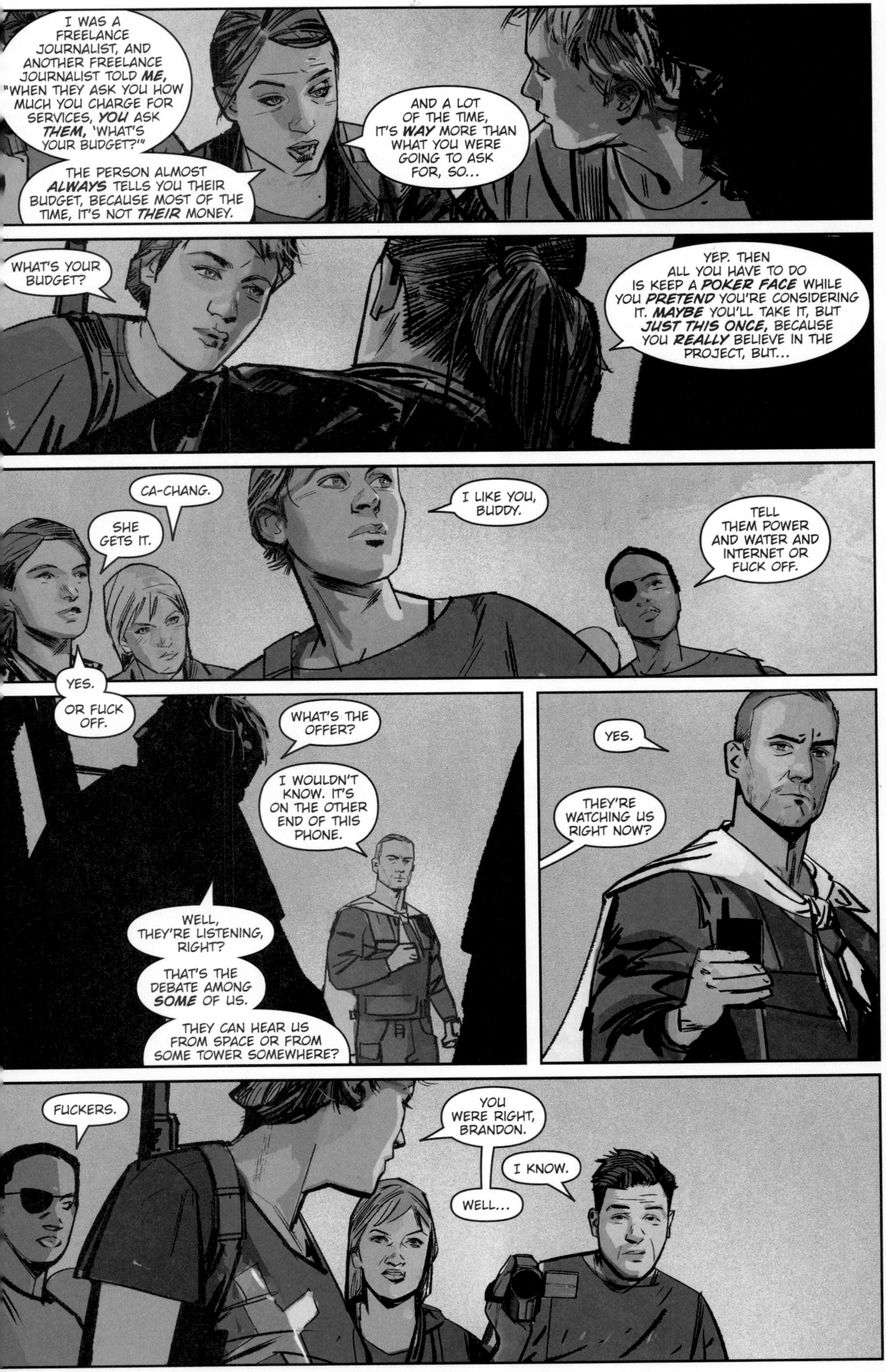
I WAS A FREELANCE JOURNALIST, AND ANOTHER FREELANCE JOURNALIST TOLD *ME*, "WHEN THEY ASK YOU HOW MUCH YOU CHARGE FOR SERVICES, *YOU* ASK *THEM*, 'WHAT'S YOUR BUDGET?'"
THE PERSON ALMOST *ALWAYS* TELLS YOU THEIR BUDGET, BECAUSE MOST OF THE TIME, IT'S NOT *THEIR* MONEY.
AND A LOT OF THE TIME, IT'S *WAY* MORE THAN WHAT YOU WERE GOING TO ASK FOR, SO...
WHAT'S YOUR BUDGET?
YEP. THEN ALL YOU HAVE TO DO IS KEEP A *POKER FACE* WHILE YOU *PRETEND* YOU'RE CONSIDERING IT. *MAYBE* YOU'LL TAKE IT, BUT *JUST THIS ONCE*, BECAUSE YOU *REALLY* BELIEVE IN THE PROJECT, BUT...
CA-CHANG.
SHE GETS IT.
I LIKE YOU, BUDDY.
TELL THEM POWER AND WATER AND INTERNET OR FUCK OFF.
YES. OR FUCK OFF.
WHAT'S THE OFFER?
I WOULDN'T KNOW. IT'S ON THE OTHER END OF THIS PHONE.
WELL, THEY'RE LISTENING, RIGHT?
THAT'S THE DEBATE AMONG *SOME* OF US.
THEY CAN HEAR US FROM SPACE OR FROM SOME TOWER SOMEWHERE?
YES.
THEY'RE WATCHING US RIGHT NOW?
FUCKERS.
YOU WERE RIGHT, BRANDON.
I KNOW.
WELL...

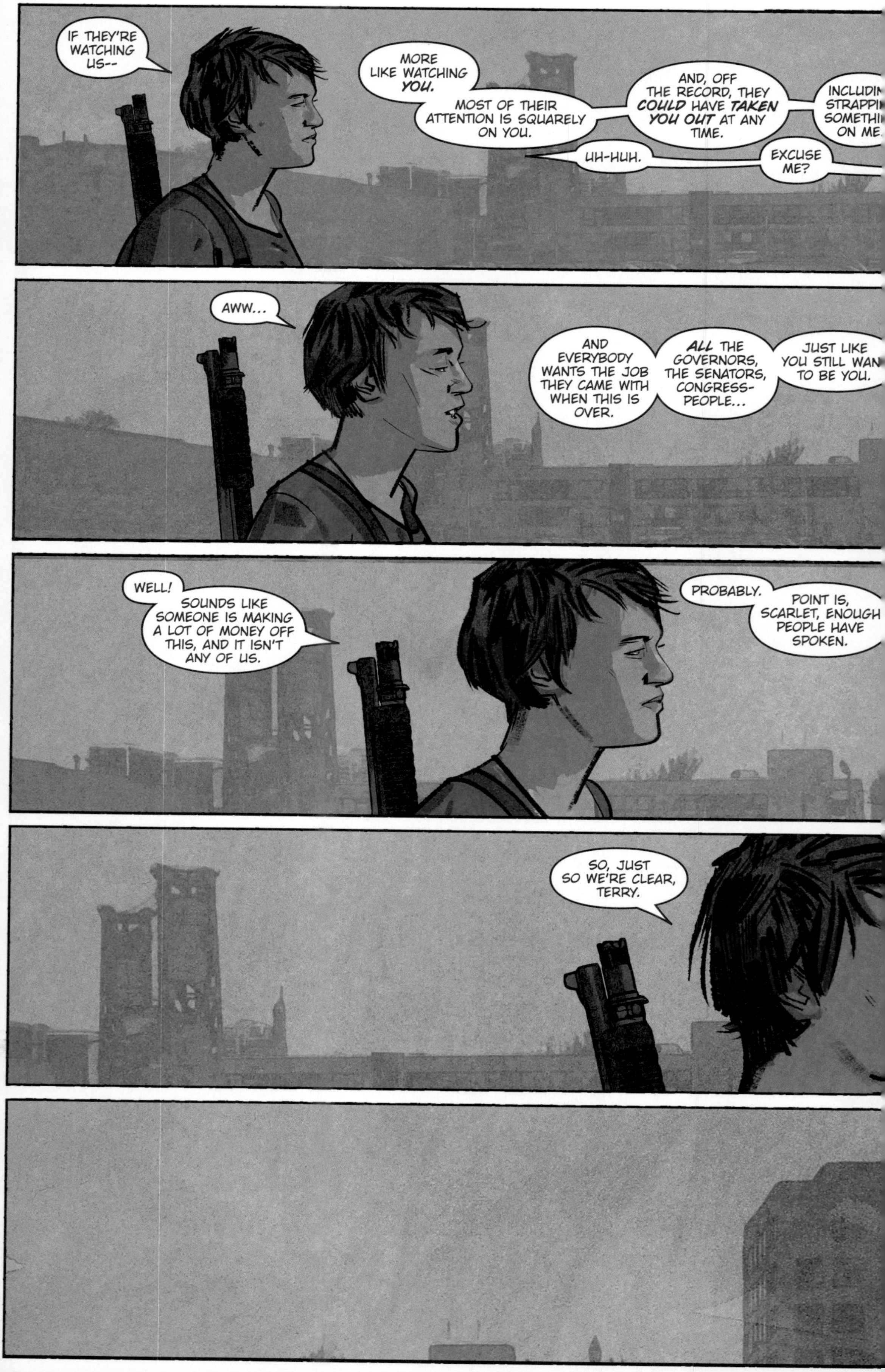
IF THEY'RE WATCHING US--
MORE LIKE WATCHING *YOU.*
MOST OF THEIR ATTENTION IS SQUARELY ON YOU.
AND, OFF THE RECORD, THEY ***COULD*** HAVE ***TAKEN YOU OUT*** AT ANY TIME.
INCLUDI STRAPPI SOMETHI ON ME.
UH-HUH.
EXCUSE ME?
AWW...
AND EVERYBODY WANTS THE JOB THEY CAME WITH WHEN THIS IS OVER.
ALL THE GOVERNORS, THE SENATORS, CONGRESS-PEOPLE...
JUST LIKE YOU STILL WAN TO BE YOU.
WELL! SOUNDS LIKE SOMEONE IS MAKING A LOT OF MONEY OFF THIS, AND IT ISN'T ANY OF US.
PROBABLY.
POINT IS, SCARLET, ENOUGH PEOPLE HAVE SPOKEN.
SO, JUST SO WE'RE CLEAR, TERRY.

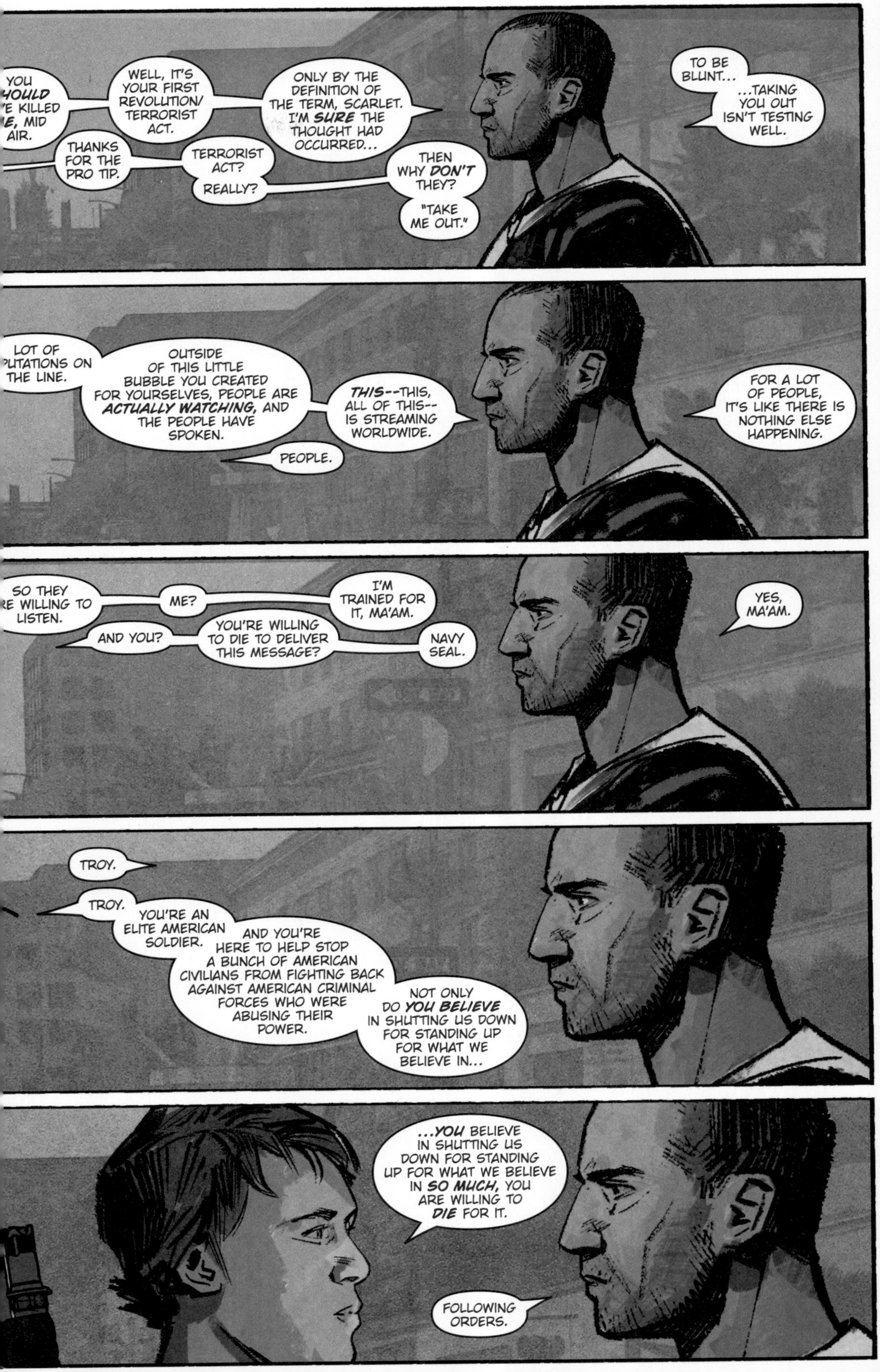
YOU SHOULD 'VE KILLED E, MID AIR.
WELL, IT'S YOUR FIRST REVOLUTION/ TERRORIST ACT.
ONLY BY THE DEFINITION OF THE TERM, SCARLET. I'M SURE THE THOUGHT HAD OCCURRED...
TO BE BLUNT...
...TAKING YOU OUT ISN'T TESTING WELL.
THANKS FOR THE PRO TIP.
TERRORIST ACT?
REALLY?
THEN WHY DON'T THEY?
"TAKE ME OUT."
LOT OF PUTATIONS ON THE LINE.
OUTSIDE OF THIS LITTLE BUBBLE YOU CREATED FOR YOURSELVES, PEOPLE ARE ACTUALLY WATCHING, AND THE PEOPLE HAVE SPOKEN.
THIS--THIS, ALL OF THIS-- IS STREAMING WORLDWIDE.
FOR A LOT OF PEOPLE, IT'S LIKE THERE IS NOTHING ELSE HAPPENING.
PEOPLE.
SO THEY RE WILLING TO LISTEN.
ME?
I'M TRAINED FOR IT, MA'AM.
YES, MA'AM.
AND YOU?
YOU'RE WILLING TO DIE TO DELIVER THIS MESSAGE?
NAVY SEAL.
TROY.
TROY.
YOU'RE AN ELITE AMERICAN SOLDIER.
AND YOU'RE HERE TO HELP STOP A BUNCH OF AMERICAN CIVILIANS FROM FIGHTING BACK AGAINST AMERICAN CRIMINAL FORCES WHO WERE ABUSING THEIR POWER.
NOT ONLY DO YOU BELIEVE IN SHUTTING US DOWN FOR STANDING UP FOR WHAT WE BELIEVE IN...
...YOU BELIEVE IN SHUTTING US DOWN FOR STANDING UP FOR WHAT WE BELIEVE IN SO MUCH, YOU ARE WILLING TO DIE FOR IT.
FOLLOWING ORDERS.

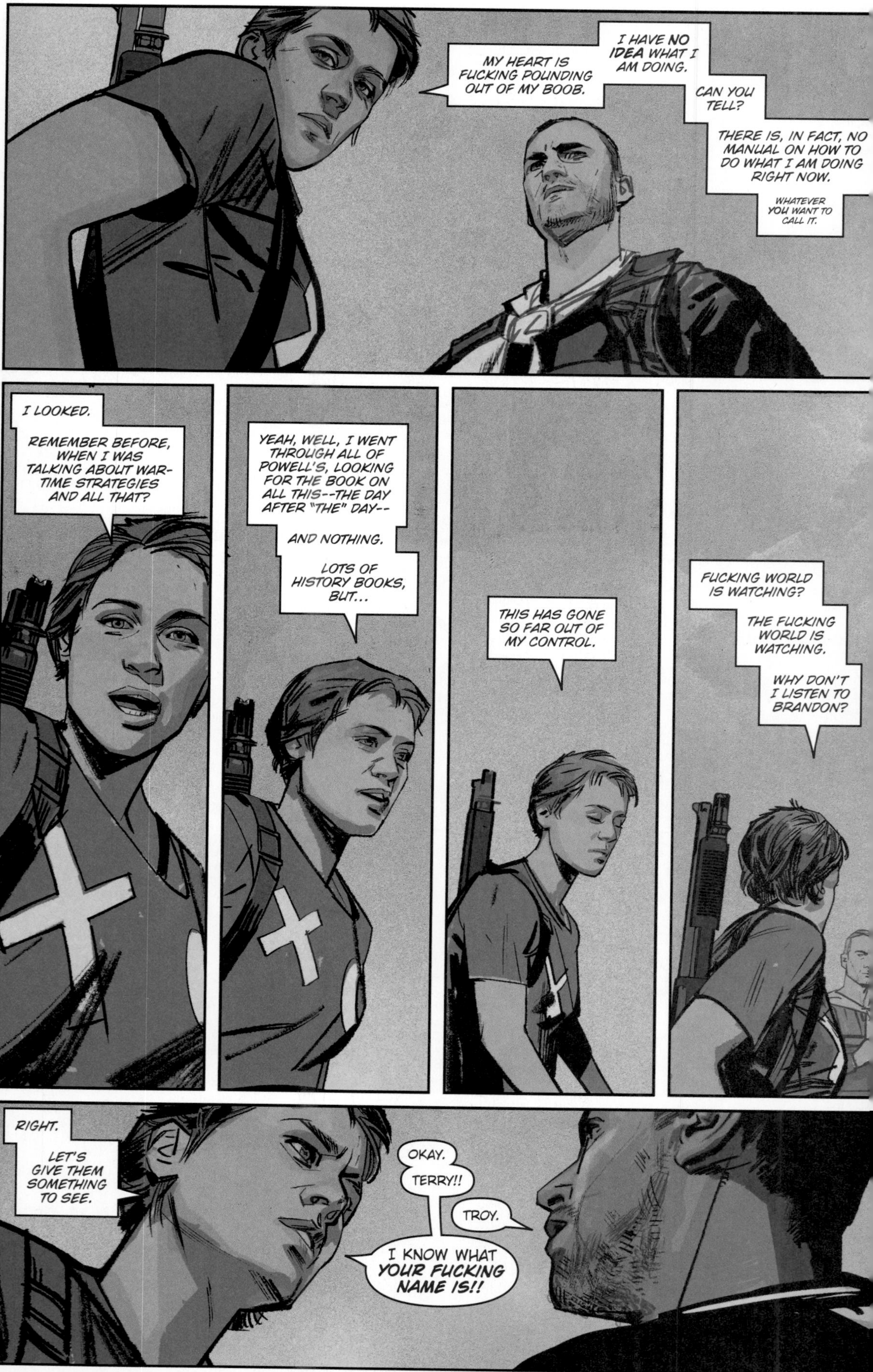
MY HEART IS FUCKING POUNDING OUT OF MY BOOB.
I HAVE NO IDEA WHAT I AM DOING.
CAN YOU TELL?
THERE IS, IN FACT, NO MANUAL ON HOW TO DO WHAT I AM DOING RIGHT NOW.
WHATEVER YOU WANT TO CALL IT.
I LOOKED.
REMEMBER BEFORE, WHEN I WAS TALKING ABOUT WAR-TIME STRATEGIES AND ALL THAT?
YEAH, WELL, I WENT THROUGH ALL OF POWELL'S, LOOKING FOR THE BOOK ON ALL THIS--THE DAY AFTER "THE" DAY--
AND NOTHING.
LOTS OF HISTORY BOOKS, BUT...
THIS HAS GONE SO FAR OUT OF MY CONTROL.
FUCKING WORLD IS WATCHING?
THE FUCKING WORLD IS WATCHING.
WHY DON'T I LISTEN TO BRANDON?
RIGHT.
LET'S GIVE THEM SOMETHING TO SEE.
OKAY.
TERRY!!
TROY.
I KNOW WHAT YOUR FUCKING NAME IS!!

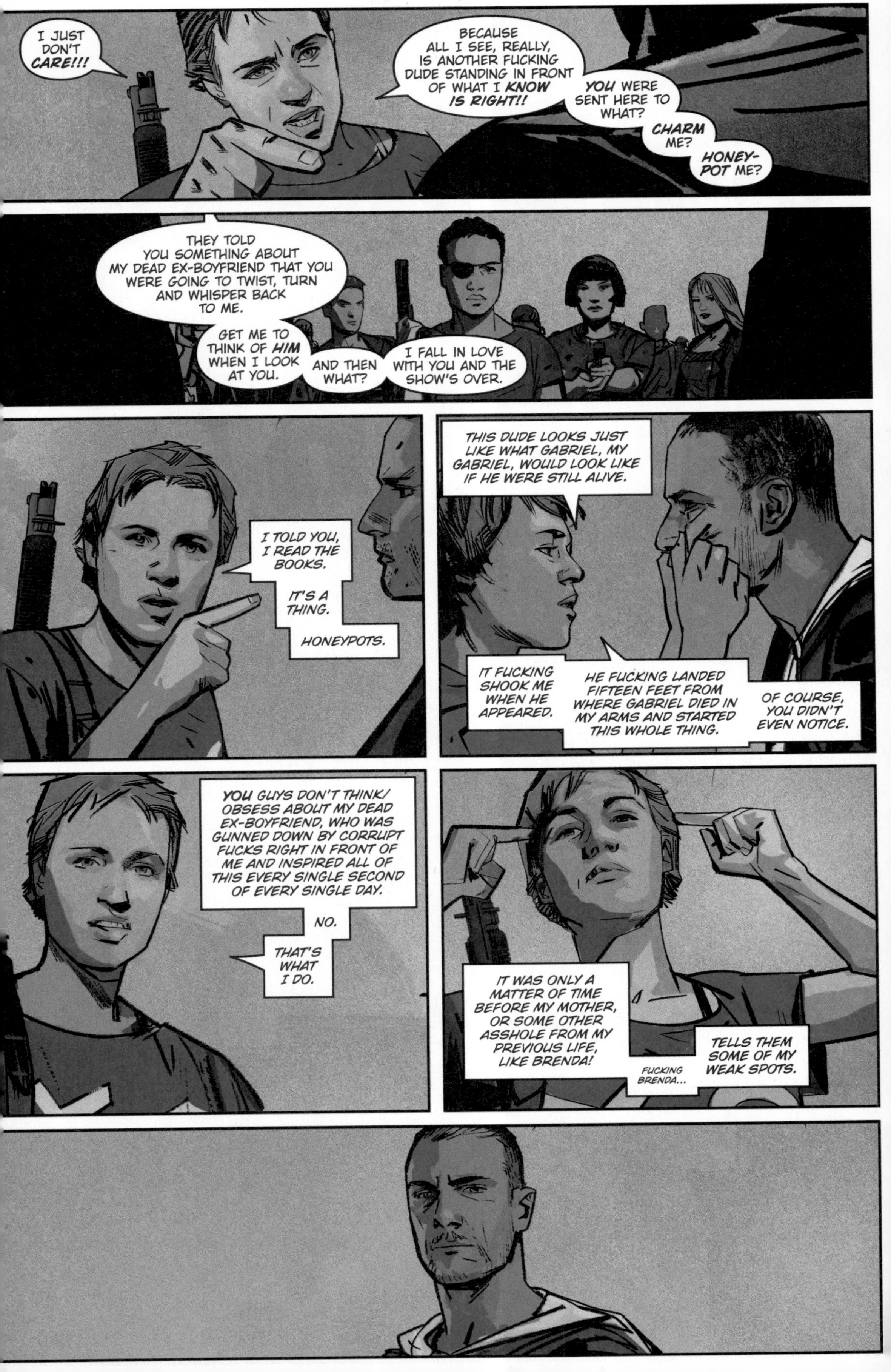
I JUST DON'T CARE!!!
BECAUSE ALL I SEE, REALLY, IS ANOTHER FUCKING DUDE STANDING IN FRONT OF WHAT I KNOW IS RIGHT!!
YOU WERE SENT HERE TO WHAT?
CHARM ME?
HONEY-POT ME?
THEY TOLD YOU SOMETHING ABOUT MY DEAD EX-BOYFRIEND THAT YOU WERE GOING TO TWIST, TURN AND WHISPER BACK TO ME.
GET ME TO THINK OF HIM WHEN I LOOK AT YOU.
AND THEN WHAT?
I FALL IN LOVE WITH YOU AND THE SHOW'S OVER.
I TOLD YOU, I READ THE BOOKS.
IT'S A THING.
HONEYPOTS.
THIS DUDE LOOKS JUST LIKE WHAT GABRIEL, MY GABRIEL, WOULD LOOK LIKE IF HE WERE STILL ALIVE.
IT FUCKING SHOOK ME WHEN HE APPEARED.
HE FUCKING LANDED FIFTEEN FEET FROM WHERE GABRIEL DIED IN MY ARMS AND STARTED THIS WHOLE THING.
OF COURSE, YOU DIDN'T EVEN NOTICE.
YOU GUYS DON'T THINK/ OBSESS ABOUT MY DEAD EX-BOYFRIEND, WHO WAS GUNNED DOWN BY CORRUPT FUCKS RIGHT IN FRONT OF ME AND INSPIRED ALL OF THIS EVERY SINGLE SECOND OF EVERY SINGLE DAY.
NO.
THAT'S WHAT I DO.
IT WAS ONLY A MATTER OF TIME BEFORE MY MOTHER, OR SOME OTHER ASSHOLE FROM MY PREVIOUS LIFE, LIKE BRENDA!
FUCKING BRENDA...
TELLS THEM SOME OF MY WEAK SPOTS.

BABY... ...YOU **CAN'T** FUCK WITH ME.

THAT'S WHAT THIS IS **ALL ABOUT.**

DON'T YOU GUYS **GET** THAT?

IT FINALLY HAPPENED!!

YOU KEPT **FUCKING** WITH US AND FUCKING WITH US AND **FUCKING** WITH US...

YOU FINALLY FUCKING FOUND THE ONE GIRL YOU CAN'T FUCKING FUCK WITH.

ALIVE **OR FUCKING DEAD!!**

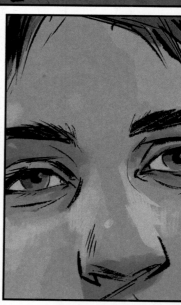

TROY, YOU'LL BE OUR GUEST FOR THE DURATION.

BUDDY, ICE? YOU GOT THIS.

GOT.

IN ABOUT AN HOUR, WHEN YOU FIGURE OUT I'M **ON YOUR SIDE,** YOU CALL.

WOW. ARRESTED IN PORTLAND AGAIN.

HEY! ARE THERE ANY DONUTS LEFT?

OH, THE DONUTS WERE GONE THE FIRST WEEK.

WEED?

OH, SHIT-TONS.

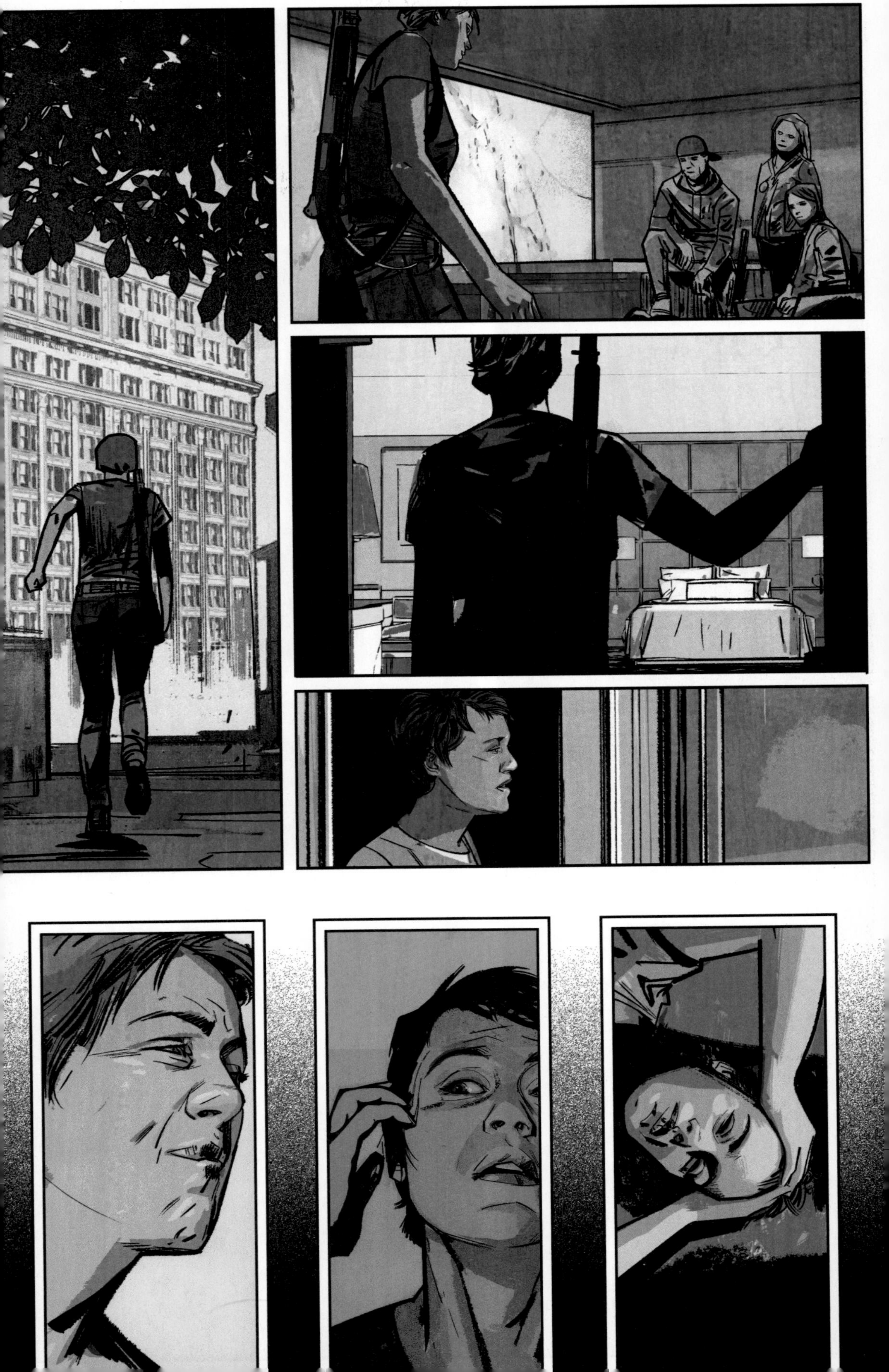

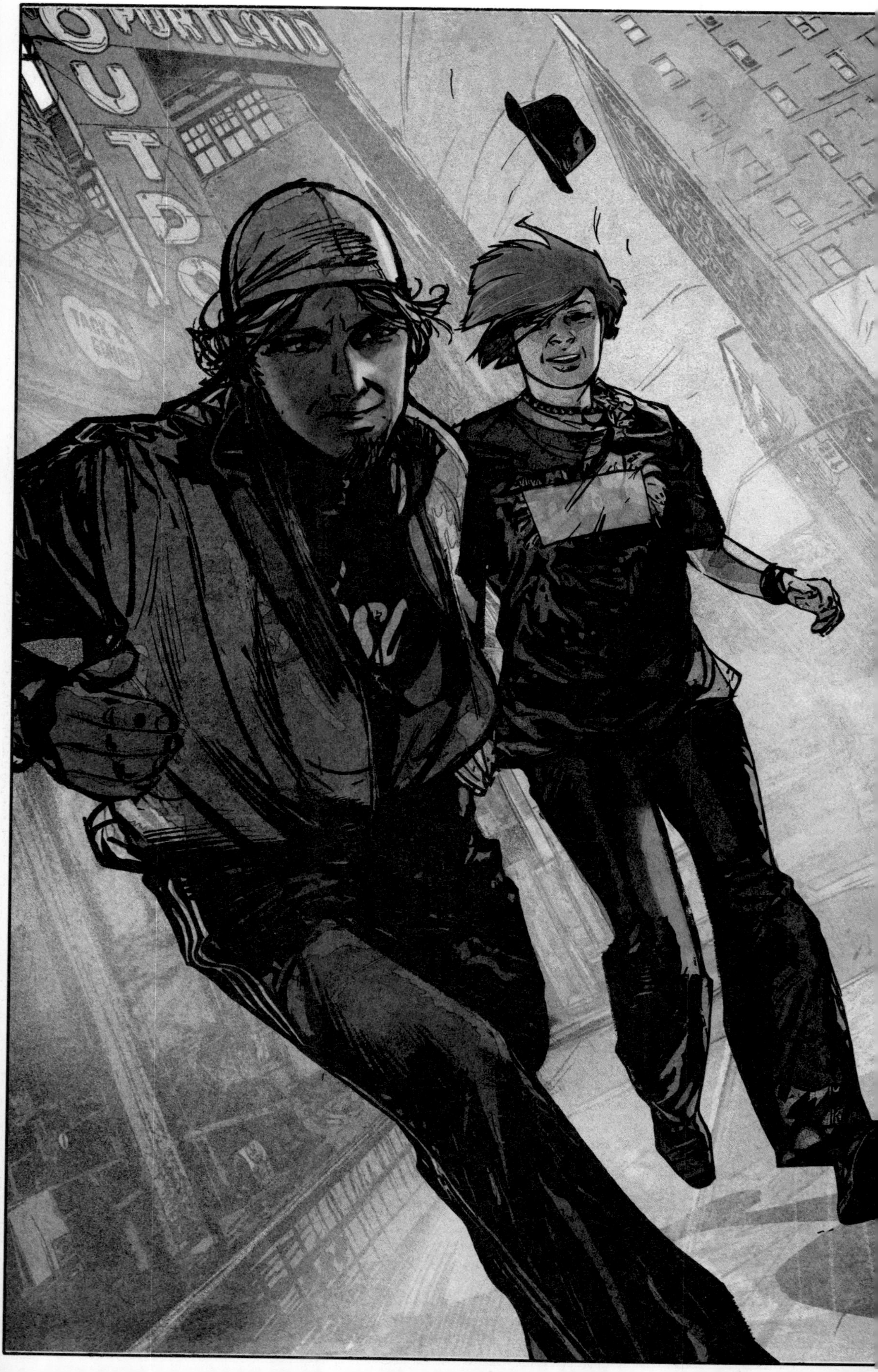
PORTLAND

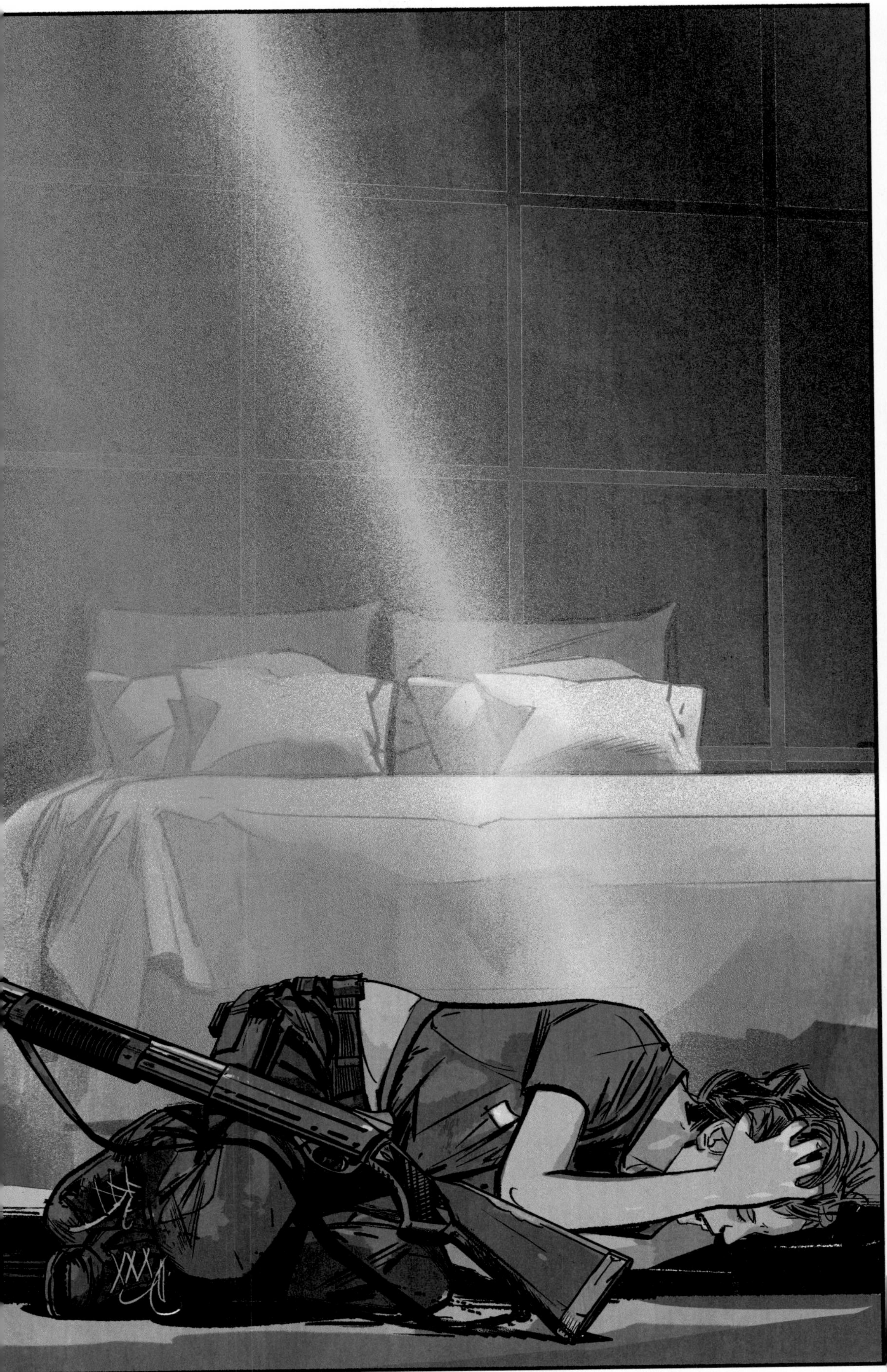

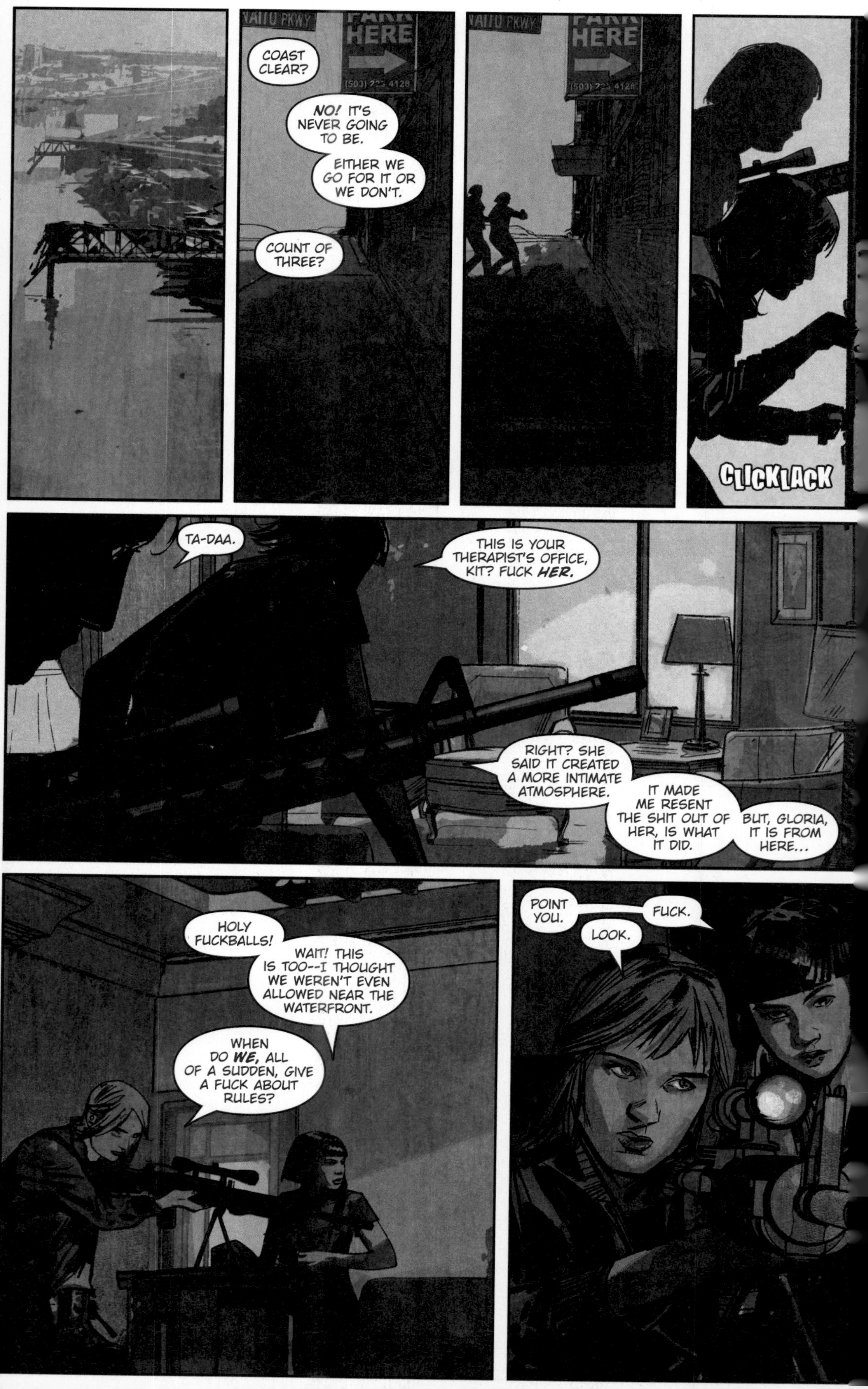

COAST CLEAR?
NO! IT'S NEVER GOING TO BE.
EITHER WE GO FOR IT OR WE DON'T.
COUNT OF THREE?
PARK HERE
CLICKLACK
TA-DAA.
THIS IS YOUR THERAPIST'S OFFICE, KIT? FUCK HER.
RIGHT? SHE SAID IT CREATED A MORE INTIMATE ATMOSPHERE.
IT MADE ME RESENT THE SHIT OUT OF HER, IS WHAT IT DID.
BUT, GLORIA, IT IS FROM HERE...
HOLY FUCKBALLS!
WAIT! THIS IS TOO--I THOUGHT WE WEREN'T EVEN ALLOWED NEAR THE WATERFRONT.
WHEN DO WE, ALL OF A SUDDEN, GIVE A FUCK ABOUT RULES?
POINT YOU.
FUCK.
LOOK.

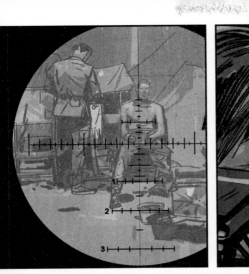

WHAT ARE THEY DOING?

SAME THING WE ARE.

WAITING FOR SOMEONE TO MAKE A MOVE.

I CAN SEE SCARLET'S POINT, THOUGH.

THESE GUYS ARE HERE TO KILL US.

SCARLET?

HEY, BABE.

EVERYTHING OKAY?

YOU ALL RIGHT?

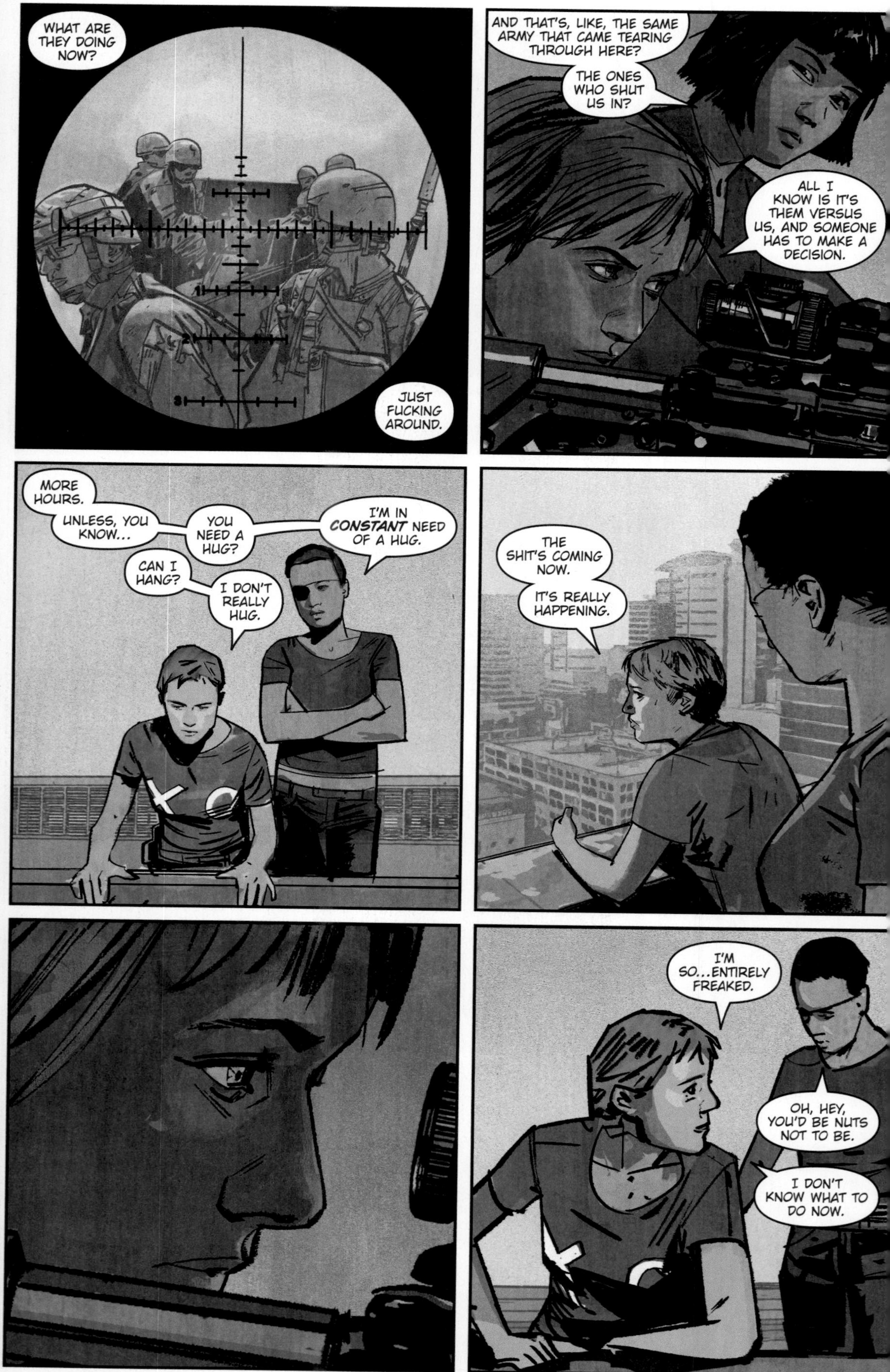
WHAT ARE THEY DOING NOW?
JUST FUCKING AROUND.
AND THAT'S, LIKE, THE SAME ARMY THAT CAME TEARING THROUGH HERE?
THE ONES WHO SHUT US IN?
ALL I KNOW IS IT'S THEM VERSUS US, AND SOMEONE HAS TO MAKE A DECISION.
MORE HOURS.
UNLESS, YOU KNOW...
YOU NEED A HUG?
I'M IN *CONSTANT* NEED OF A HUG.
CAN I HANG?
I DON'T REALLY HUG.
THE SHIT'S COMING NOW.
IT'S REALLY HAPPENING.
I'M SO...ENTIRELY FREAKED.
OH, HEY, YOU'D BE NUTS NOT TO BE.
I DON'T KNOW WHAT TO DO NOW.

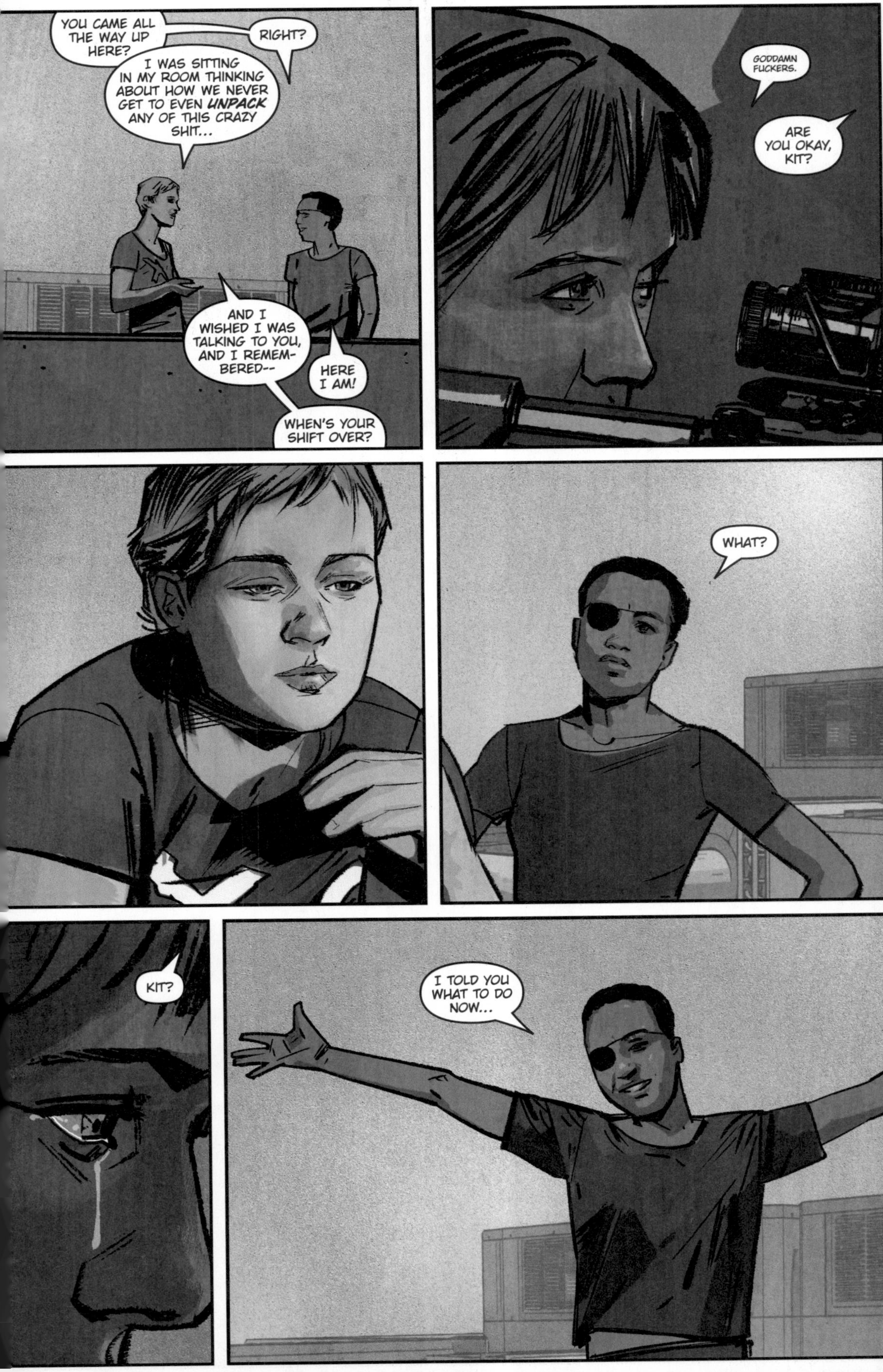
YOU CAME ALL THE WAY UP HERE?
RIGHT?
I WAS SITTING IN MY ROOM THINKING ABOUT HOW WE NEVER GET TO EVEN UNPACK ANY OF THIS CRAZY SHIT...
AND I WISHED I WAS TALKING TO YOU, AND I REMEMBERED--
HERE I AM!
WHEN'S YOUR SHIFT OVER?
GODDAMN FUCKERS.
ARE YOU OKAY, KIT?
WHAT?
KIT?
I TOLD YOU WHAT TO DO NOW...

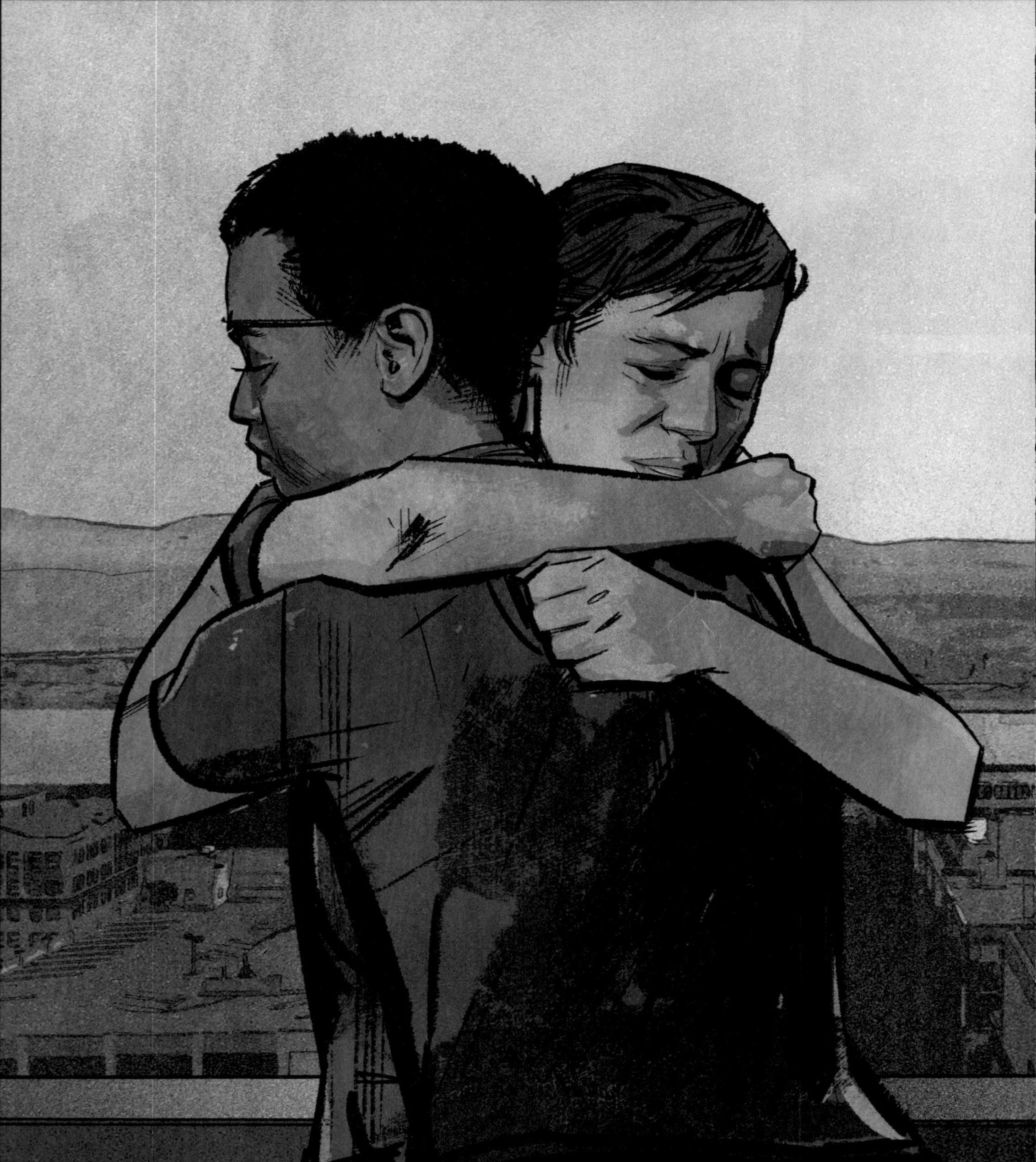

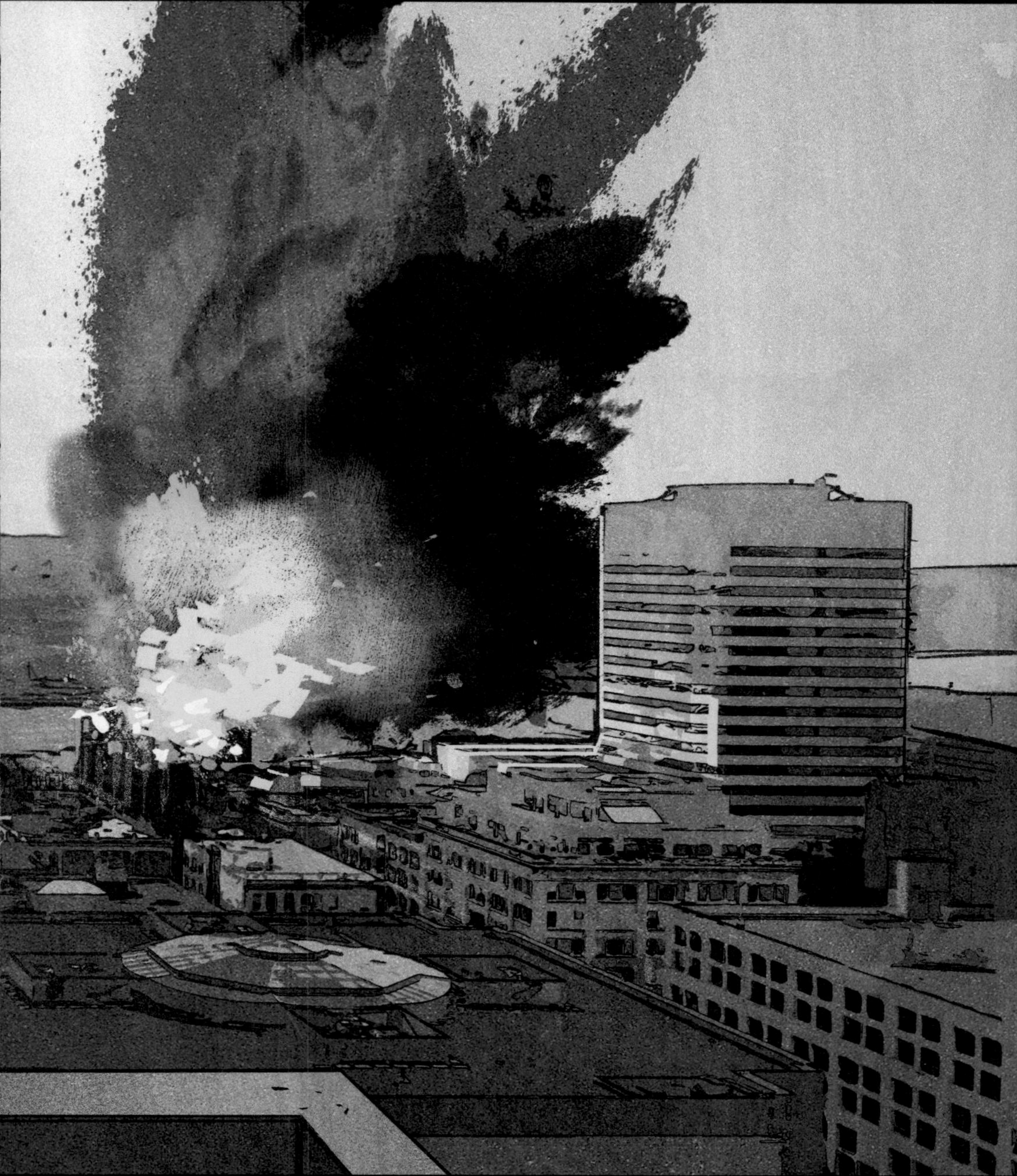

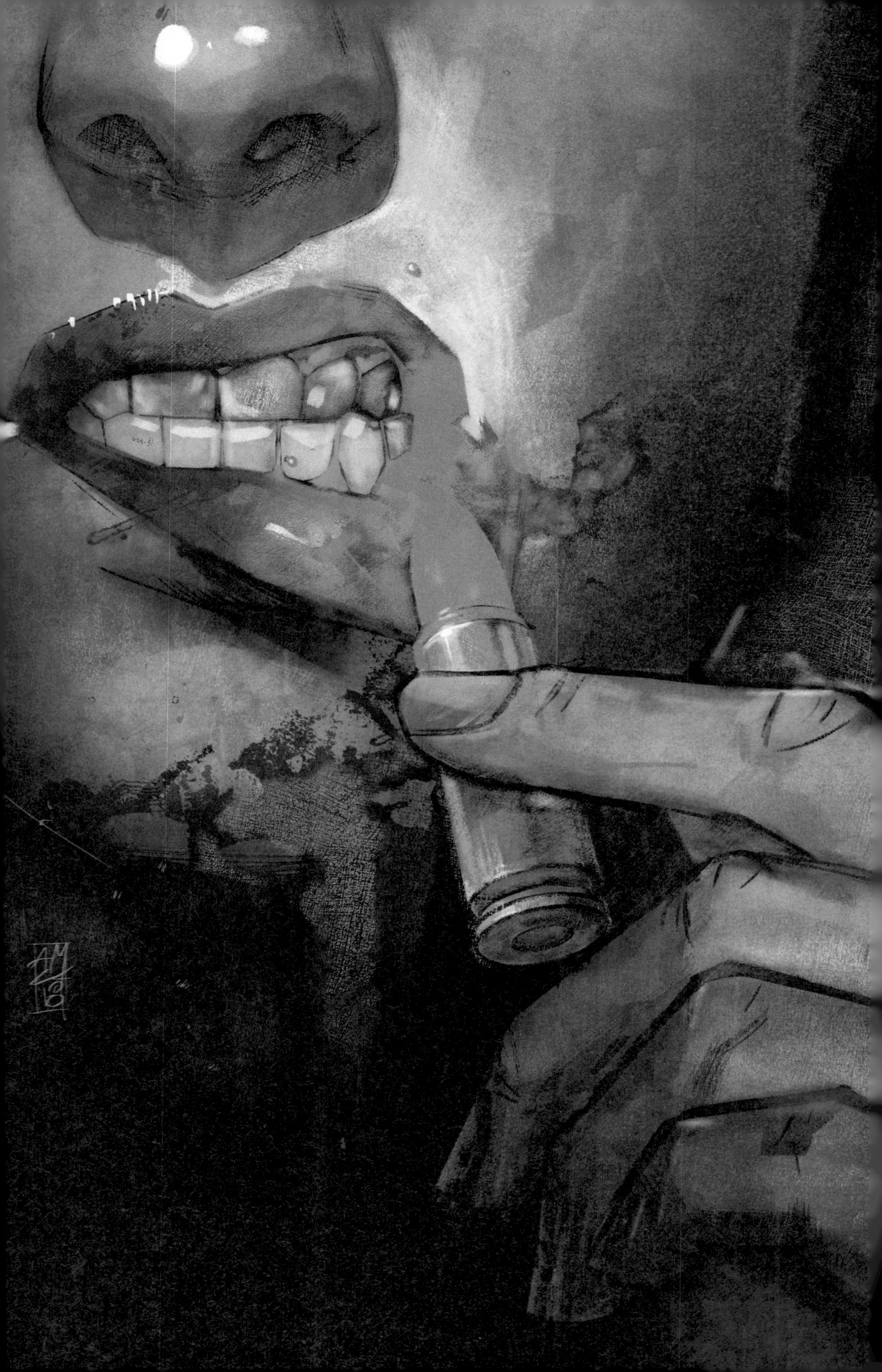

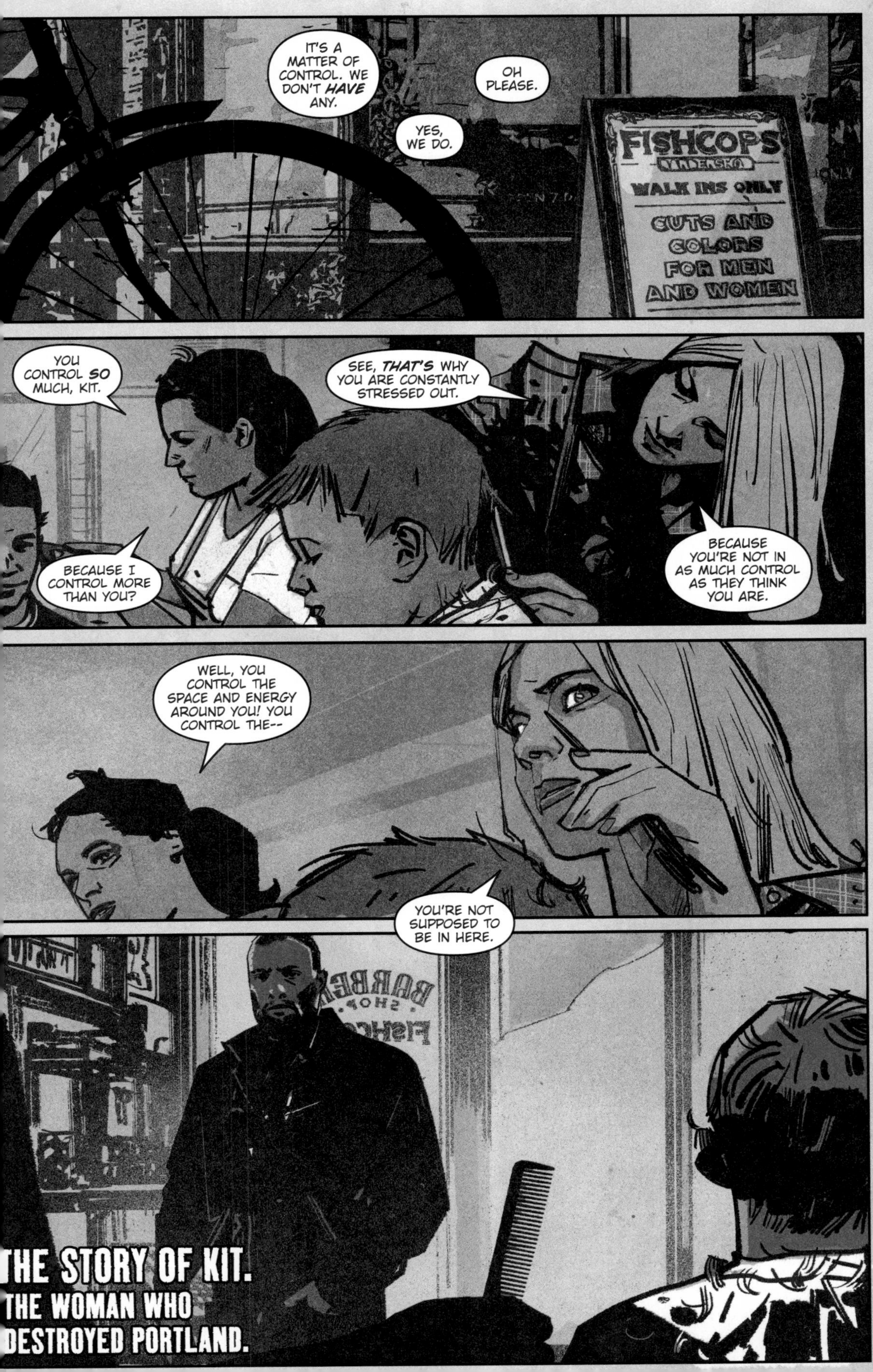
IT'S A MATTER OF CONTROL. WE DON'T HAVE ANY.
OH PLEASE.
YES, WE DO.
FISHCOPS
WALK INS ONLY
CUTS AND COLORS FOR MEN AND WOMEN
YOU CONTROL SO MUCH, KIT.
SEE, THAT'S WHY YOU ARE CONSTANTLY STRESSED OUT.
BECAUSE I CONTROL MORE THAN YOU?
BECAUSE YOU'RE NOT IN AS MUCH CONTROL AS THEY THINK YOU ARE.
WELL, YOU CONTROL THE SPACE AND ENERGY AROUND YOU! YOU CONTROL THE--
YOU'RE NOT SUPPOSED TO BE IN HERE.
BARBER SHOP FISHCOPS
THE STORY OF KIT.
THE WOMAN WHO DESTROYED PORTLAND.

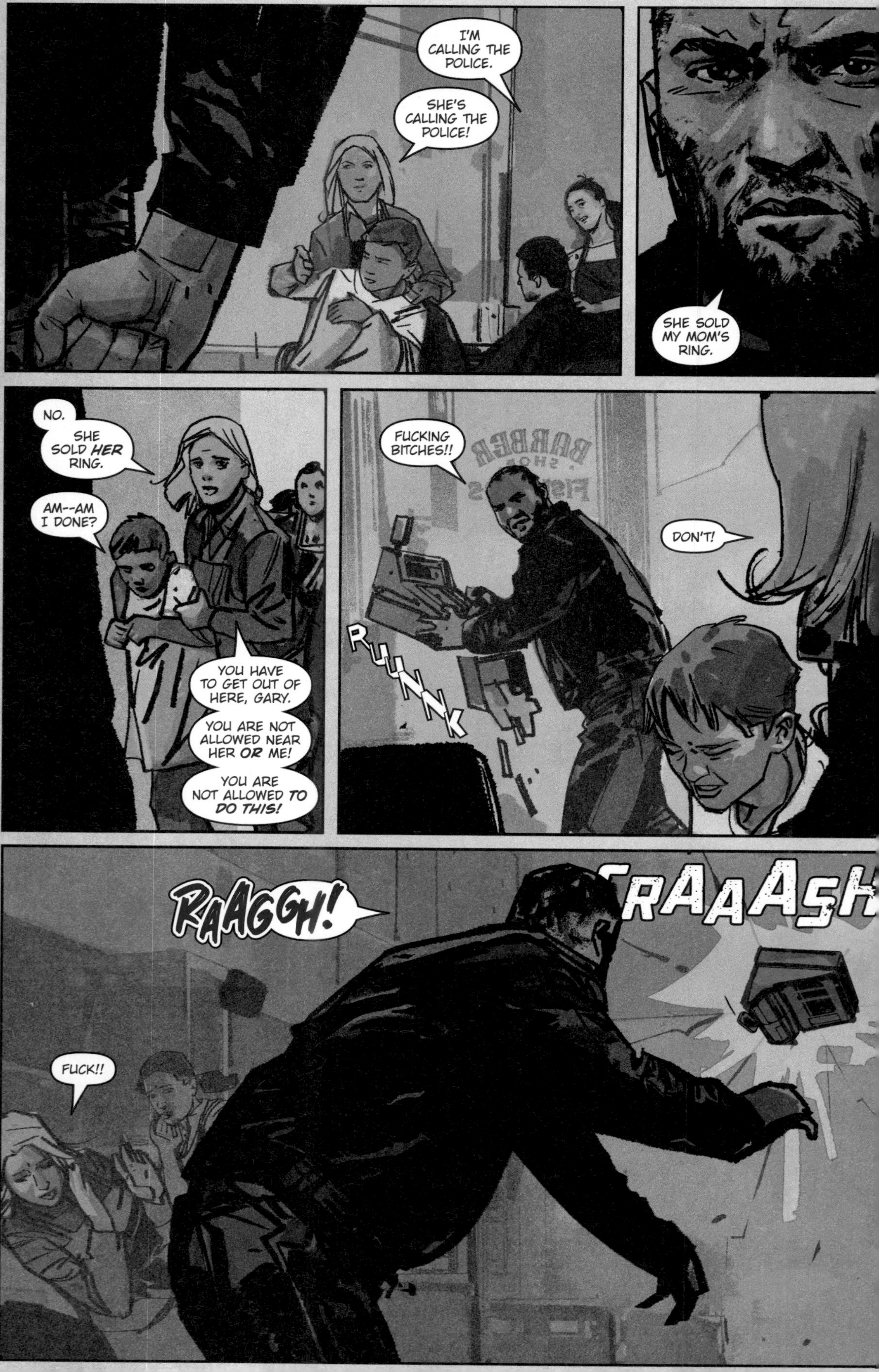

I'M CALLING THE POLICE.
SHE'S CALLING THE POLICE!
SHE SOLD MY MOM'S RING.
NO.
SHE SOLD HER RING.
AM--AM I DONE?
YOU HAVE TO GET OUT OF HERE, GARY.
YOU ARE NOT ALLOWED NEAR HER OR ME!
YOU ARE NOT ALLOWED TO DO THIS!
FUCKING BITCHES!!
BARBER SHOP
RUUNNK
DON'T!
RAAGGH!
CRAAASH
FUCK!!

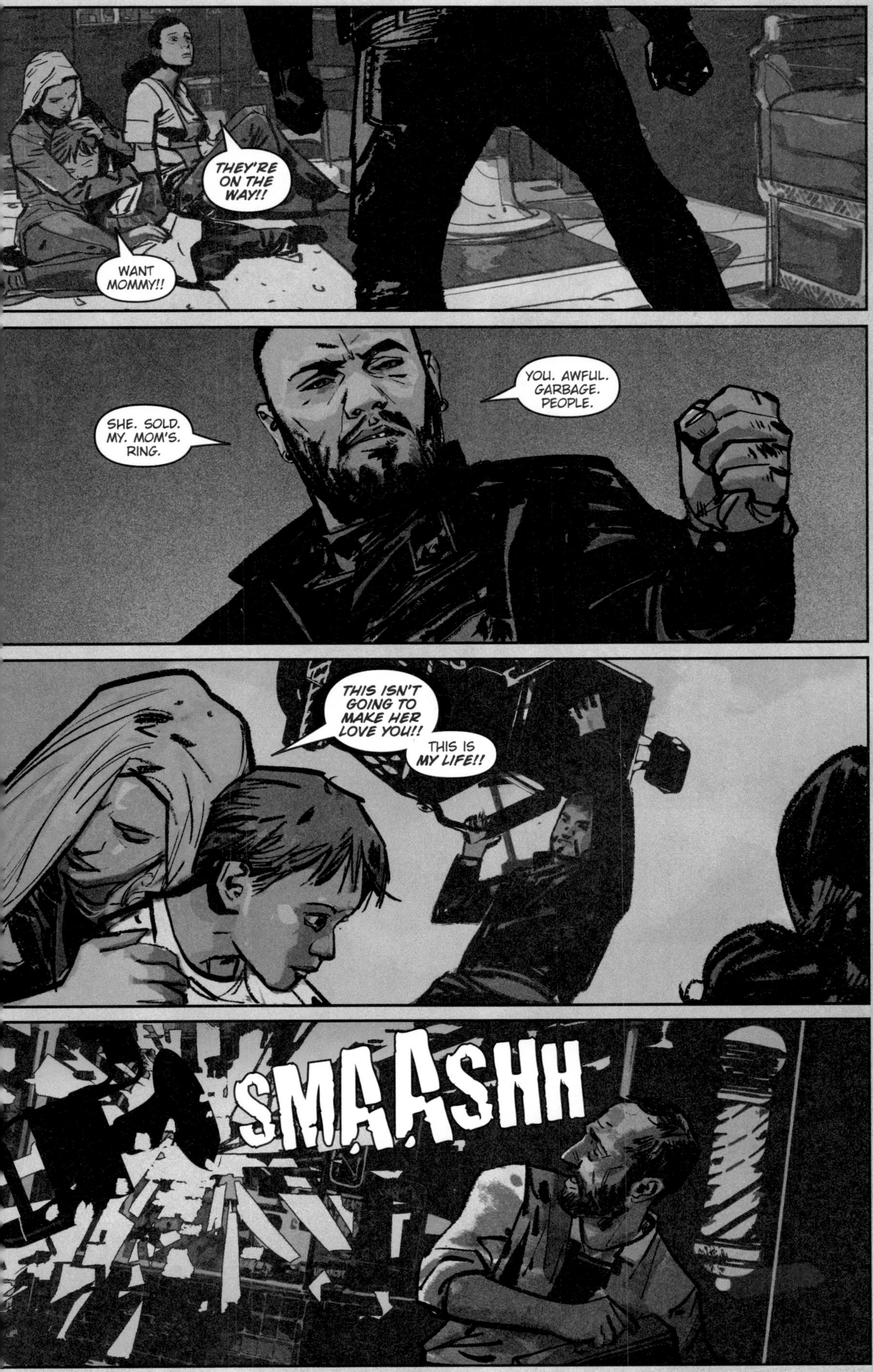
THEY'RE ON THE WAY!!
WANT MOMMY!!
SHE. SOLD. MY. MOM'S. RING.
YOU. AWFUL. GARBAGE. PEOPLE.
THIS ISN'T GOING TO MAKE HER LOVE YOU!!
THIS IS MY LIFE!!
SMAASHH

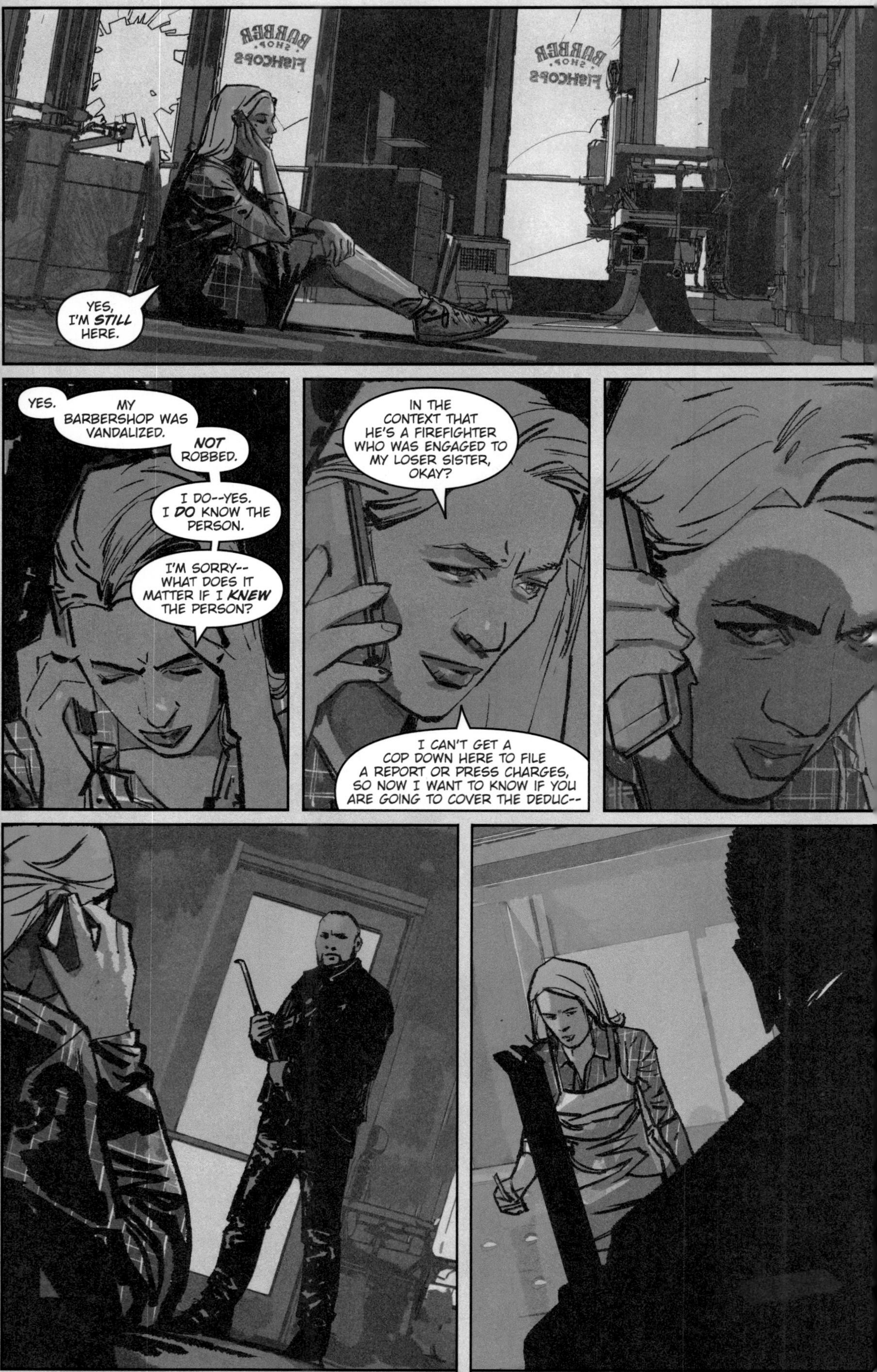
BARBER SHOP FISHCOPS
YES, I'M STILL HERE.
YES.
MY BARBERSHOP WAS VANDALIZED.
NOT ROBBED.
I DO--YES. I DO KNOW THE PERSON.
I'M SORRY-- WHAT DOES IT MATTER IF I KNEW THE PERSON?
IN THE CONTEXT THAT HE'S A FIREFIGHTER WHO WAS ENGAGED TO MY LOSER SISTER, OKAY?
I CAN'T GET A COP DOWN HERE TO FILE A REPORT OR PRESS CHARGES, SO NOW I WANT TO KNOW IF YOU ARE GOING TO COVER THE DEDUC--

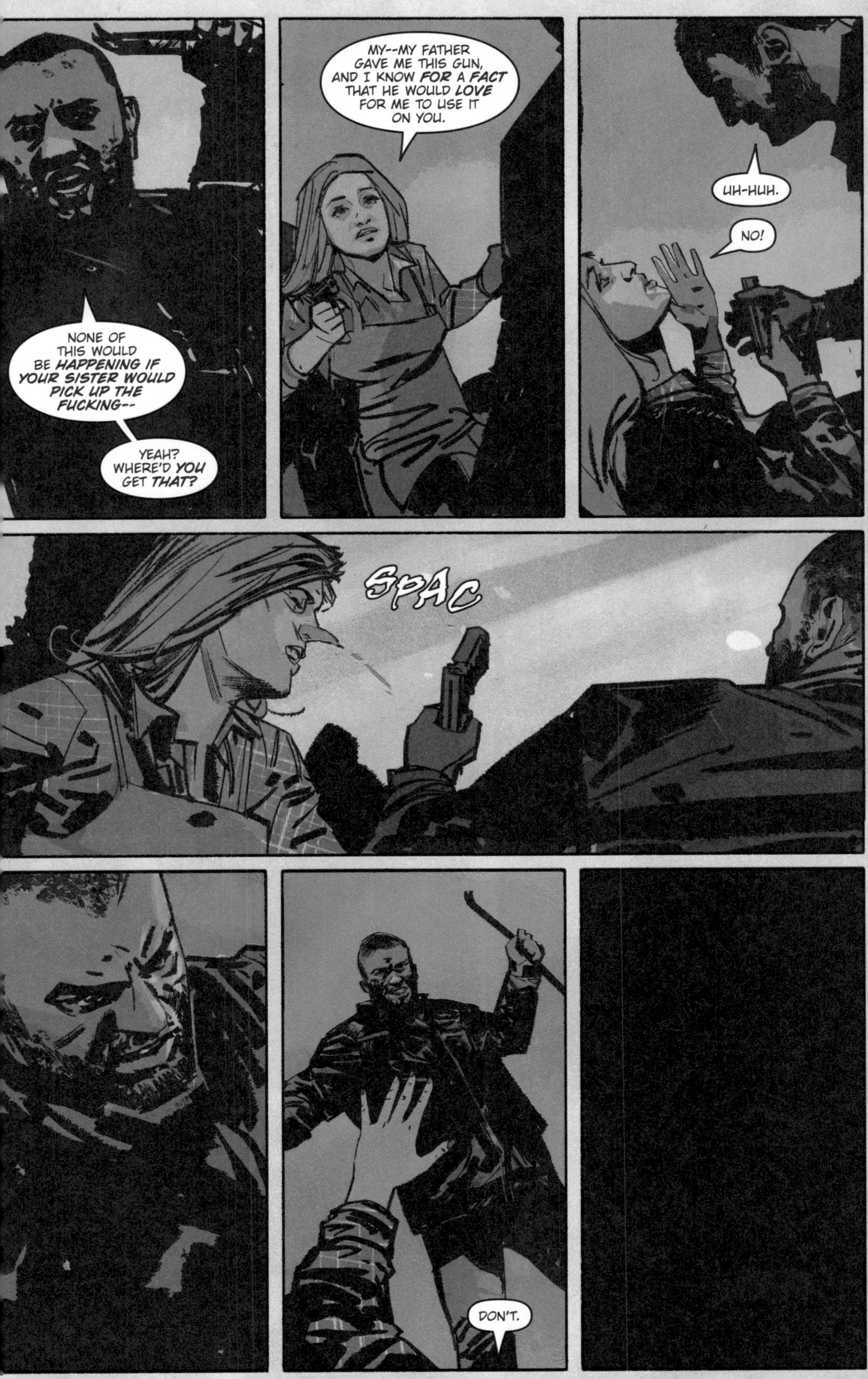
MY--MY FATHER GAVE ME THIS GUN, AND I KNOW FOR A FACT THAT HE WOULD LOVE FOR ME TO USE IT ON YOU.
NONE OF THIS WOULD BE HAPPENING IF YOUR SISTER WOULD PICK UP THE FUCKING--
YEAH? WHERE'D YOU GET THAT?
UH-HUH.
NO!
SPAC
DON'T.

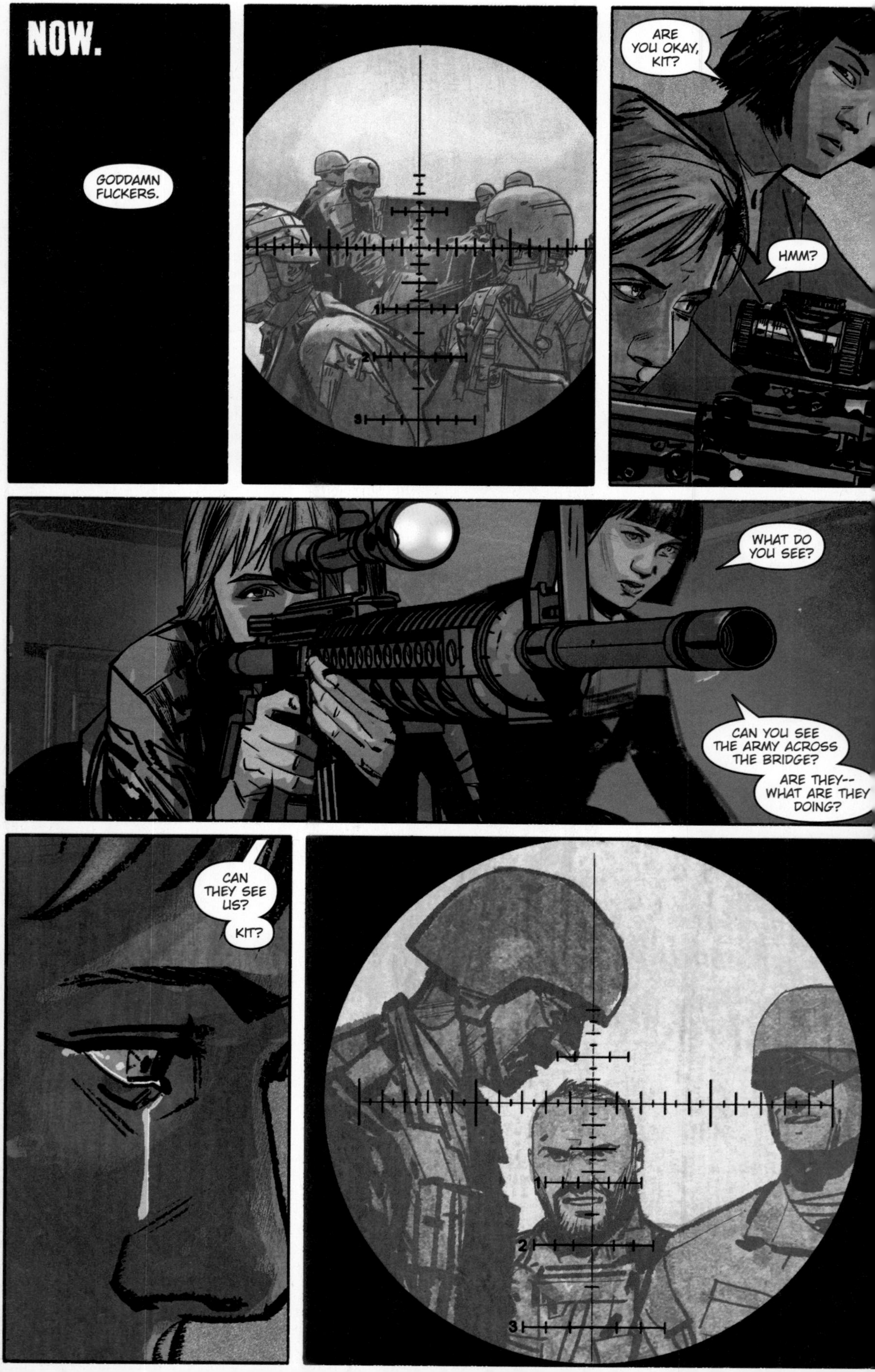
NOW.
GODDAMN FUCKERS.
1
2
3
ARE YOU OKAY, KIT?
HMM?
WHAT DO YOU SEE?
CAN YOU SEE THE ARMY ACROSS THE BRIDGE?
ARE THEY-- WHAT ARE THEY DOING?
CAN THEY SEE US?
KIT?
1
2
3

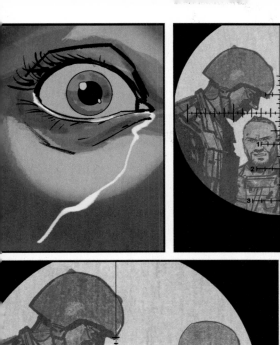

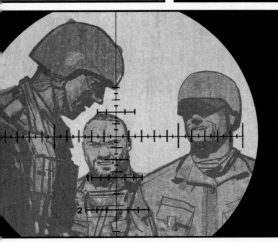

KIT!! WHAT DID YOU JUST DO?!

WHAT?

YOU JUST-- YOU JUST *FIRED THE GUN!!*

NO, I DIDN'T.

KIT.

OH... OH MY GOD...

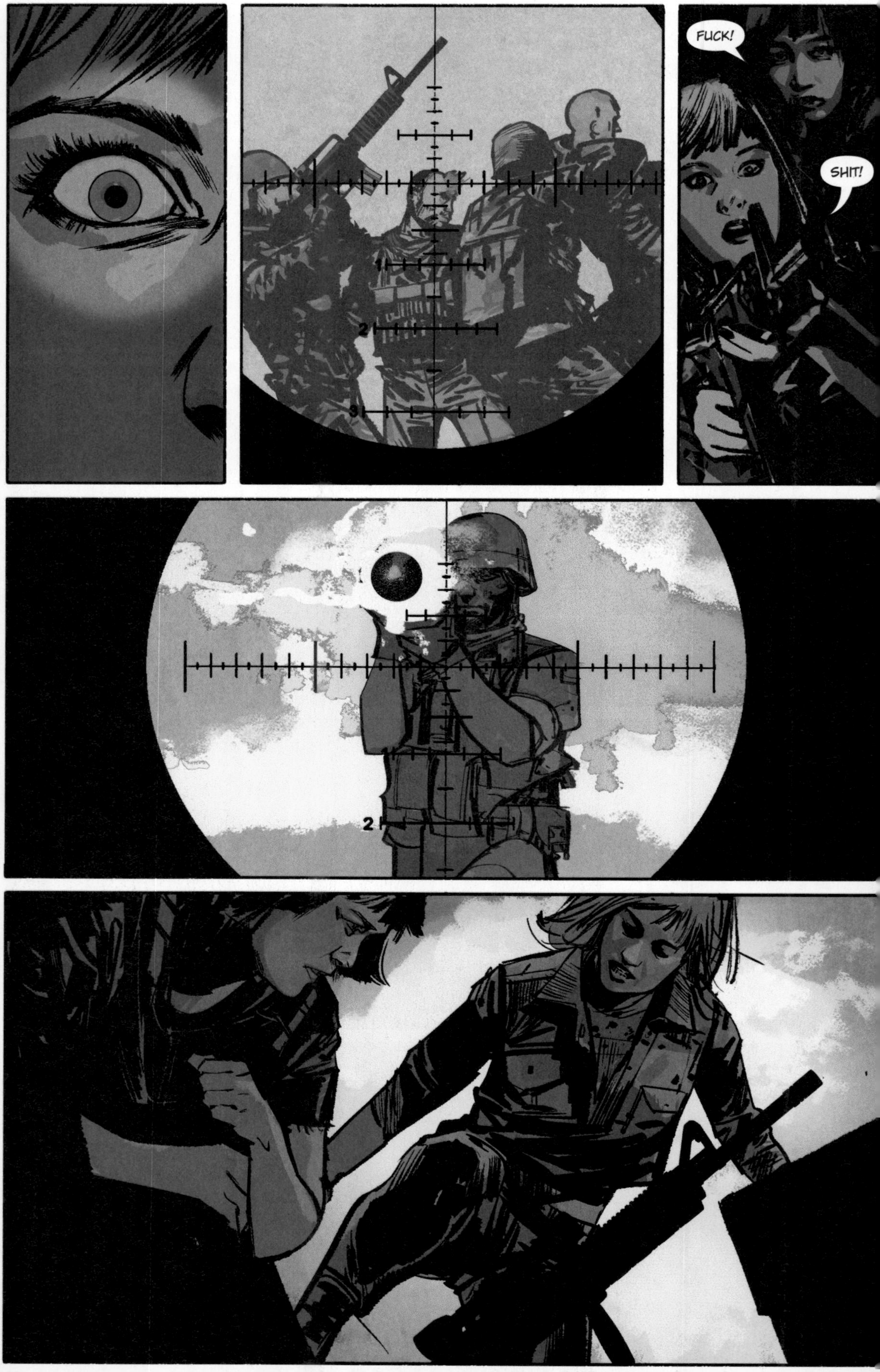
FUCK!
SHIT!

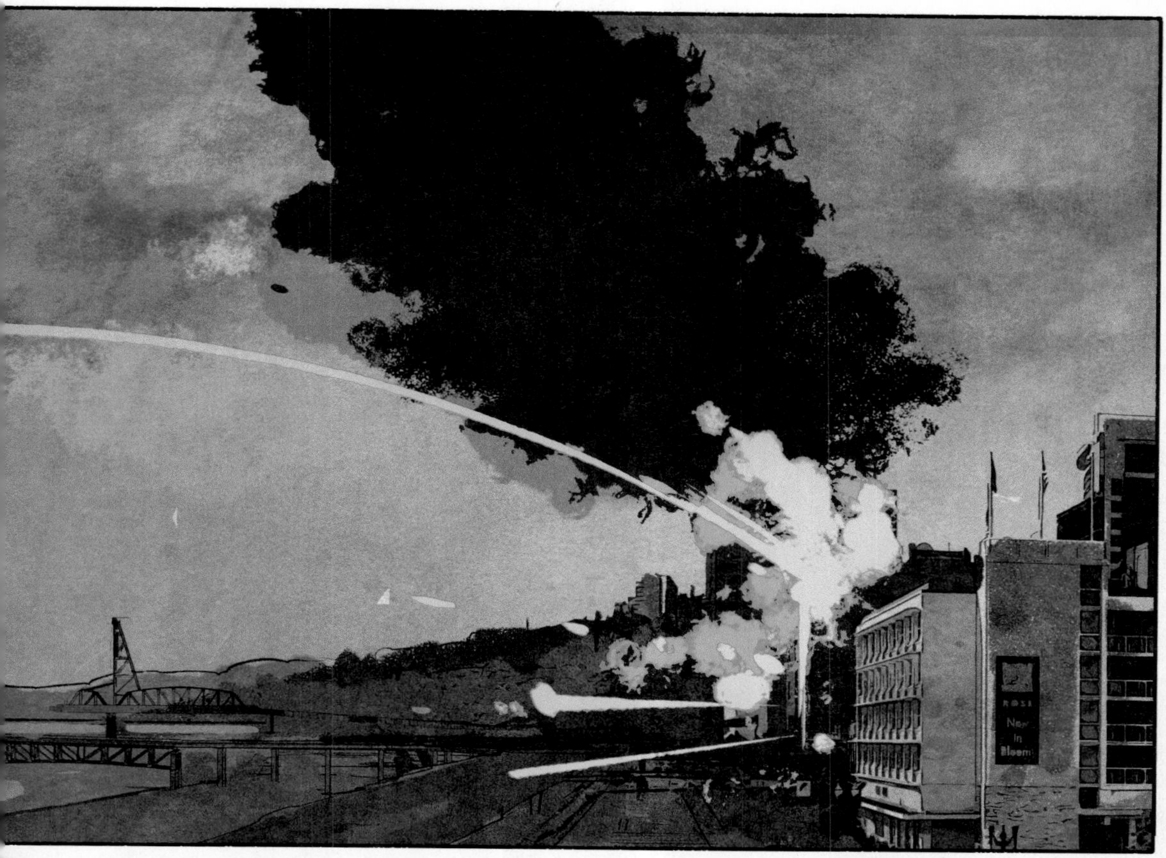

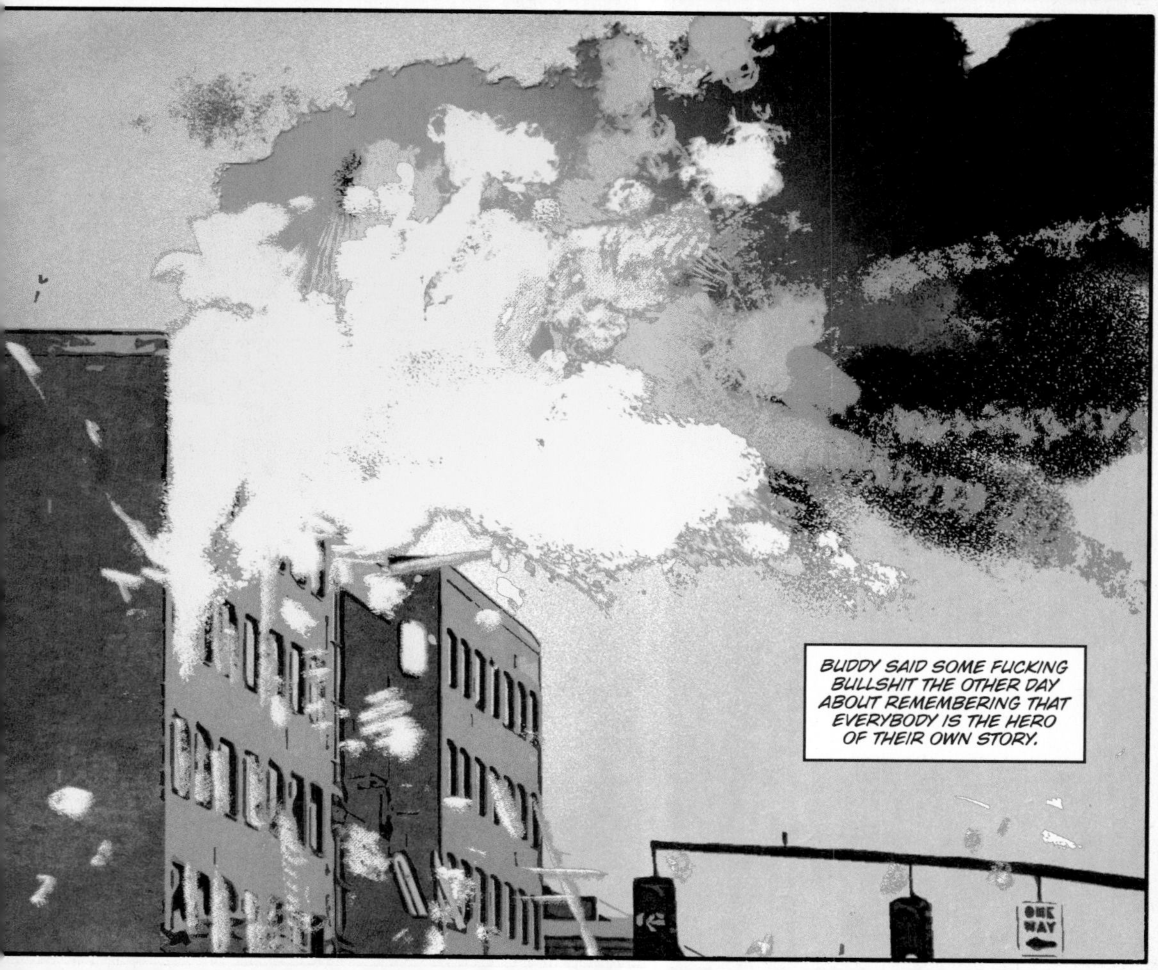
BUDDY SAID SOME FUCKING BULLSHIT THE OTHER DAY ABOUT REMEMBERING THAT EVERYBODY IS THE HERO OF THEIR OWN STORY.
ONE WAY

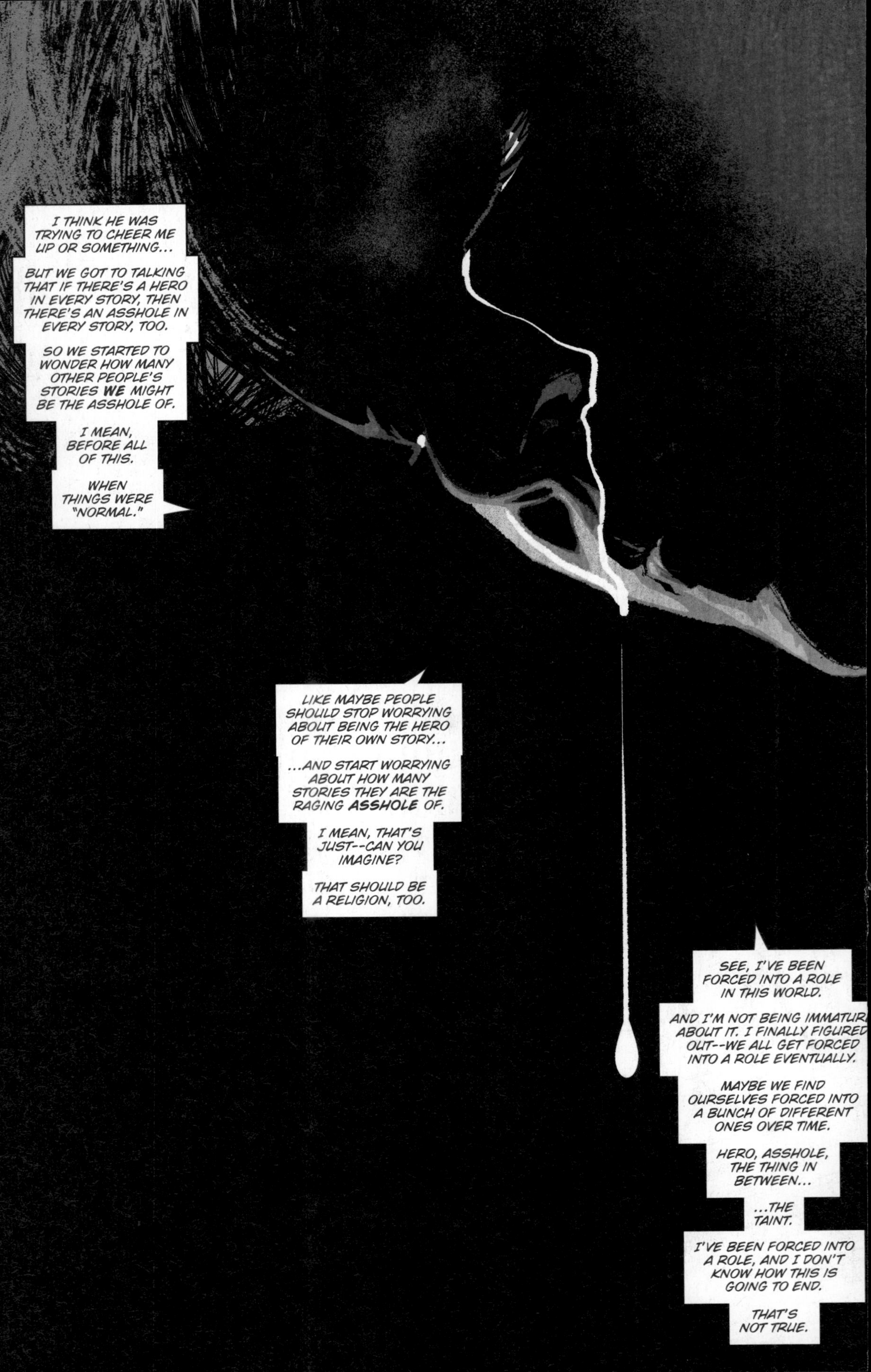
I THINK HE WAS TRYING TO CHEER ME UP OR SOMETHING...
BUT WE GOT TO TALKING THAT IF THERE'S A HERO IN EVERY STORY, THEN THERE'S AN ASSHOLE IN EVERY STORY, TOO.
SO WE STARTED TO WONDER HOW MANY OTHER PEOPLE'S STORIES **WE** MIGHT BE THE ASSHOLE OF.
I MEAN, BEFORE ALL OF THIS.
WHEN THINGS WERE "NORMAL."
LIKE MAYBE PEOPLE SHOULD STOP WORRYING ABOUT BEING THE HERO OF THEIR OWN STORY...
...AND START WORRYING ABOUT HOW MANY STORIES THEY ARE THE RAGING **ASSHOLE** OF.
I MEAN, THAT'S JUST--CAN YOU IMAGINE?
THAT SHOULD BE A RELIGION, TOO.
SEE, I'VE BEEN FORCED INTO A ROLE IN THIS WORLD.
AND I'M NOT BEING IMMATURE ABOUT IT. I FINALLY FIGURED OUT--WE ALL GET FORCED INTO A ROLE EVENTUALLY.
MAYBE WE FIND OURSELVES FORCED INTO A BUNCH OF DIFFERENT ONES OVER TIME.
HERO, ASSHOLE, THE THING IN BETWEEN...
...THE TAINT.
I'VE BEEN FORCED INTO A ROLE, AND I DON'T KNOW HOW THIS IS GOING TO END.
THAT'S NOT TRUE.

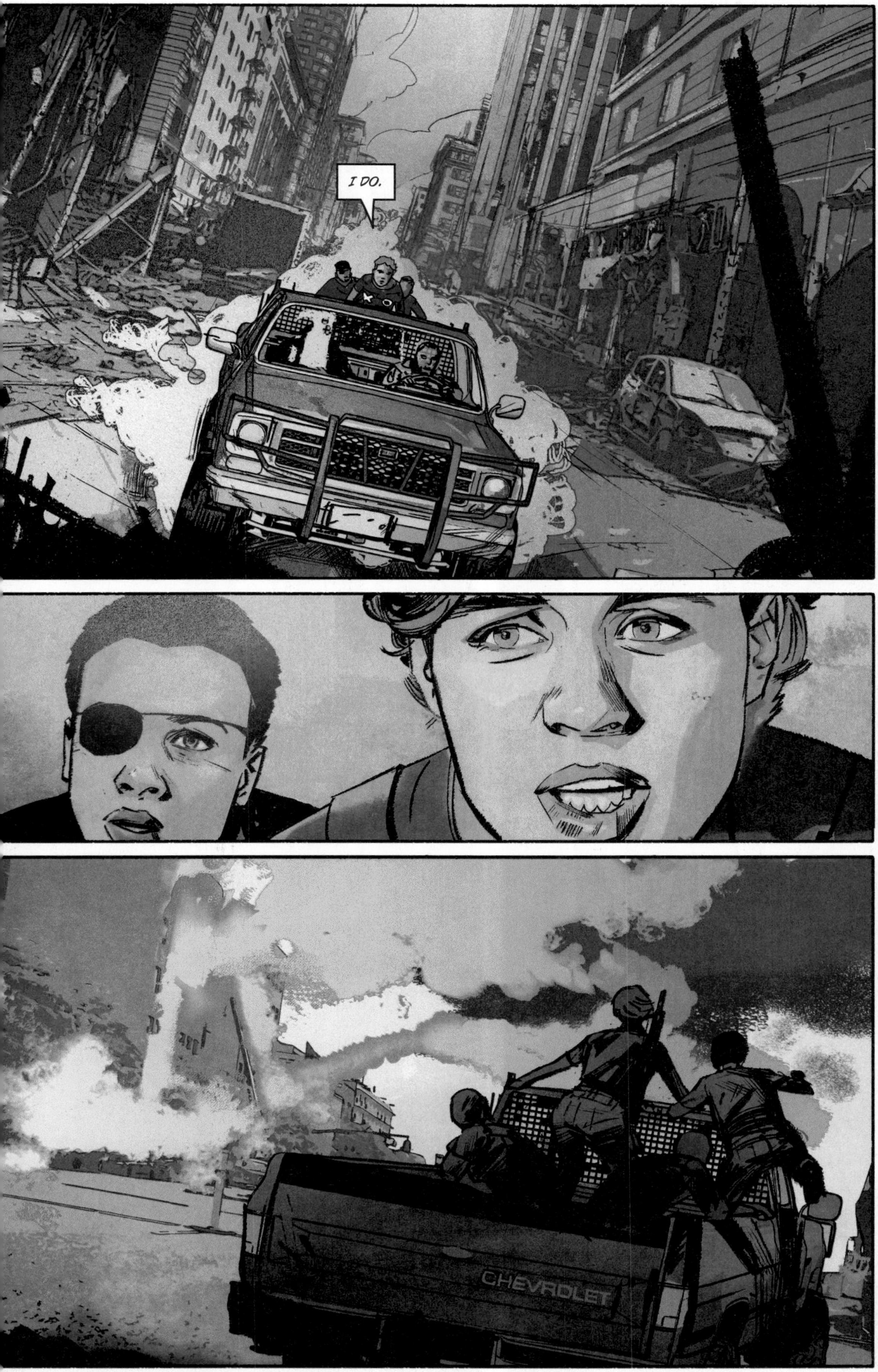
I DO.
CHEVROLET

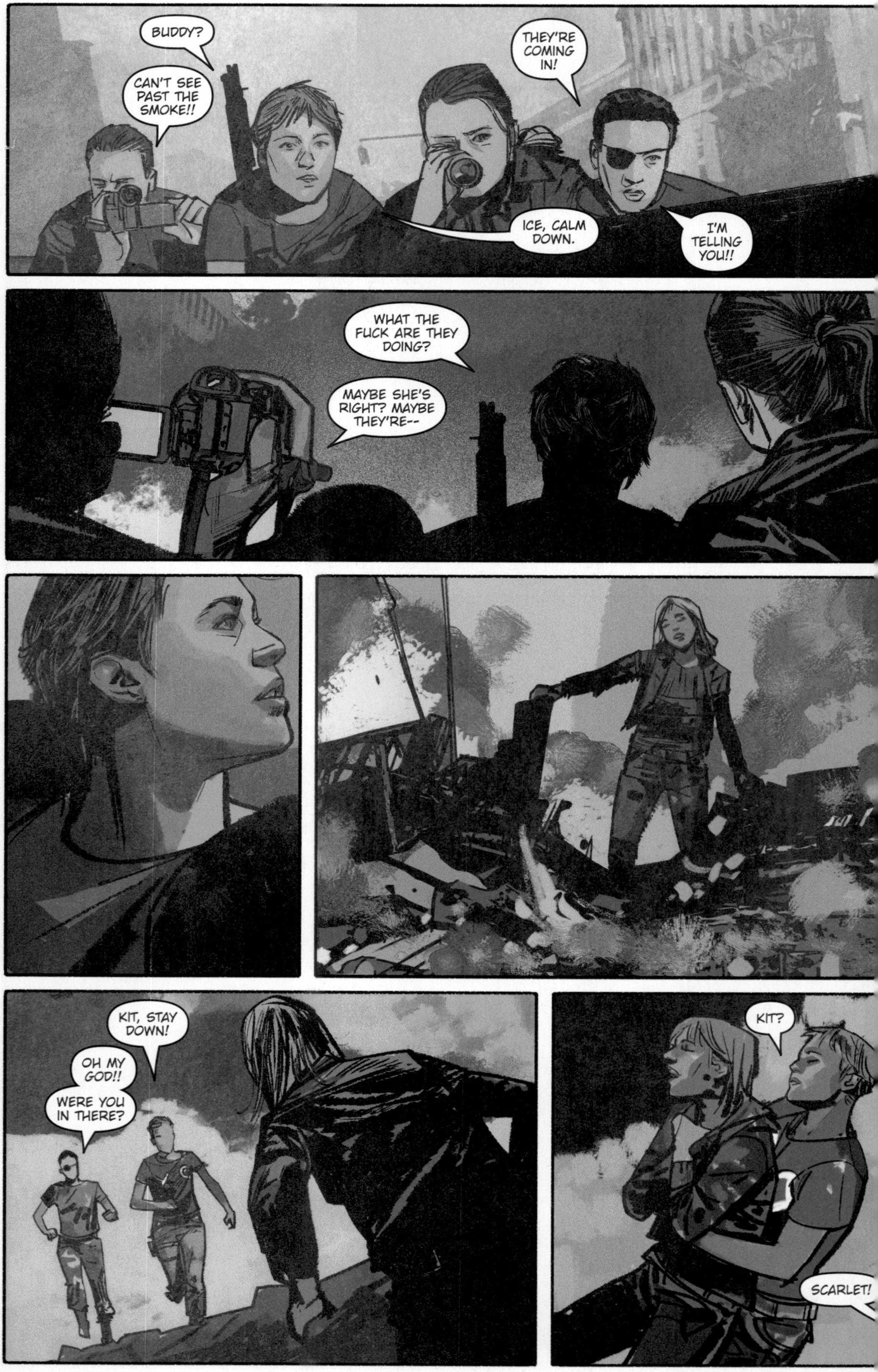
BUDDY?
CAN'T SEE PAST THE SMOKE!!
THEY'RE COMING IN!
ICE, CALM DOWN.
I'M TELLING YOU!!
WHAT THE FUCK ARE THEY DOING?
MAYBE SHE'S RIGHT? MAYBE THEY'RE--
KIT, STAY DOWN!
OH MY GOD!!
WERE YOU IN THERE?
KIT?
SCARLET!

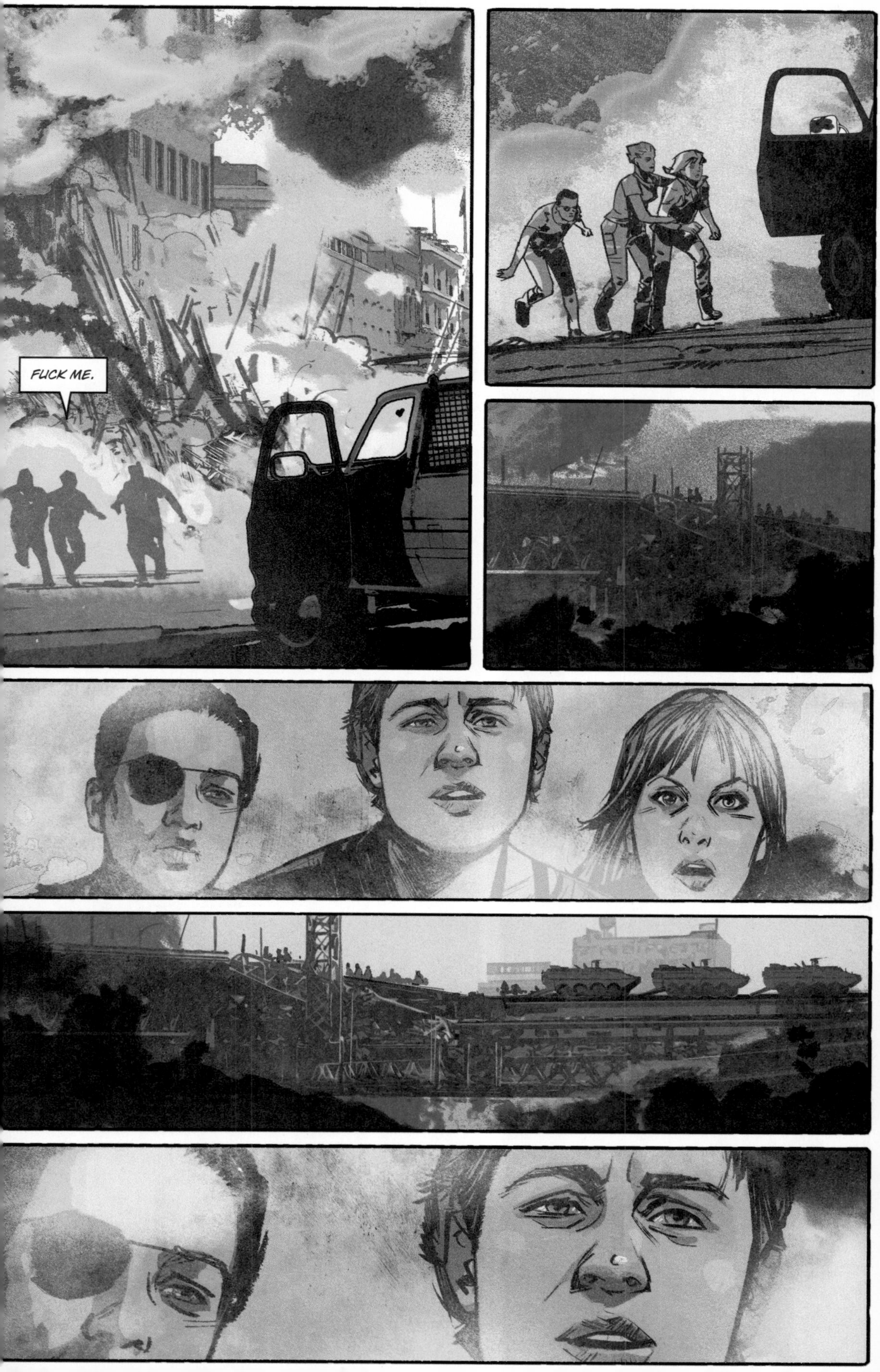
FUCK ME.

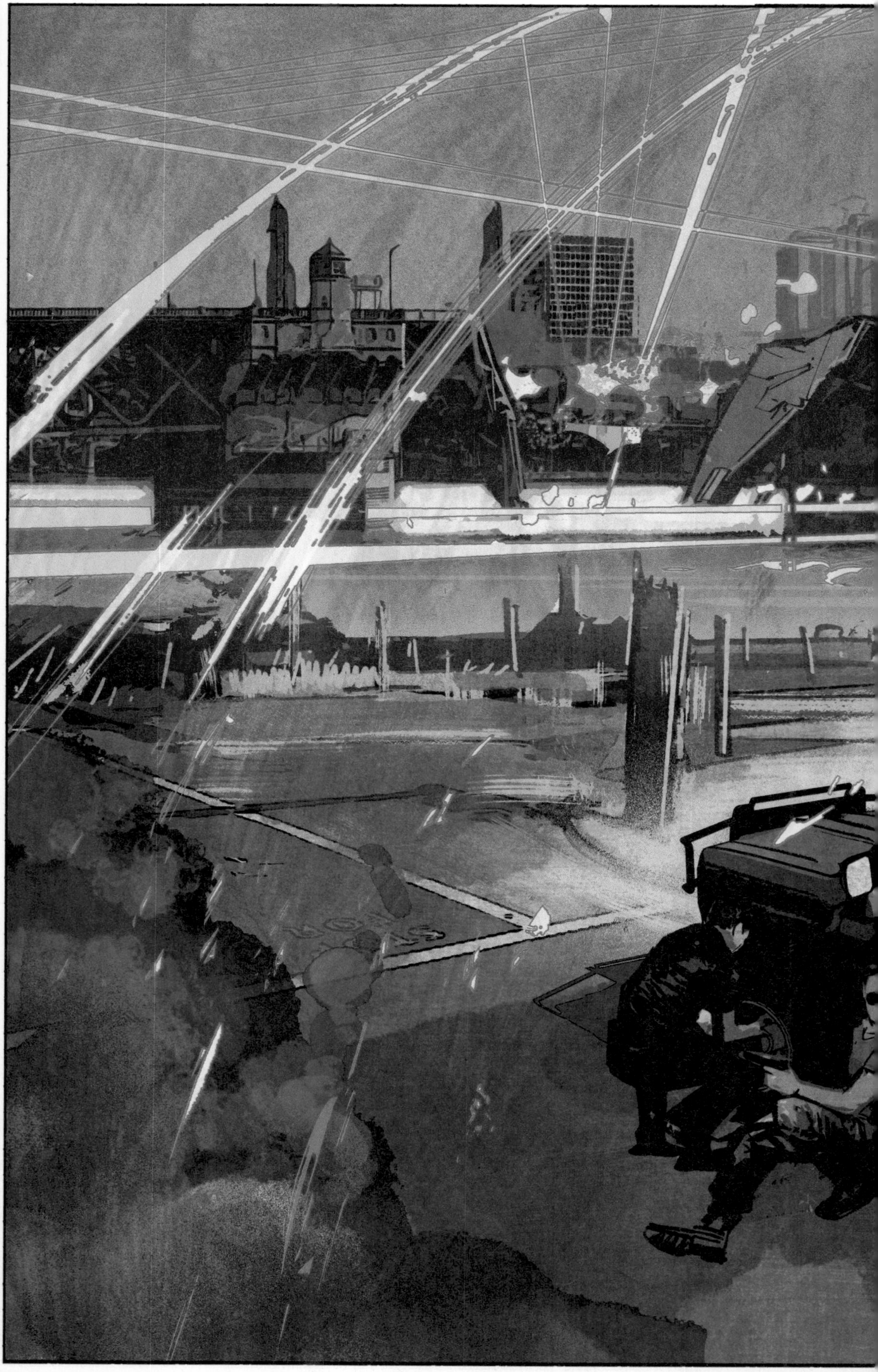

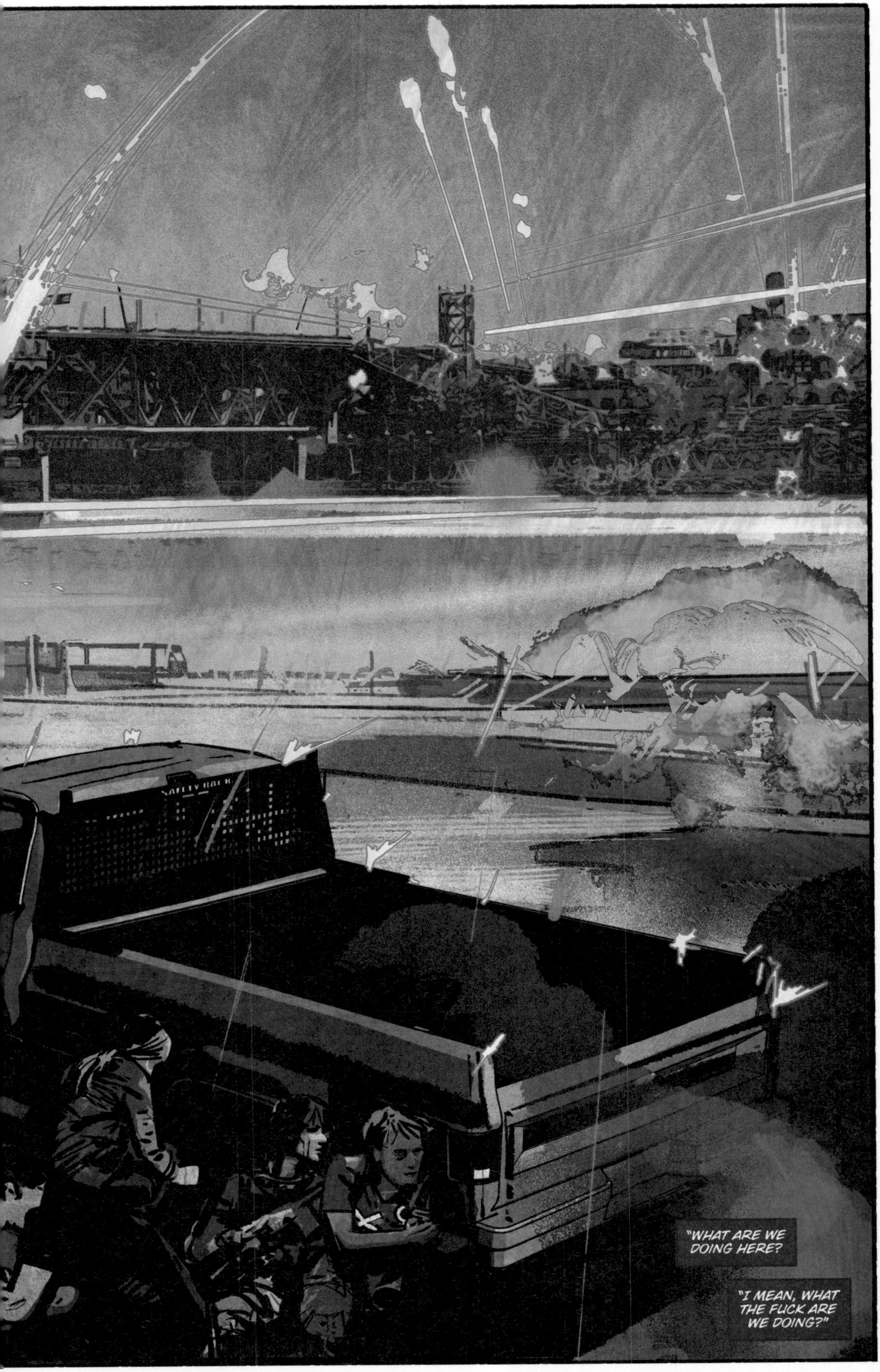
"WHAT ARE WE DOING HERE?
"I MEAN, WHAT THE FUCK ARE WE DOING?"

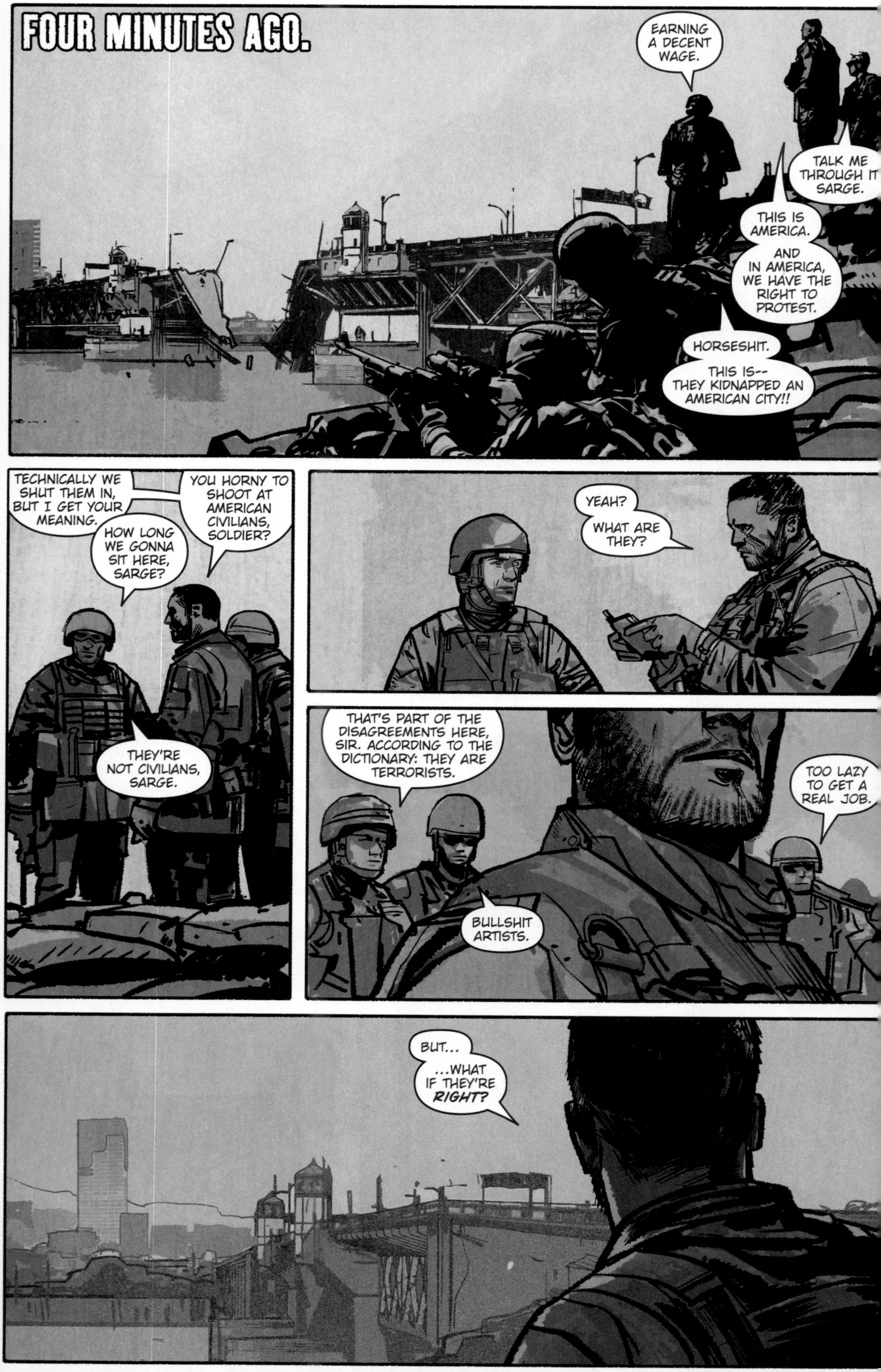
FOUR MINUTES AGO.
EARNING A DECENT WAGE.
TALK ME THROUGH IT SARGE.
THIS IS AMERICA.
AND IN AMERICA, WE HAVE THE RIGHT TO PROTEST.
HORSESHIT.
THIS IS-- THEY KIDNAPPED AN AMERICAN CITY!!
TECHNICALLY WE SHUT THEM IN, BUT I GET YOUR MEANING.
YOU HORNY TO SHOOT AT AMERICAN CIVILIANS, SOLDIER?
HOW LONG WE GONNA SIT HERE, SARGE?
THEY'RE NOT CIVILIANS, SARGE.
YEAH?
WHAT ARE THEY?
THAT'S PART OF THE DISAGREEMENTS HERE, SIR. ACCORDING TO THE DICTIONARY: THEY ARE TERRORISTS.
TOO LAZY TO GET A REAL JOB.
BULLSHIT ARTISTS.
BUT...
...WHAT IF THEY'RE *RIGHT?*

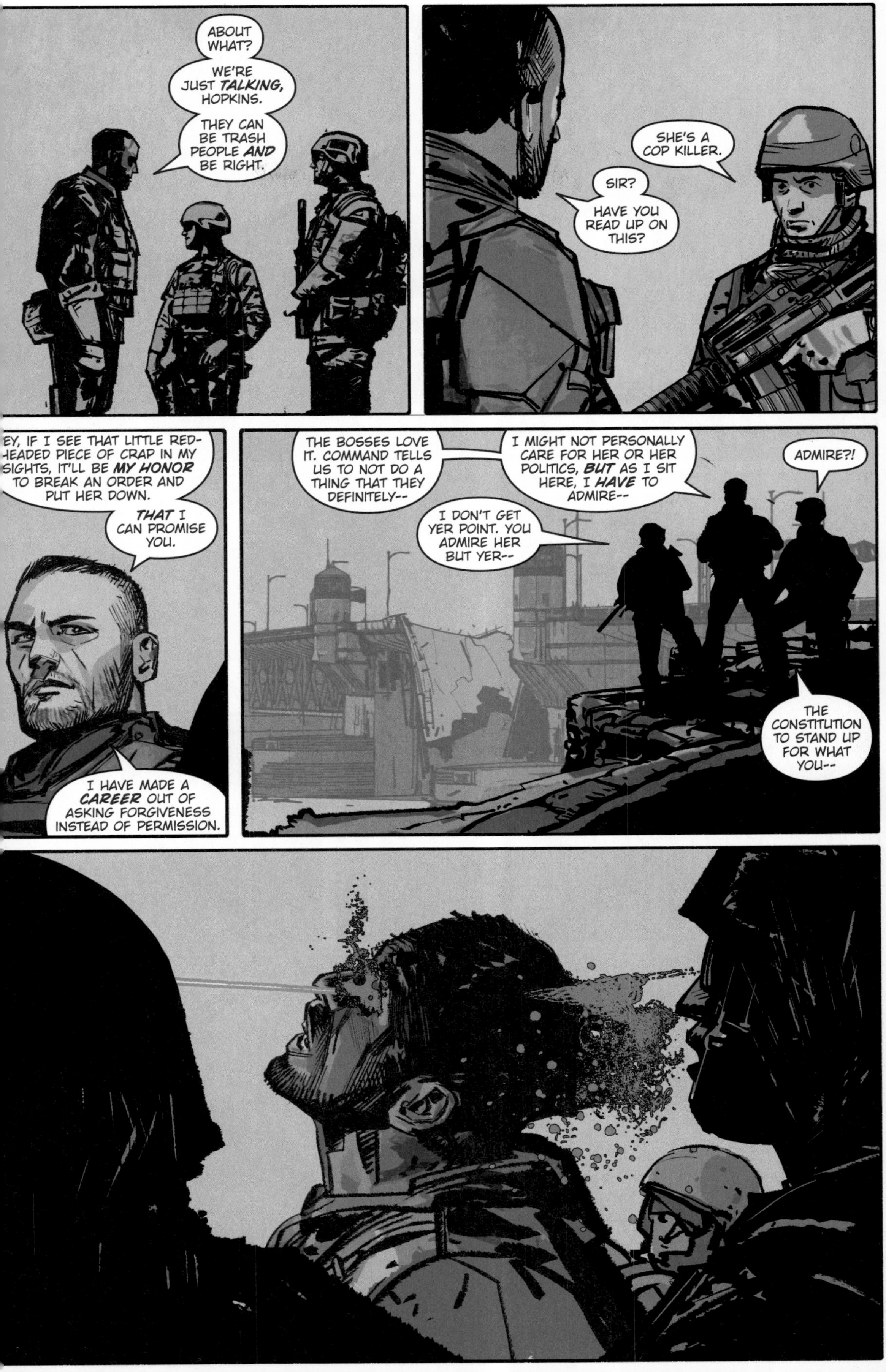
ABOUT WHAT?
WE'RE JUST TALKING, HOPKINS.
THEY CAN BE TRASH PEOPLE AND BE RIGHT.
SHE'S A COP KILLER.
SIR?
HAVE YOU READ UP ON THIS?
EY, IF I SEE THAT LITTLE RED-HEADED PIECE OF CRAP IN MY SIGHTS, IT'LL BE MY HONOR TO BREAK AN ORDER AND PUT HER DOWN.
THAT I CAN PROMISE YOU.
I HAVE MADE A CAREER OUT OF ASKING FORGIVENESS INSTEAD OF PERMISSION.
THE BOSSES LOVE IT. COMMAND TELLS US TO NOT DO A THING THAT THEY DEFINITELY--
I MIGHT NOT PERSONALLY CARE FOR HER OR HER POLITICS, BUT AS I SIT HERE, I HAVE TO ADMIRE--
ADMIRE?!
I DON'T GET YER POINT. YOU ADMIRE HER BUT YER--
THE CONSTITUTION TO STAND UP FOR WHAT YOU--

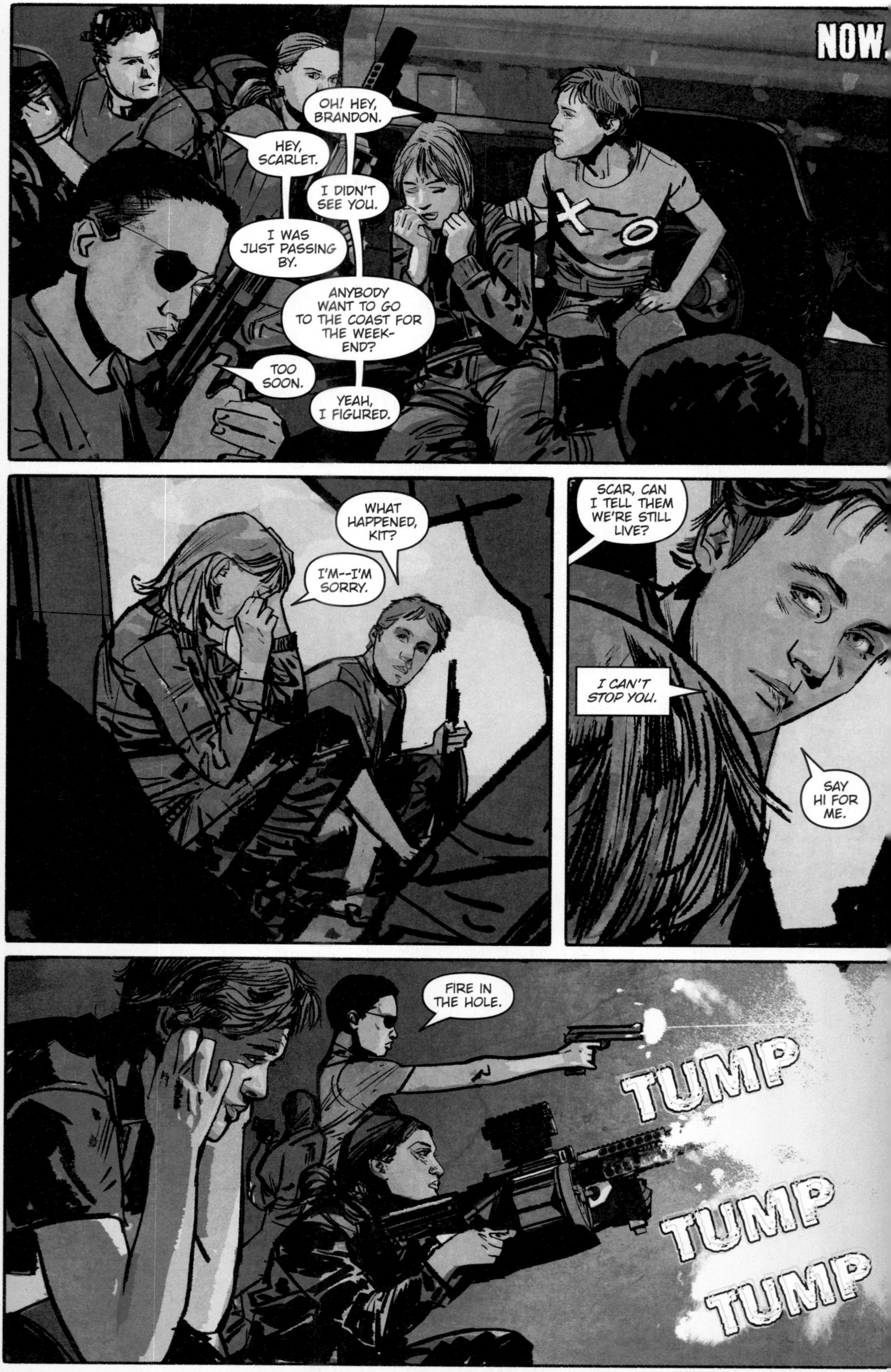
NOW.
HEY, SCARLET.
OH! HEY, BRANDON.
I DIDN'T SEE YOU.
I WAS JUST PASSING BY.
ANYBODY WANT TO GO TO THE COAST FOR THE WEEK-END?
TOO SOON.
YEAH, I FIGURED.
WHAT HAPPENED, KIT?
I'M--I'M SORRY.
SCAR, CAN I TELL THEM WE'RE STILL LIVE?
I CAN'T STOP YOU.
SAY HI FOR ME.
FIRE IN THE HOLE.
TUMP
TUMP
TUMP

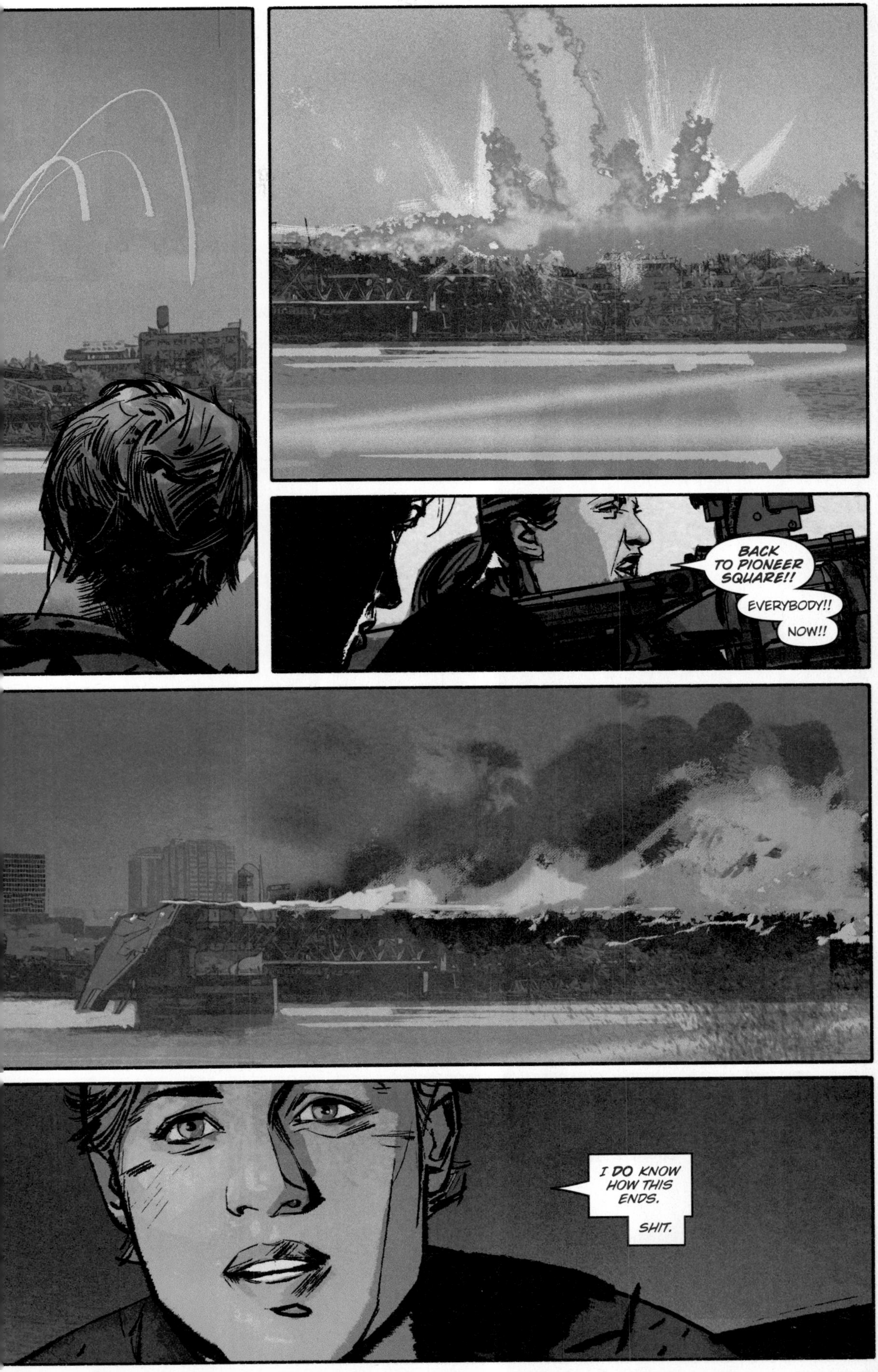
BACK TO PIONEER SQUARE!!
EVERYBODY!!
NOW!!
I DO KNOW HOW THIS ENDS.
SHIT.

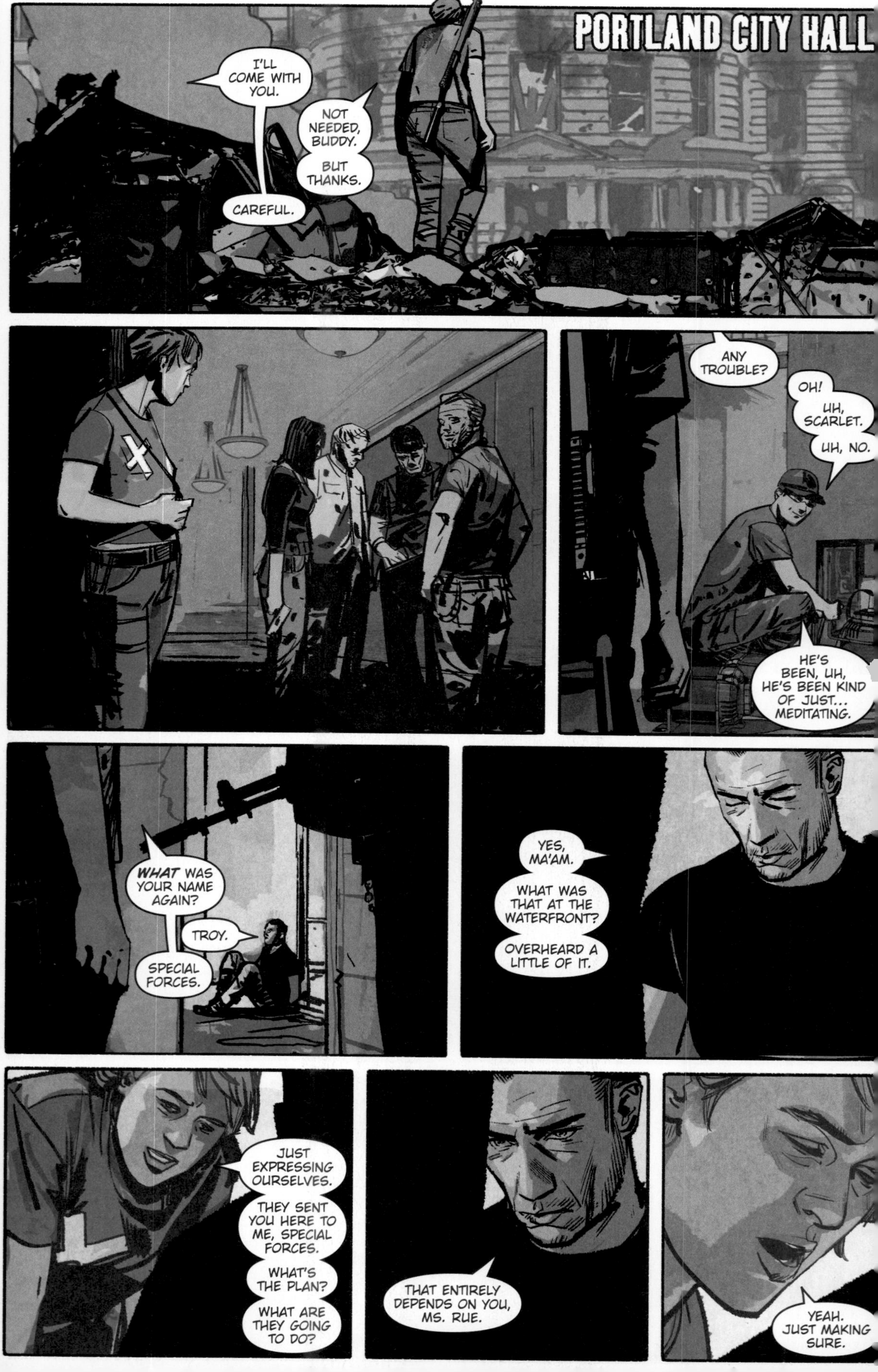
PORTLAND CITY HALL
I'LL COME WITH YOU.
NOT NEEDED, BUDDY.
BUT THANKS.
CAREFUL.
ANY TROUBLE?
OH!
UH, SCARLET.
UH, NO.
HE'S BEEN, UH, HE'S BEEN KIND OF JUST... MEDITATING.
WHAT WAS YOUR NAME AGAIN?
TROY.
SPECIAL FORCES.
YES, MA'AM.
WHAT WAS THAT AT THE WATERFRONT?
OVERHEARD A LITTLE OF IT.
JUST EXPRESSING OURSELVES.
THEY SENT YOU HERE TO ME, SPECIAL FORCES.
WHAT'S THE PLAN?
WHAT ARE THEY GOING TO DO?
THAT ENTIRELY DEPENDS ON YOU, MS. RUE.
YEAH. JUST MAKING SURE.

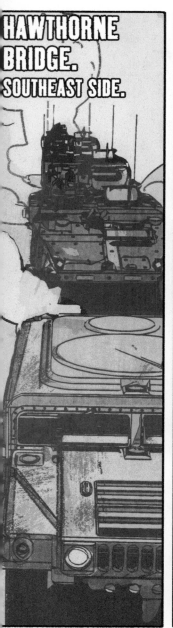

HAWTHORNE BRIDGE. SOUTHEAST SIDE.

COMMAND IS HERE.

EVERYONE UP!

EVERYONE IN PLACES!

OH, COLONEL ORLANDO, SIR.

THERE'S BEEN A DEVELOPMENT.

SHOW ME.

HOW LONG?

FIVE MINUTES.

IT'S LIKE THEY KNEW YOU WERE COMING.

HMM.

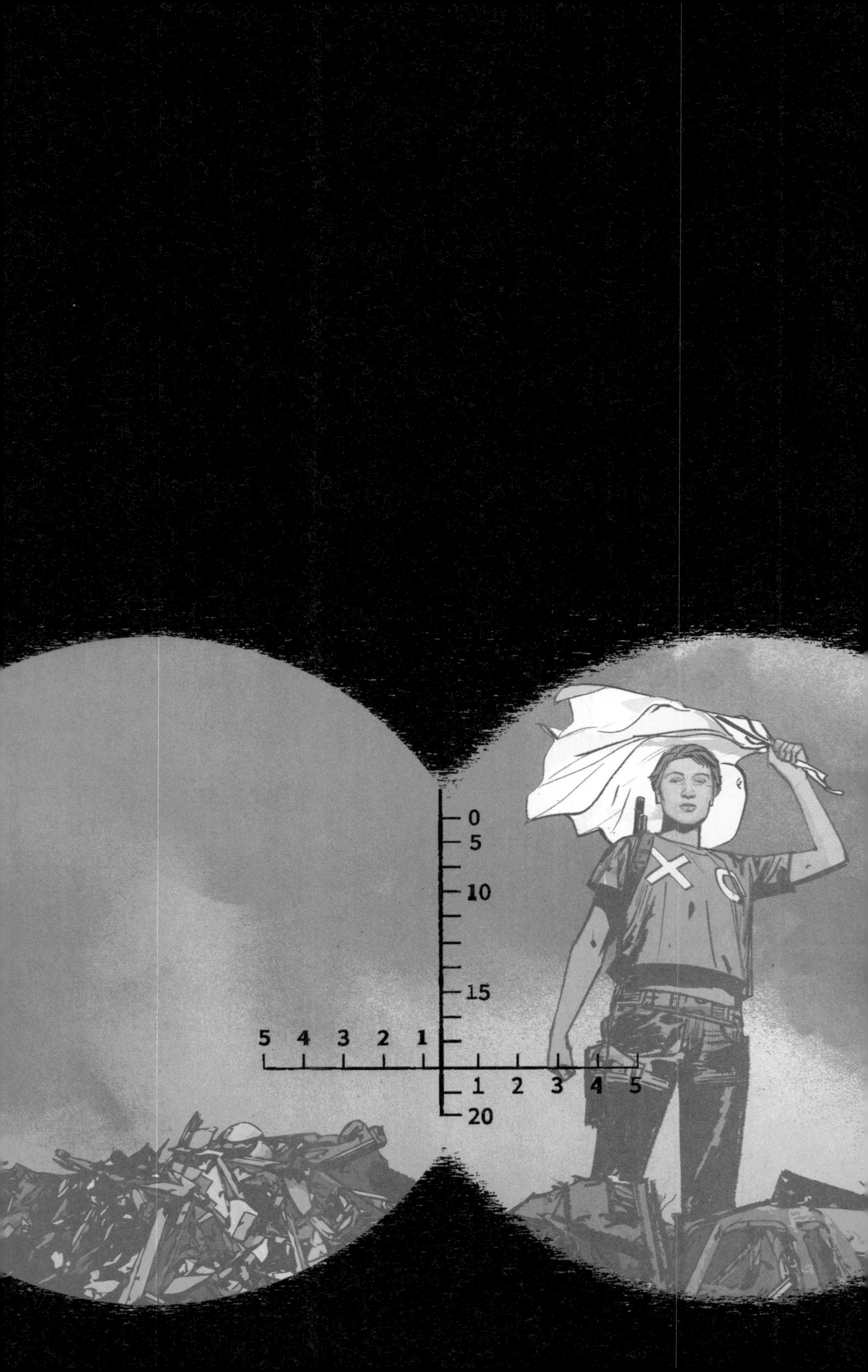
0
5
10
15
20
5 4 3 2 1
1 2 3 4 5

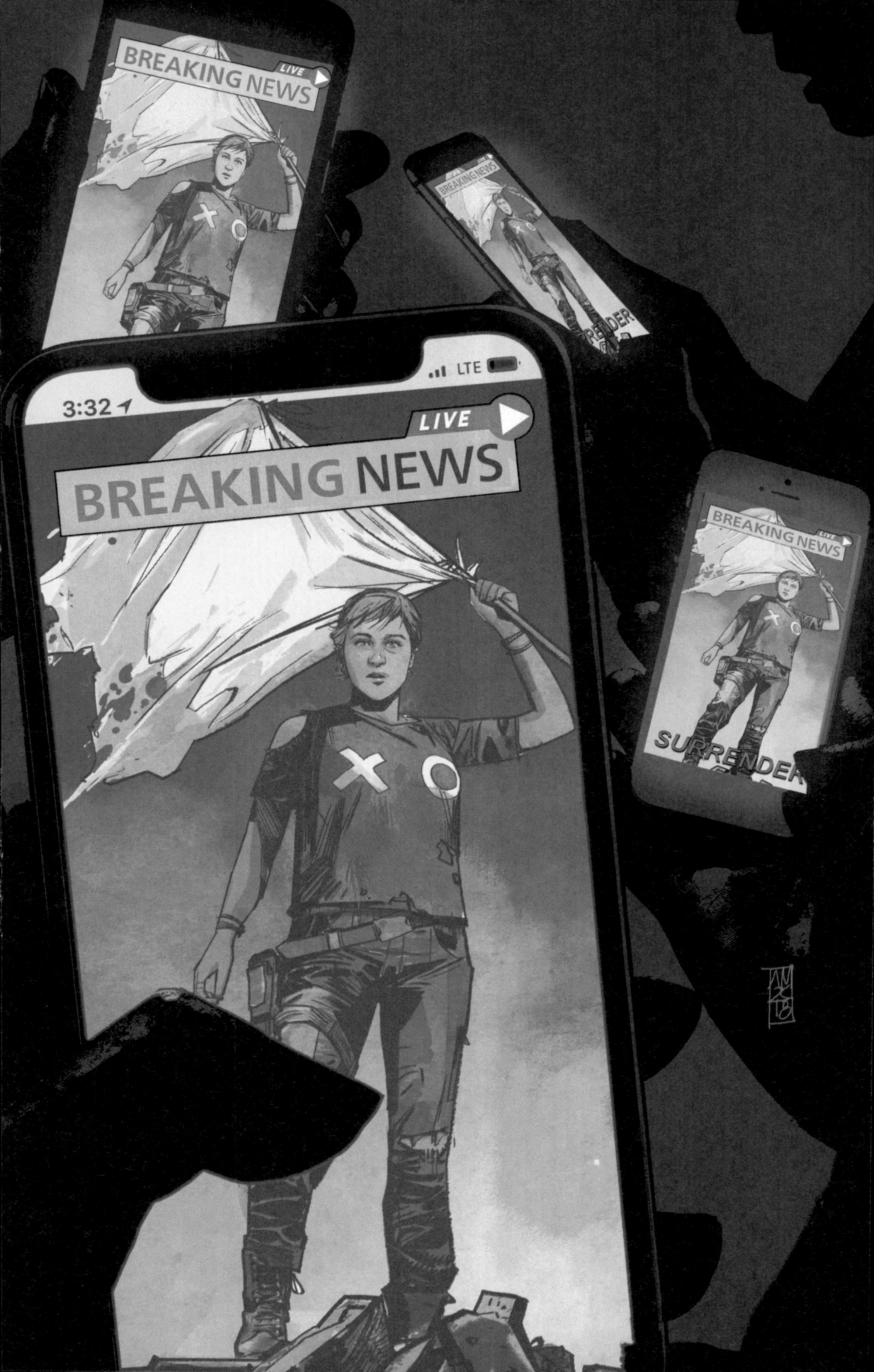
BREAKING NEWS
LIVE
BREAKING NEWS
SURRENDER
3:32
LTE
LIVE
BREAKING NEWS
BREAKING NEWS
LIVE
SURRENDER

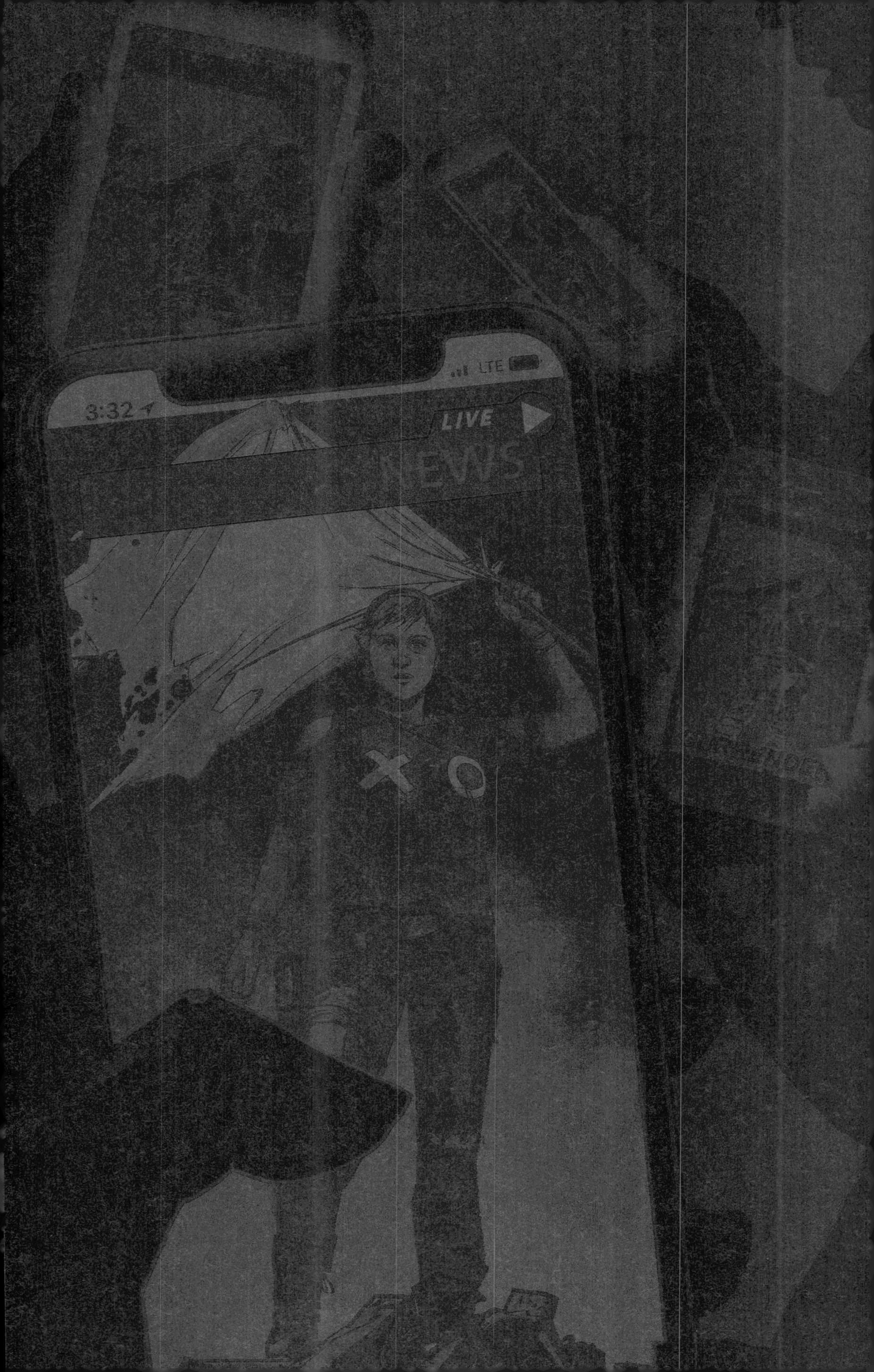
3:32
LTE
LIVE
NEWS

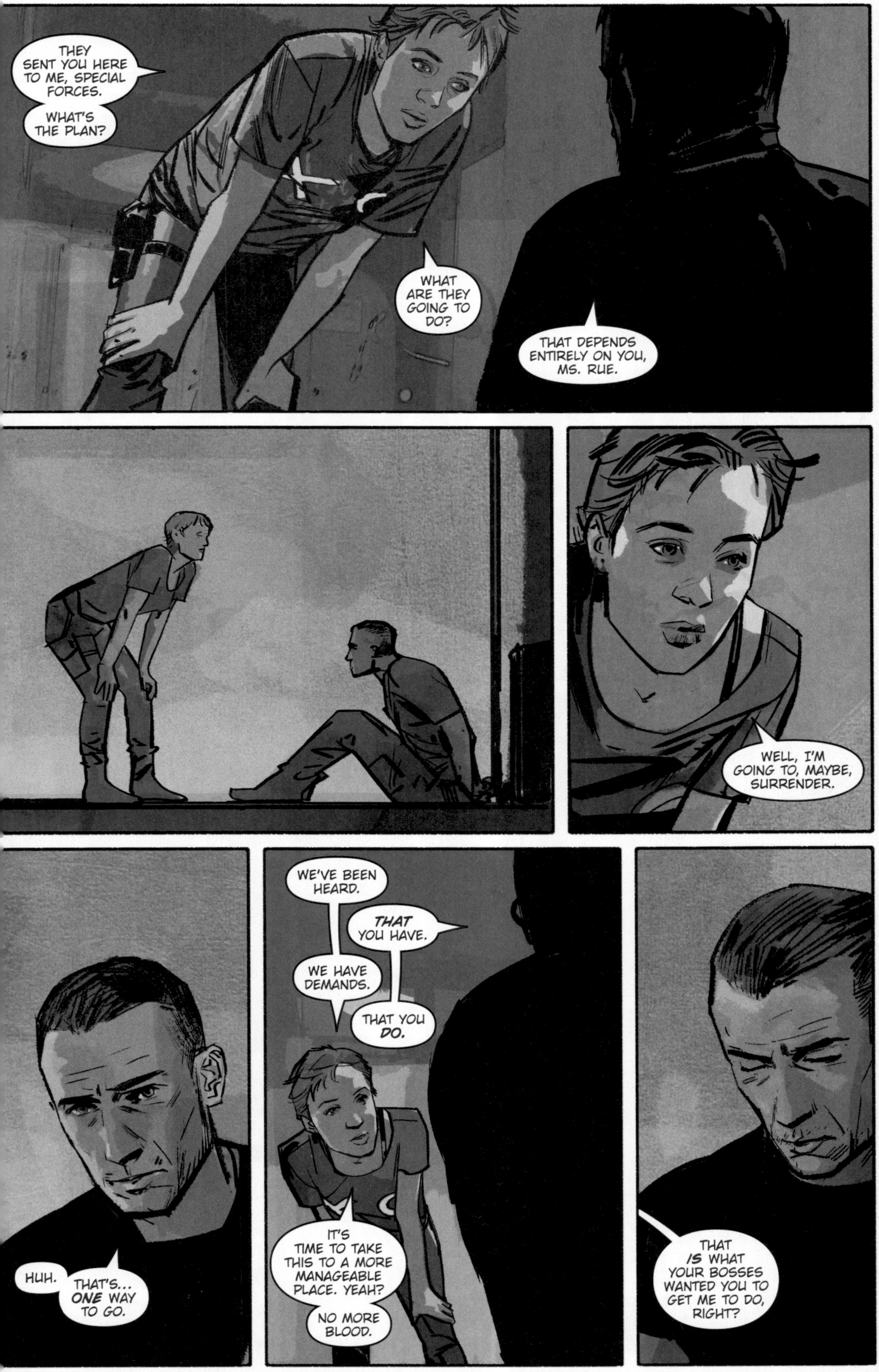
THEY SENT YOU HERE TO ME, SPECIAL FORCES.
WHAT'S THE PLAN?
WHAT ARE THEY GOING TO DO?
THAT DEPENDS ENTIRELY ON YOU, MS. RUE.
WELL, I'M GOING TO, MAYBE, SURRENDER.
HUH.
THAT'S... ONE WAY TO GO.
WE'VE BEEN HEARD.
THAT YOU HAVE.
WE HAVE DEMANDS.
THAT YOU DO.
IT'S TIME TO TAKE THIS TO A MORE MANAGEABLE PLACE. YEAH?
NO MORE BLOOD.
THAT IS WHAT YOUR BOSSES WANTED YOU TO GET ME TO DO, RIGHT?

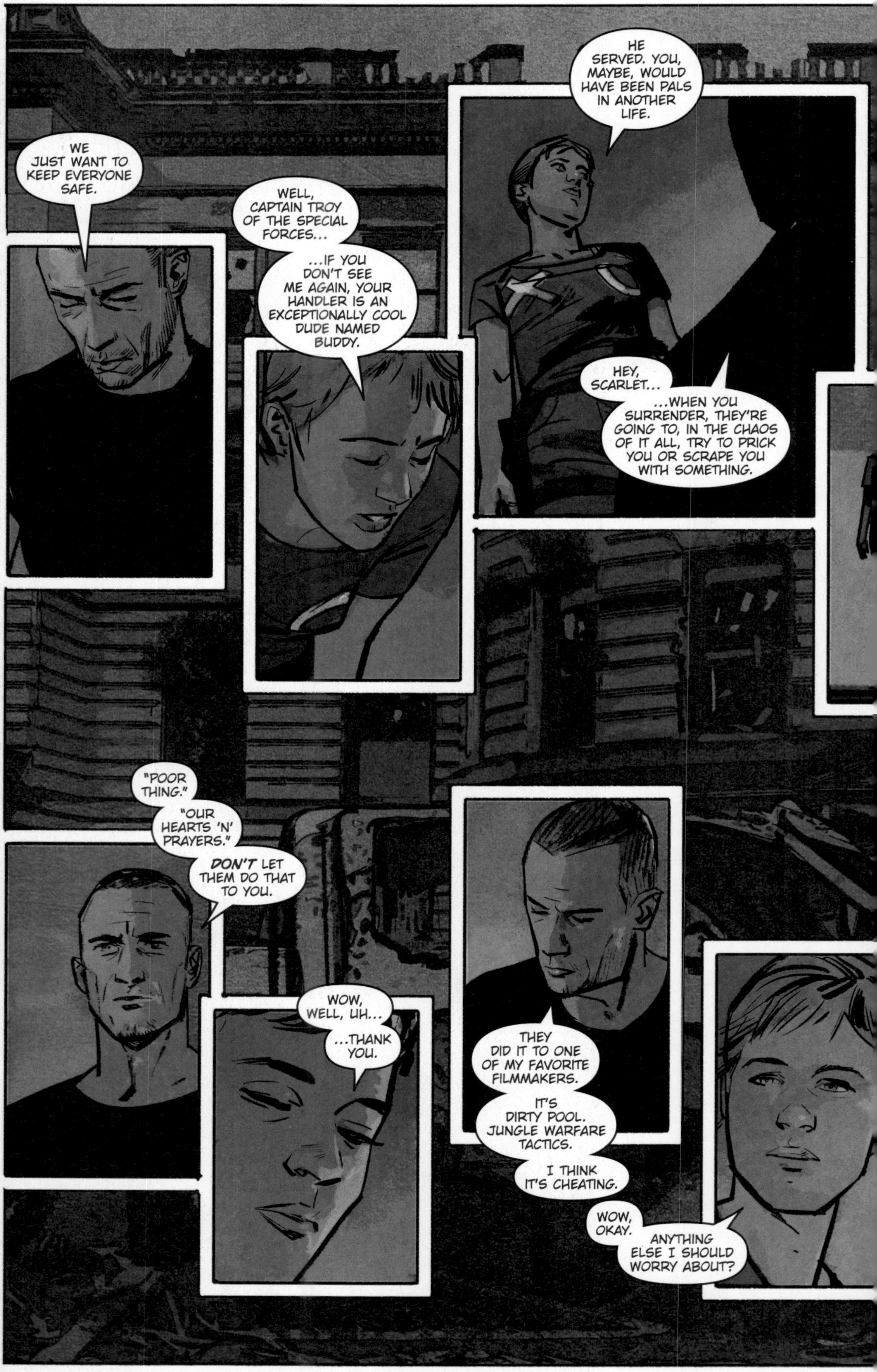
WE JUST WANT TO KEEP EVERYONE SAFE.
WELL, CAPTAIN TROY OF THE SPECIAL FORCES...
...IF YOU DON'T SEE ME AGAIN, YOUR HANDLER IS AN EXCEPTIONALLY COOL DUDE NAMED BUDDY.
HE SERVED. YOU, MAYBE, WOULD HAVE BEEN PALS IN ANOTHER LIFE.
HEY, SCARLET...
...WHEN YOU SURRENDER, THEY'RE GOING TO, IN THE CHAOS OF IT ALL, TRY TO PRICK YOU OR SCRAPE YOU WITH SOMETHING.
"POOR THING."
"OUR HEARTS 'N' PRAYERS."
DON'T LET THEM DO THAT TO YOU.
WOW, WELL, UH...
...THANK YOU.
THEY DID IT TO ONE OF MY FAVORITE FILMMAKERS.
IT'S DIRTY POOL. JUNGLE WARFARE TACTICS.
I THINK IT'S CHEATING.
WOW, OKAY.
ANYTHING ELSE I SHOULD WORRY ABOUT?

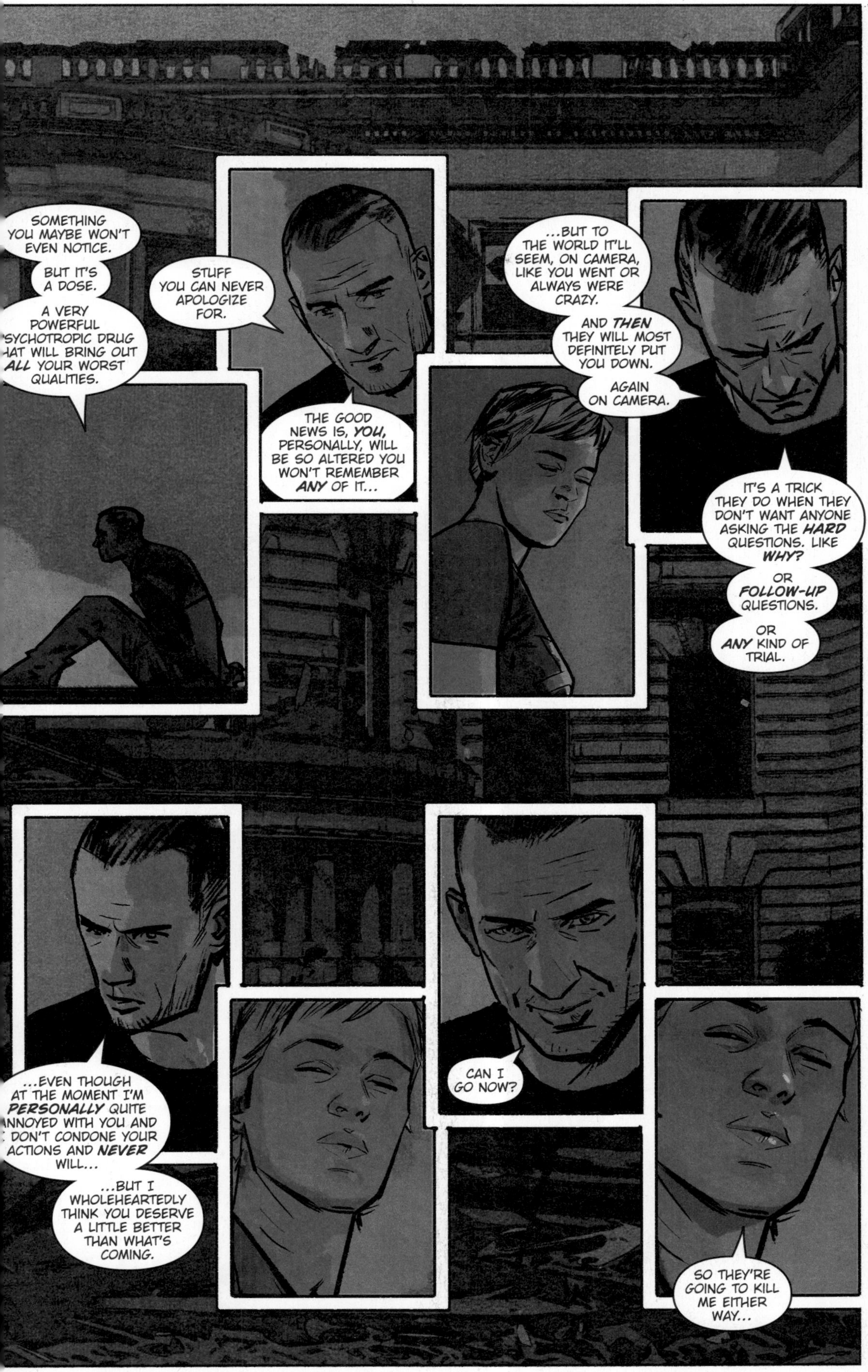
SOMETHING YOU MAYBE WON'T EVEN NOTICE.
BUT IT'S A DOSE.
A VERY POWERFUL SYCHOTROPIC DRUG HAT WILL BRING OUT ALL YOUR WORST QUALITIES.
STUFF YOU CAN NEVER APOLOGIZE FOR.
THE GOOD NEWS IS, YOU, PERSONALLY, WILL BE SO ALTERED YOU WON'T REMEMBER ANY OF IT...
...BUT TO THE WORLD IT'LL SEEM, ON CAMERA, LIKE YOU WENT OR ALWAYS WERE CRAZY.
AND THEN THEY WILL MOST DEFINITELY PUT YOU DOWN.
AGAIN ON CAMERA.
IT'S A TRICK THEY DO WHEN THEY DON'T WANT ANYONE ASKING THE HARD QUESTIONS. LIKE WHY?
OR FOLLOW-UP QUESTIONS.
OR ANY KIND OF TRIAL.
...EVEN THOUGH AT THE MOMENT I'M PERSONALLY QUITE ANNOYED WITH YOU AND DON'T CONDONE YOUR ACTIONS AND NEVER WILL...
...BUT I WHOLEHEARTEDLY THINK YOU DESERVE A LITTLE BETTER THAN WHAT'S COMING.
CAN I GO NOW?
SO THEY'RE GOING TO KILL ME EITHER WAY...

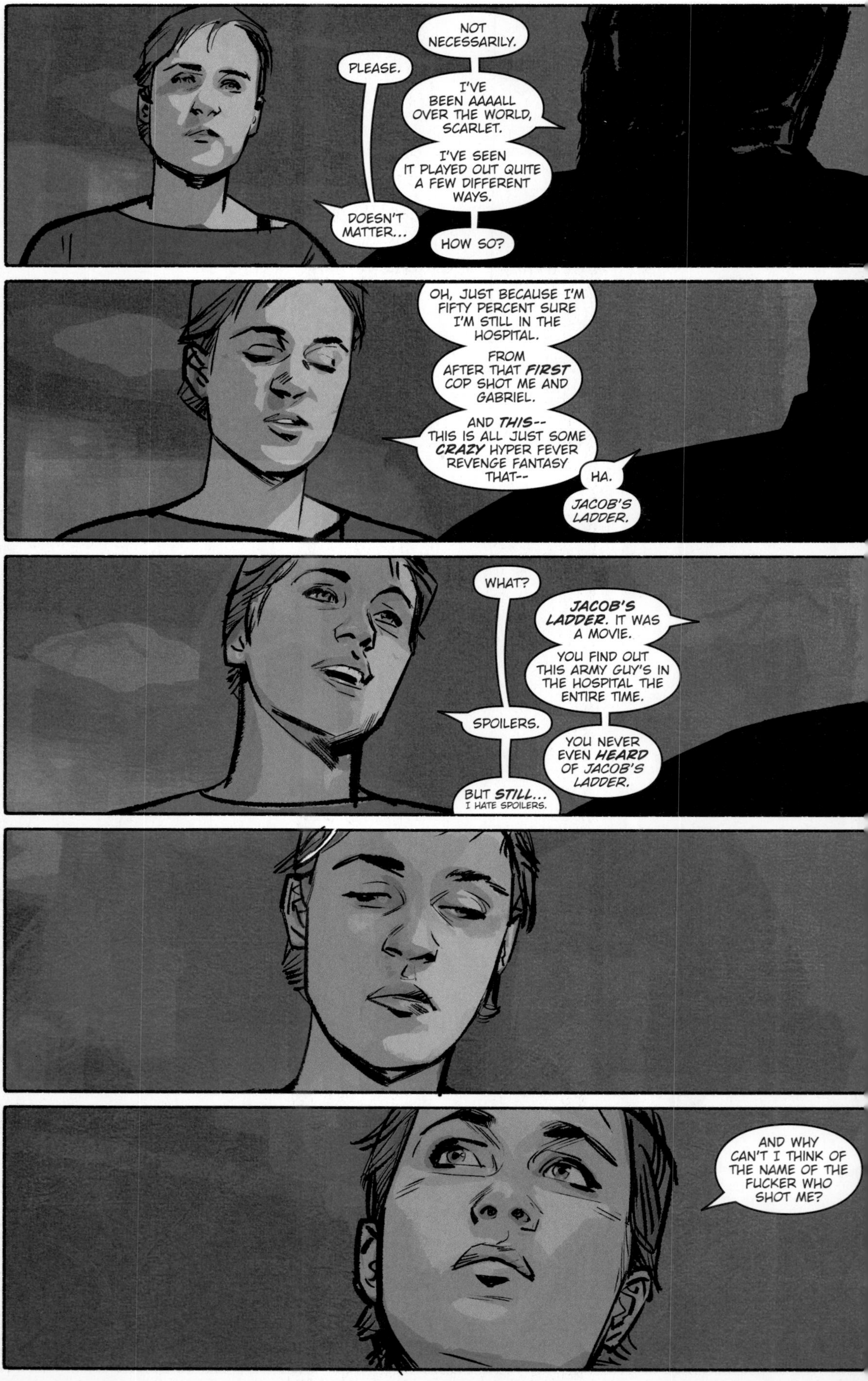
NOT NECESSARILY.
PLEASE.
I'VE BEEN AAAALL OVER THE WORLD, SCARLET.
I'VE SEEN IT PLAYED OUT QUITE A FEW DIFFERENT WAYS.
DOESN'T MATTER...
HOW SO?
OH, JUST BECAUSE I'M FIFTY PERCENT SURE I'M STILL IN THE HOSPITAL.
FROM AFTER THAT FIRST COP SHOT ME AND GABRIEL.
AND THIS-- THIS IS ALL JUST SOME CRAZY HYPER FEVER REVENGE FANTASY THAT--
HA.
JACOB'S LADDER.
WHAT?
JACOB'S LADDER. IT WAS A MOVIE.
YOU FIND OUT THIS ARMY GUY'S IN THE HOSPITAL THE ENTIRE TIME.
SPOILERS.
YOU NEVER EVEN HEARD OF JACOB'S LADDER.
BUT STILL... I HATE SPOILERS.
AND WHY CAN'T I THINK OF THE NAME OF THE FUCKER WHO SHOT ME?

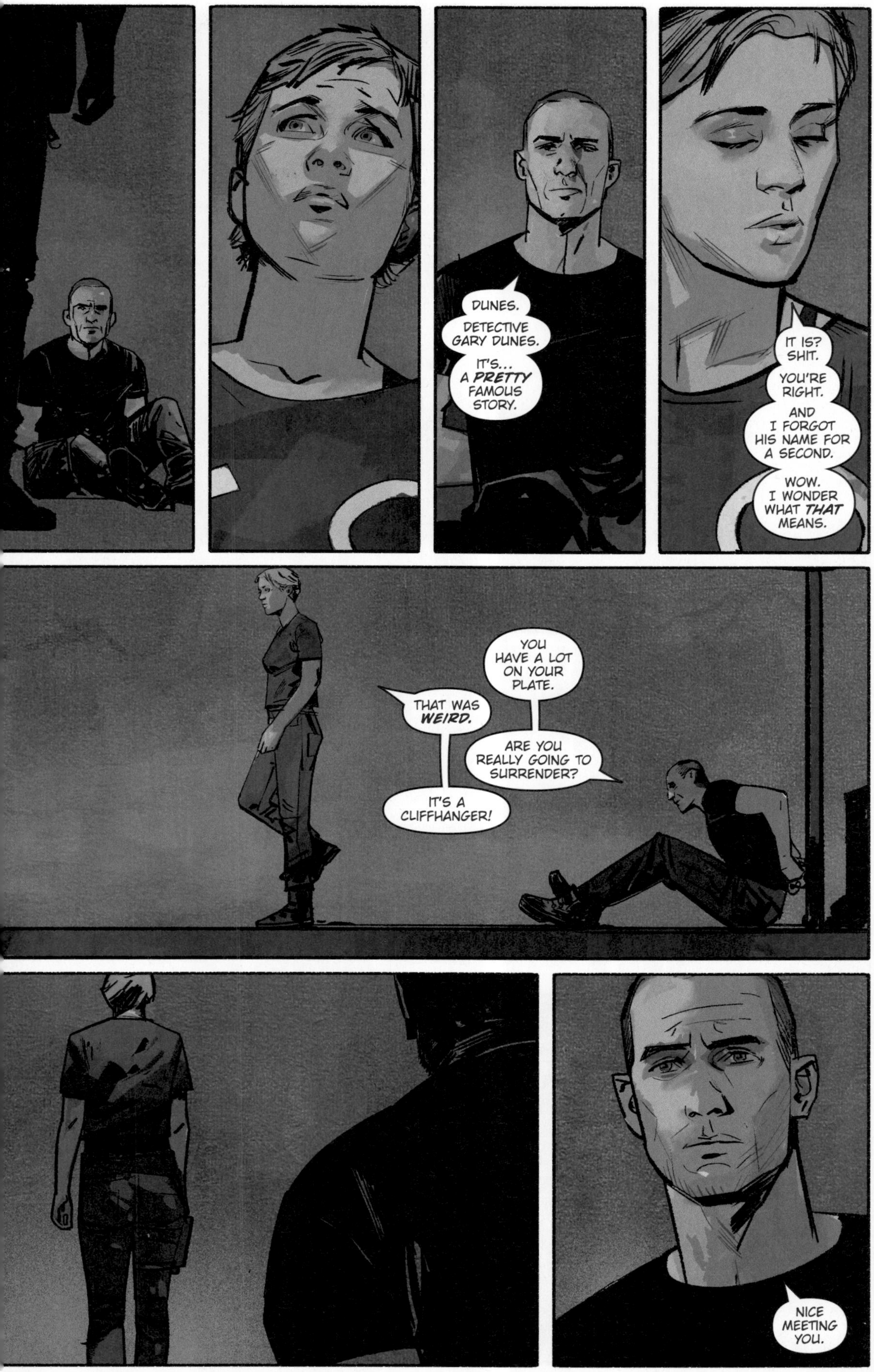
DUNES.
DETECTIVE GARY DUNES.
IT'S... A PRETTY FAMOUS STORY.
IT IS? SHIT.
YOU'RE RIGHT.
AND I FORGOT HIS NAME FOR A SECOND.
WOW. I WONDER WHAT THAT MEANS.
THAT WAS WEIRD.
YOU HAVE A LOT ON YOUR PLATE.
ARE YOU REALLY GOING TO SURRENDER?
IT'S A CLIFFHANGER!
NICE MEETING YOU.

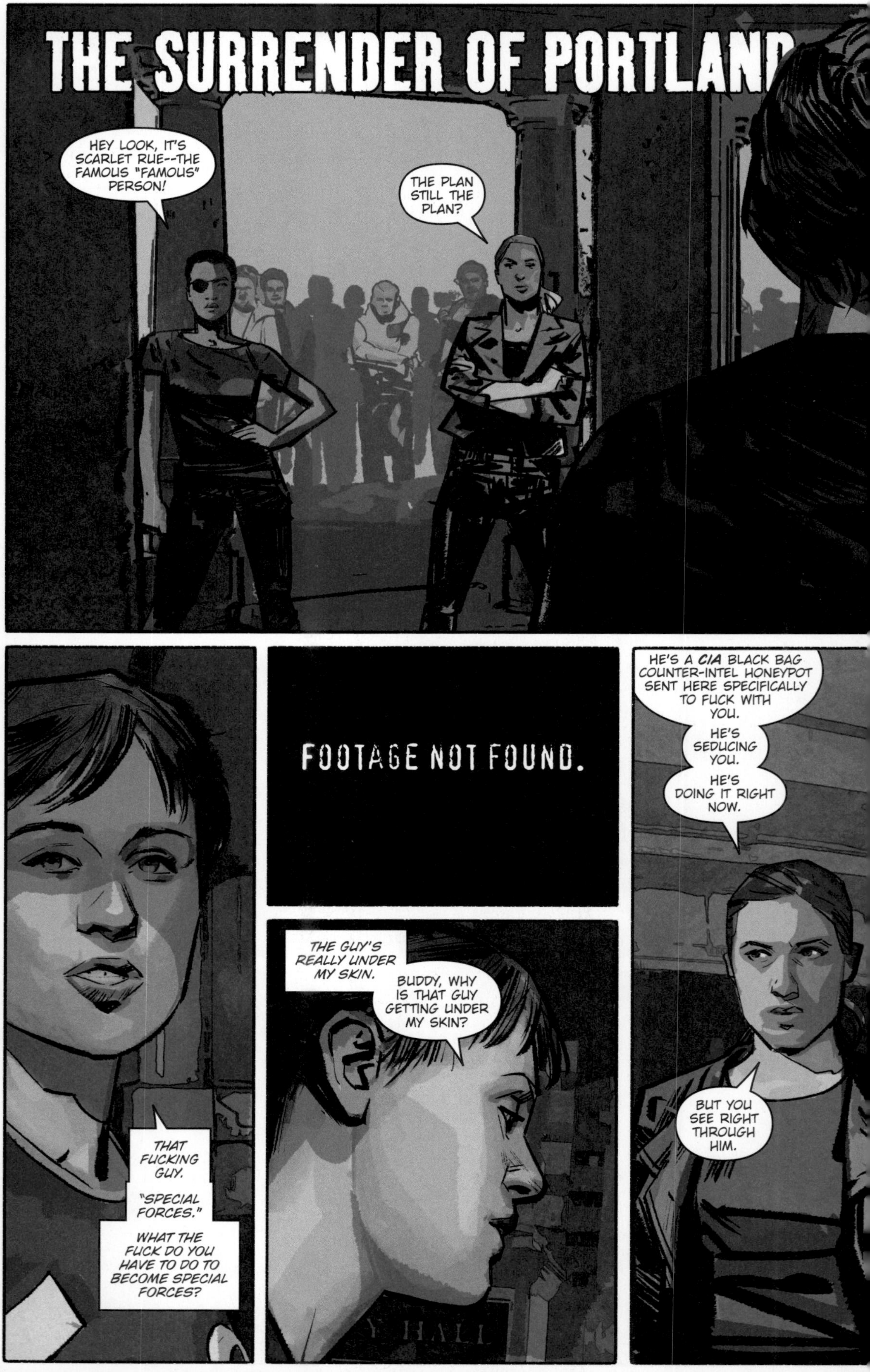
THE SURRENDER OF PORTLAND
HEY LOOK, IT'S SCARLET RUE--THE FAMOUS "FAMOUS" PERSON!
THE PLAN STILL THE PLAN?
THAT FUCKING GUY.
"SPECIAL FORCES."
WHAT THE FUCK DO YOU HAVE TO DO TO BECOME SPECIAL FORCES?
FOOTAGE NOT FOUND.
THE GUY'S REALLY UNDER MY SKIN.
BUDDY, WHY IS THAT GUY GETTING UNDER MY SKIN?
HE'S A CIA BLACK BAG COUNTER-INTEL HONEYPOT SENT HERE SPECIFICALLY TO FUCK WITH YOU.
HE'S SEDUCING YOU.
HE'S DOING IT RIGHT NOW.
BUT YOU SEE RIGHT THROUGH HIM.

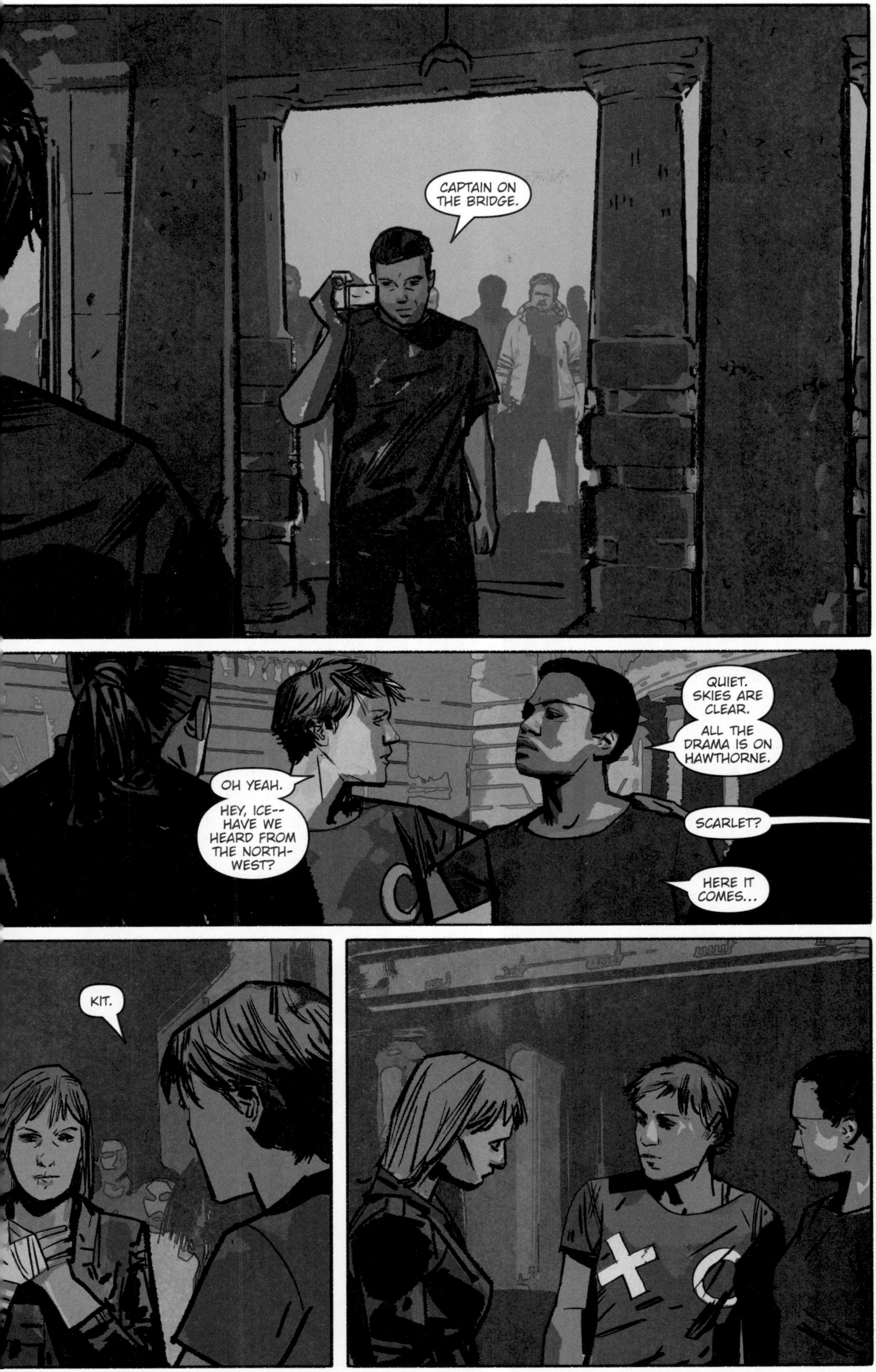
CAPTAIN ON THE BRIDGE.
OH YEAH.
HEY, ICE-- HAVE WE HEARD FROM THE NORTH-WEST?
QUIET. SKIES ARE CLEAR.
ALL THE DRAMA IS ON HAWTHORNE.
SCARLET?
HERE IT COMES...
KIT.

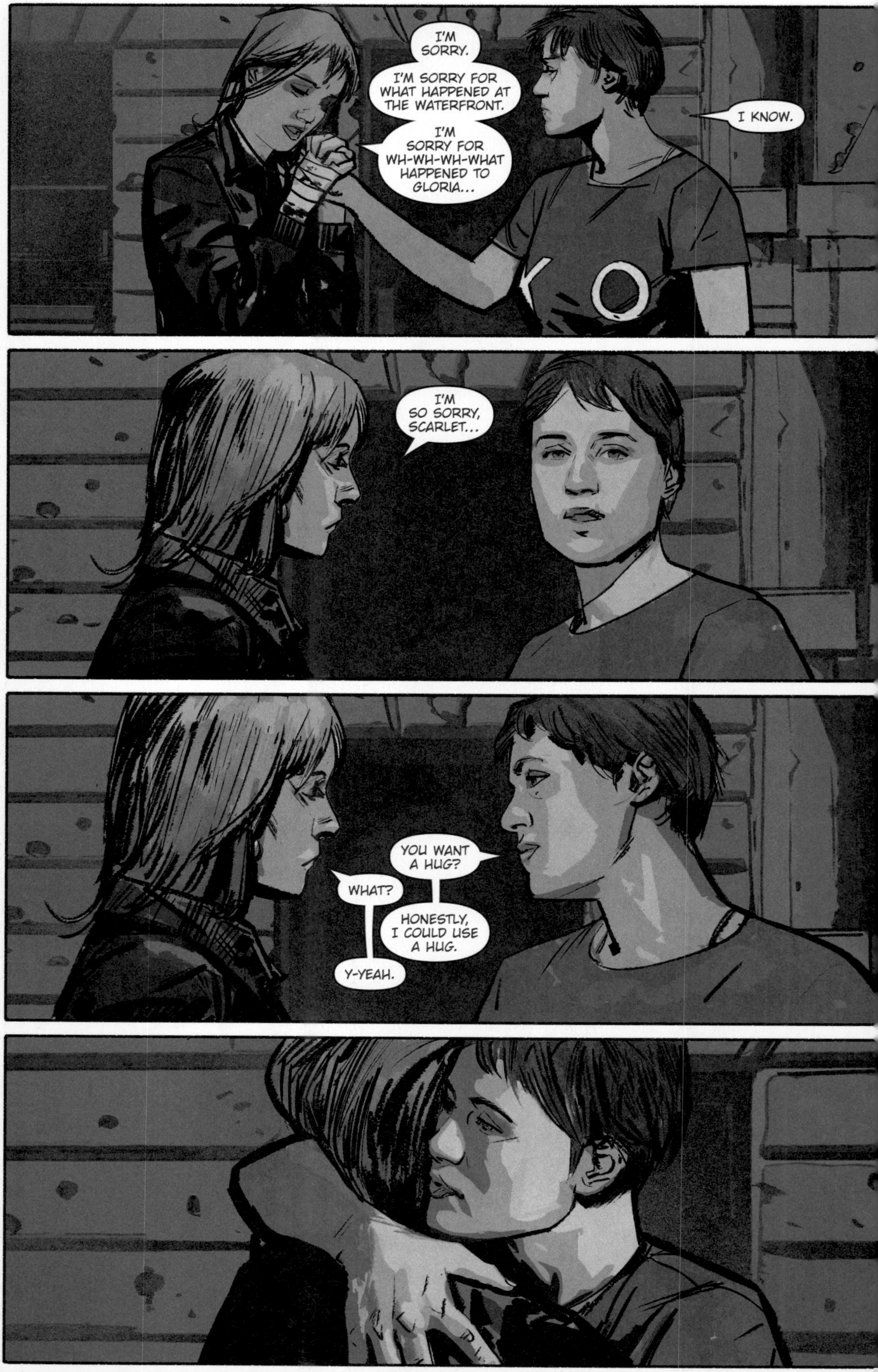
I'M SORRY.
I'M SORRY FOR WHAT HAPPENED AT THE WATERFRONT.
I'M SORRY FOR WH-WH-WH-WHAT HAPPENED TO GLORIA...
I KNOW.
I'M SO SORRY, SCARLET...
YOU WANT A HUG?
WHAT?
HONESTLY, I COULD USE A HUG.
Y-YEAH.

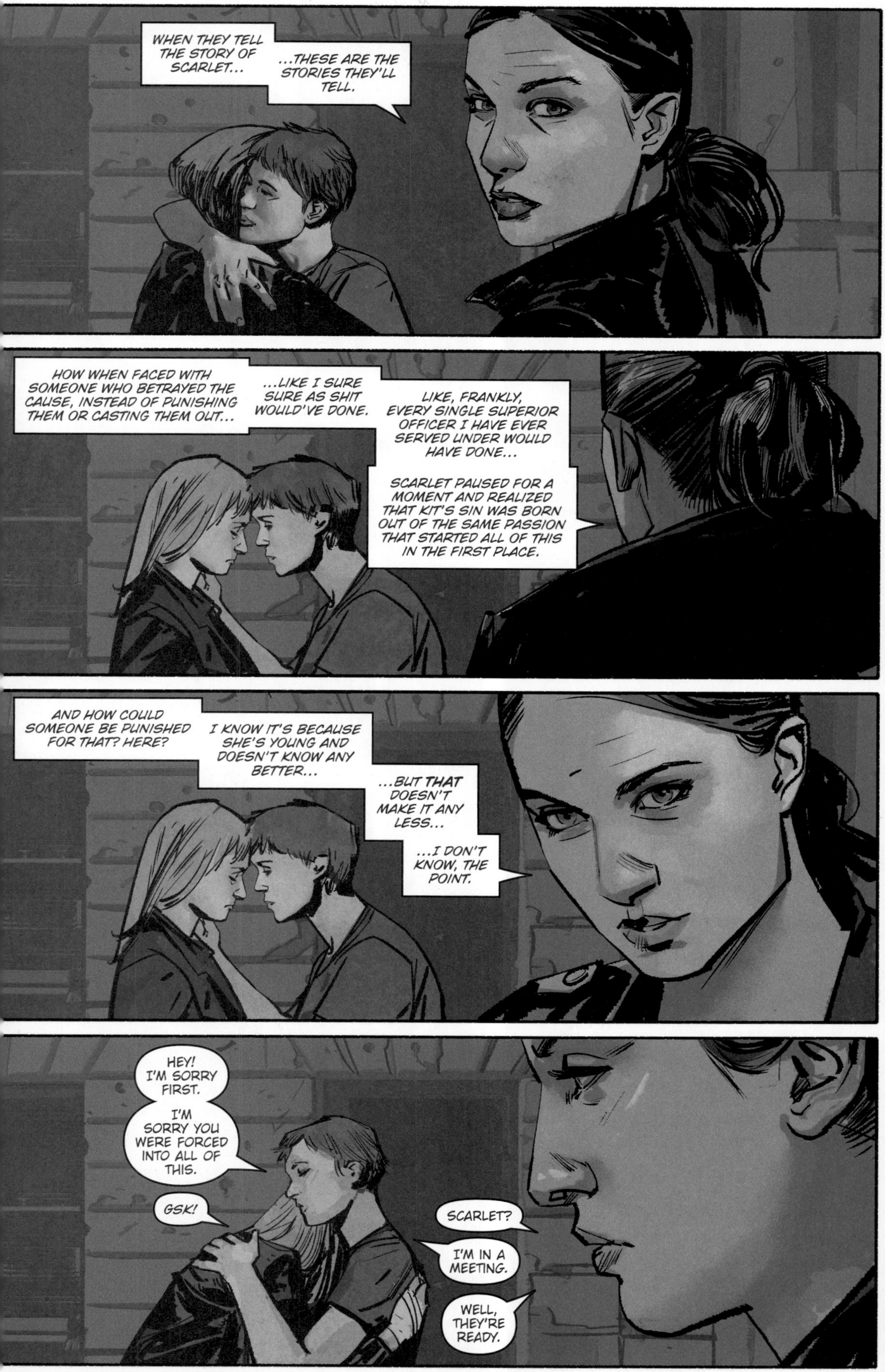
WHEN THEY TELL THE STORY OF SCARLET...
...THESE ARE THE STORIES THEY'LL TELL.
HOW WHEN FACED WITH SOMEONE WHO BETRAYED THE CAUSE, INSTEAD OF PUNISHING THEM OR CASTING THEM OUT...
...LIKE I SURE SURE AS SHIT WOULD'VE DONE.
LIKE, FRANKLY, EVERY SINGLE SUPERIOR OFFICER I HAVE EVER SERVED UNDER WOULD HAVE DONE...
SCARLET PAUSED FOR A MOMENT AND REALIZED THAT KIT'S SIN WAS BORN OUT OF THE SAME PASSION THAT STARTED ALL OF THIS IN THE FIRST PLACE.
AND HOW COULD SOMEONE BE PUNISHED FOR THAT? HERE?
I KNOW IT'S BECAUSE SHE'S YOUNG AND DOESN'T KNOW ANY BETTER...
...BUT THAT DOESN'T MAKE IT ANY LESS...
...I DON'T KNOW, THE POINT.
HEY! I'M SORRY FIRST.
I'M SORRY YOU WERE FORCED INTO ALL OF THIS.
GSK!
SCARLET?
I'M IN A MEETING.
WELL, THEY'RE READY.

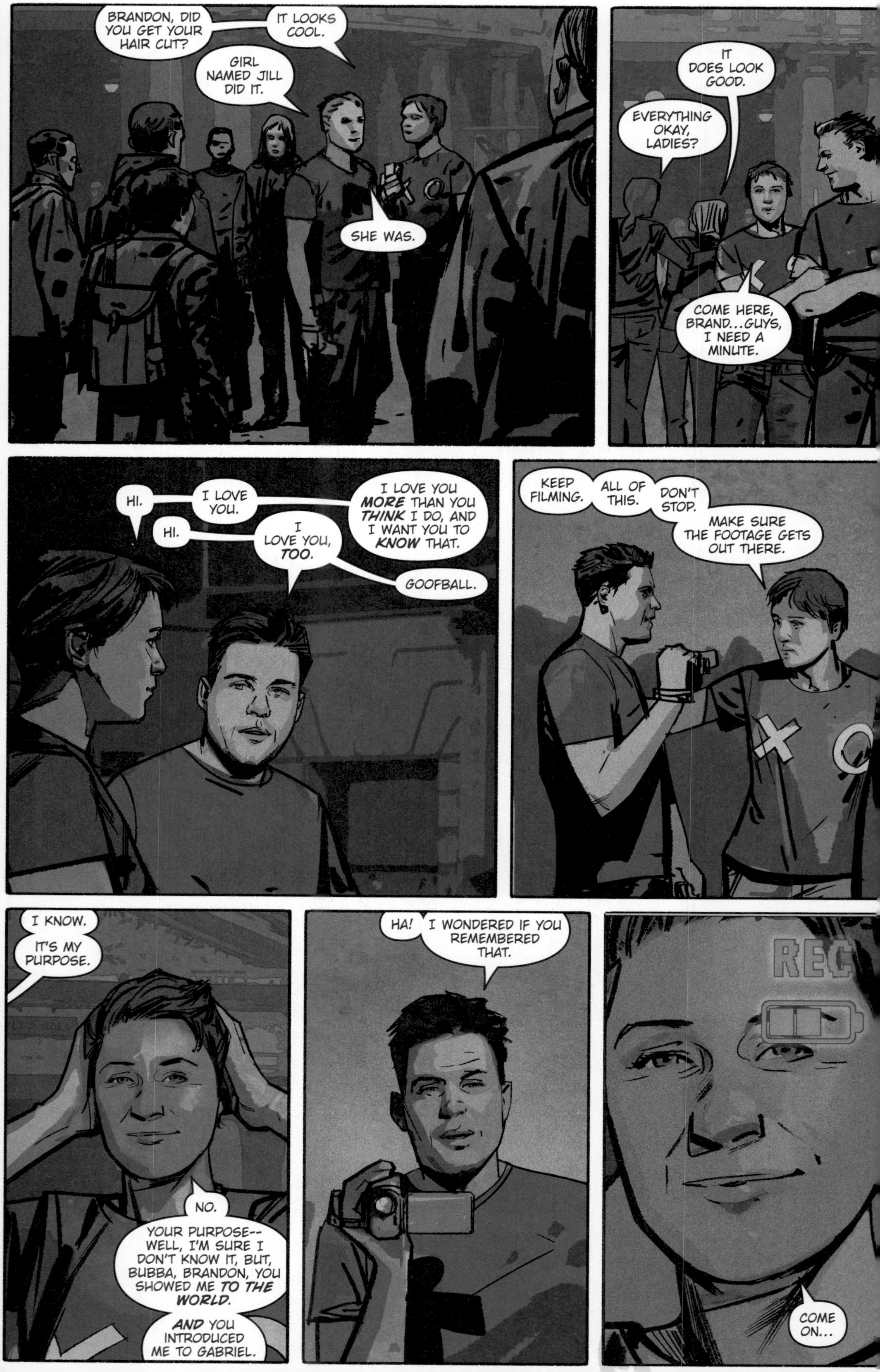
BRANDON, DID YOU GET YOUR HAIR CUT?
IT LOOKS COOL.
GIRL NAMED JILL DID IT.
SHE WAS.
IT DOES LOOK GOOD.
EVERYTHING OKAY, LADIES?
COME HERE, BRAND...GUYS, I NEED A MINUTE.
HI.
I LOVE YOU.
I LOVE YOU MORE THAN YOU THINK I DO, AND I WANT YOU TO KNOW THAT.
HI.
I LOVE YOU, TOO.
GOOFBALL.
KEEP FILMING.
ALL OF THIS.
DON'T STOP.
MAKE SURE THE FOOTAGE GETS OUT THERE.
I KNOW.
IT'S MY PURPOSE.
NO.
YOUR PURPOSE--WELL, I'M SURE I DON'T KNOW IT, BUT, BUBBA, BRANDON, YOU SHOWED ME TO THE WORLD.
AND YOU INTRODUCED ME TO GABRIEL.
HA!
I WONDERED IF YOU REMEMBERED THAT.
REC
COME ON...

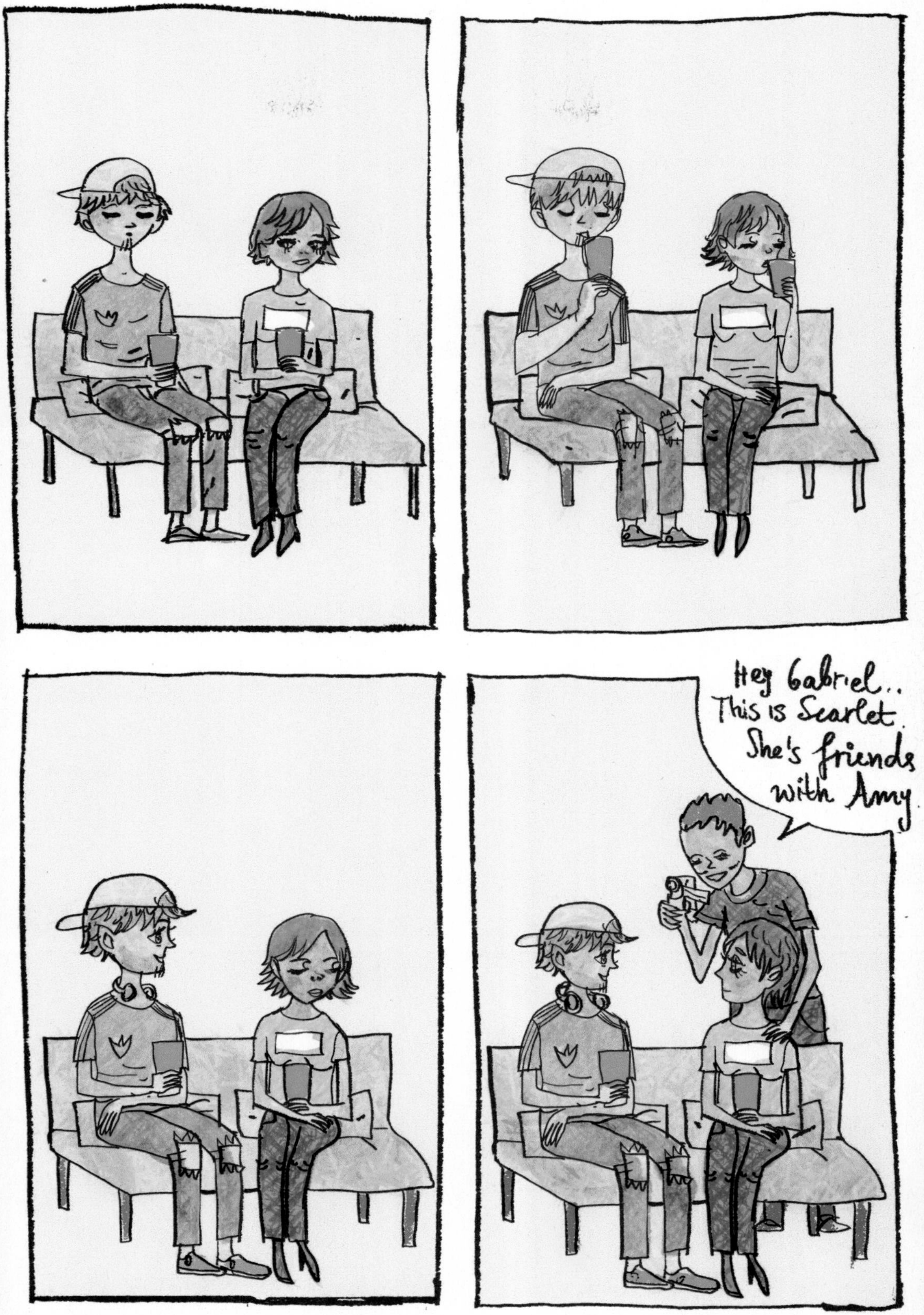
Hey Gabriel.. This is Scarlet. She's friends with Amy.

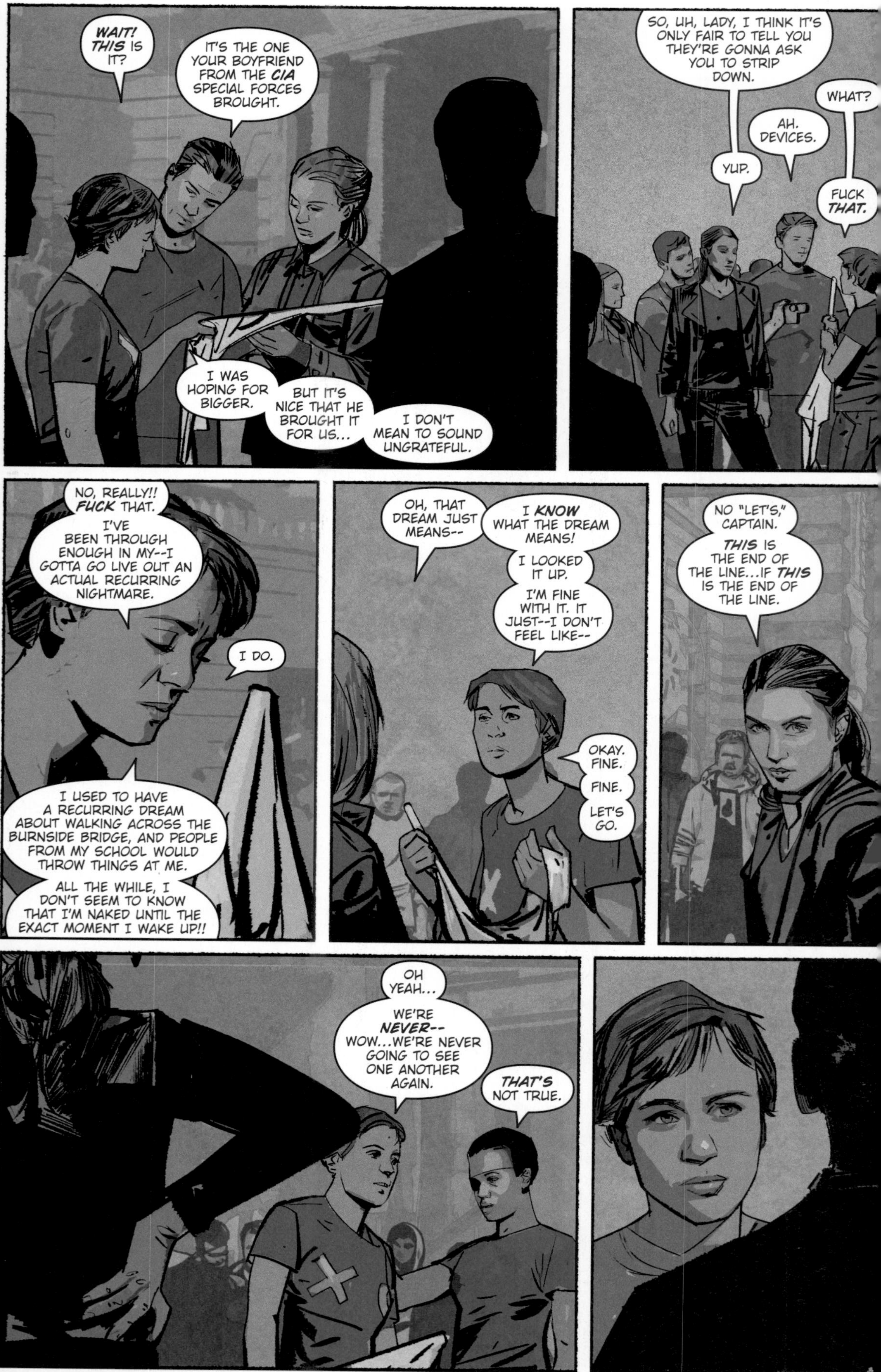
WAIT! THIS IS IT?
IT'S THE ONE YOUR BOYFRIEND FROM THE CIA SPECIAL FORCES BROUGHT.
I WAS HOPING FOR BIGGER.
BUT IT'S NICE THAT HE BROUGHT IT FOR US...
I DON'T MEAN TO SOUND UNGRATEFUL.
SO, UH, LADY, I THINK IT'S ONLY FAIR TO TELL YOU THEY'RE GONNA ASK YOU TO STRIP DOWN.
YUP.
AH. DEVICES.
WHAT?
FUCK THAT.
NO, REALLY!! FUCK THAT.
I'VE BEEN THROUGH ENOUGH IN MY--I GOTTA GO LIVE OUT AN ACTUAL RECURRING NIGHTMARE.
I DO.
I USED TO HAVE A RECURRING DREAM ABOUT WALKING ACROSS THE BURNSIDE BRIDGE, AND PEOPLE FROM MY SCHOOL WOULD THROW THINGS AT ME.
ALL THE WHILE, I DON'T SEEM TO KNOW THAT I'M NAKED UNTIL THE EXACT MOMENT I WAKE UP!!
OH, THAT DREAM JUST MEANS--
I KNOW WHAT THE DREAM MEANS!
I LOOKED IT UP.
I'M FINE WITH IT. IT JUST--I DON'T FEEL LIKE--
OKAY. FINE.
FINE.
LET'S GO.
NO "LET'S," CAPTAIN.
THIS IS THE END OF THE LINE...IF THIS IS THE END OF THE LINE.
OH YEAH...
WE'RE NEVER--
WOW...WE'RE NEVER GOING TO SEE ONE ANOTHER AGAIN.
THAT'S NOT TRUE.

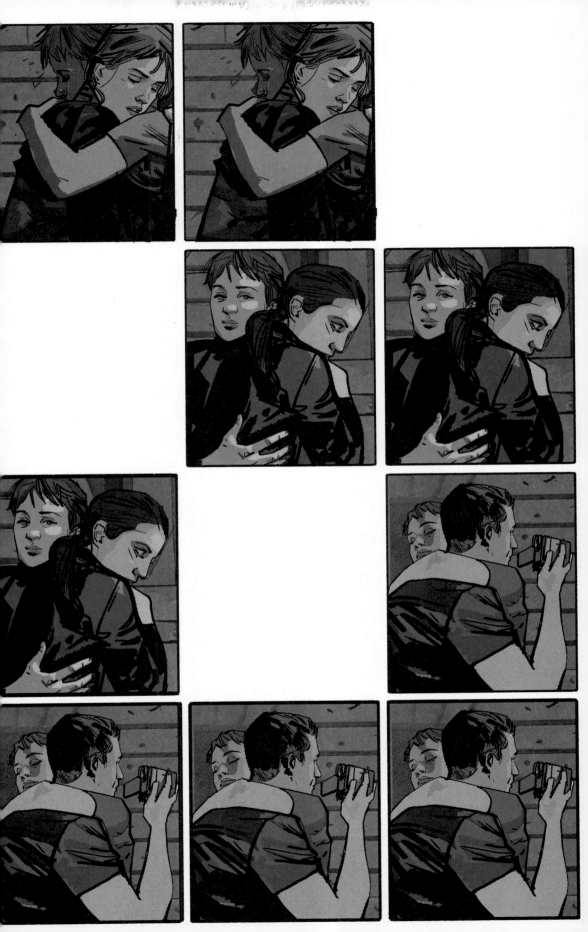

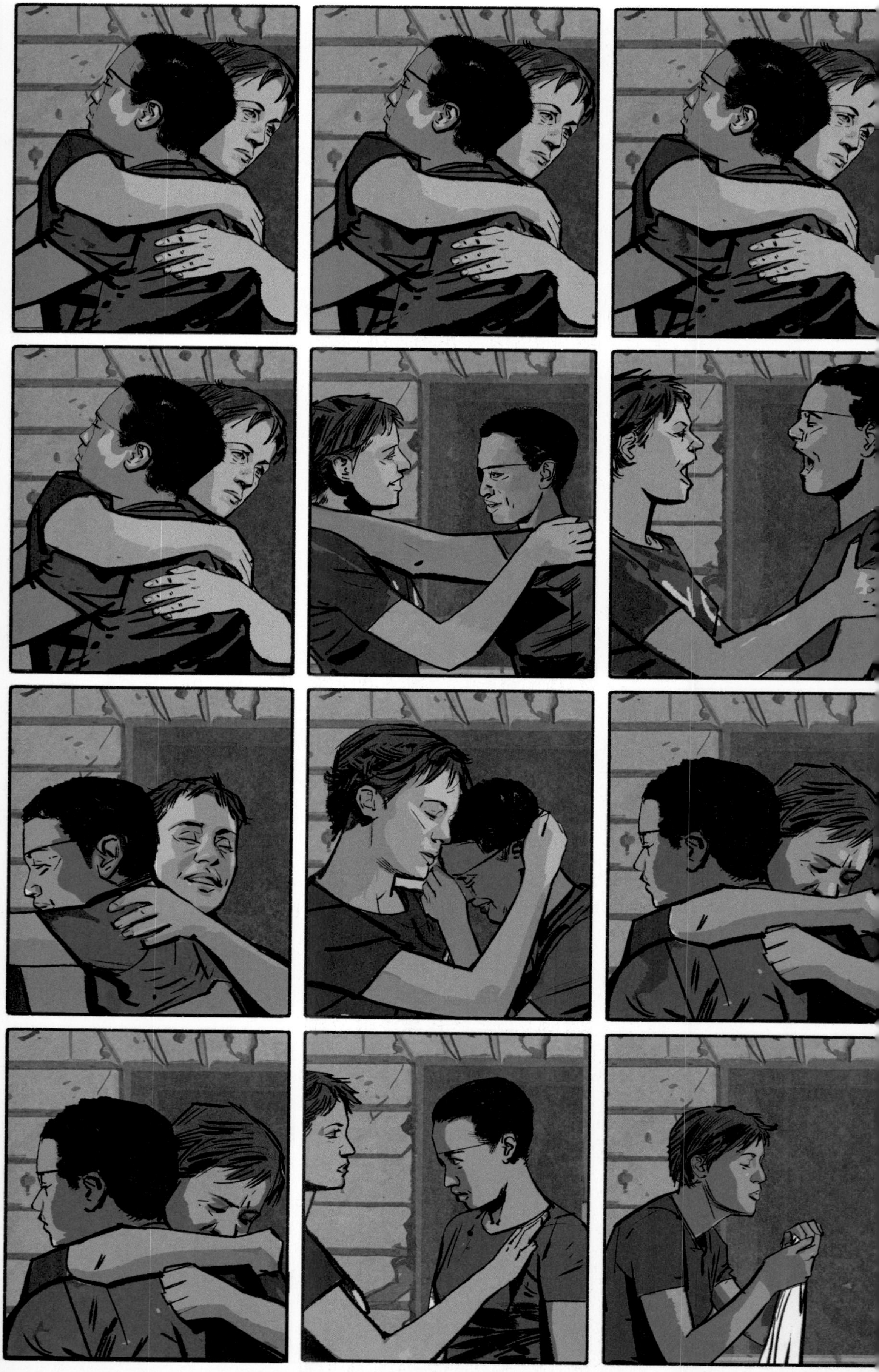

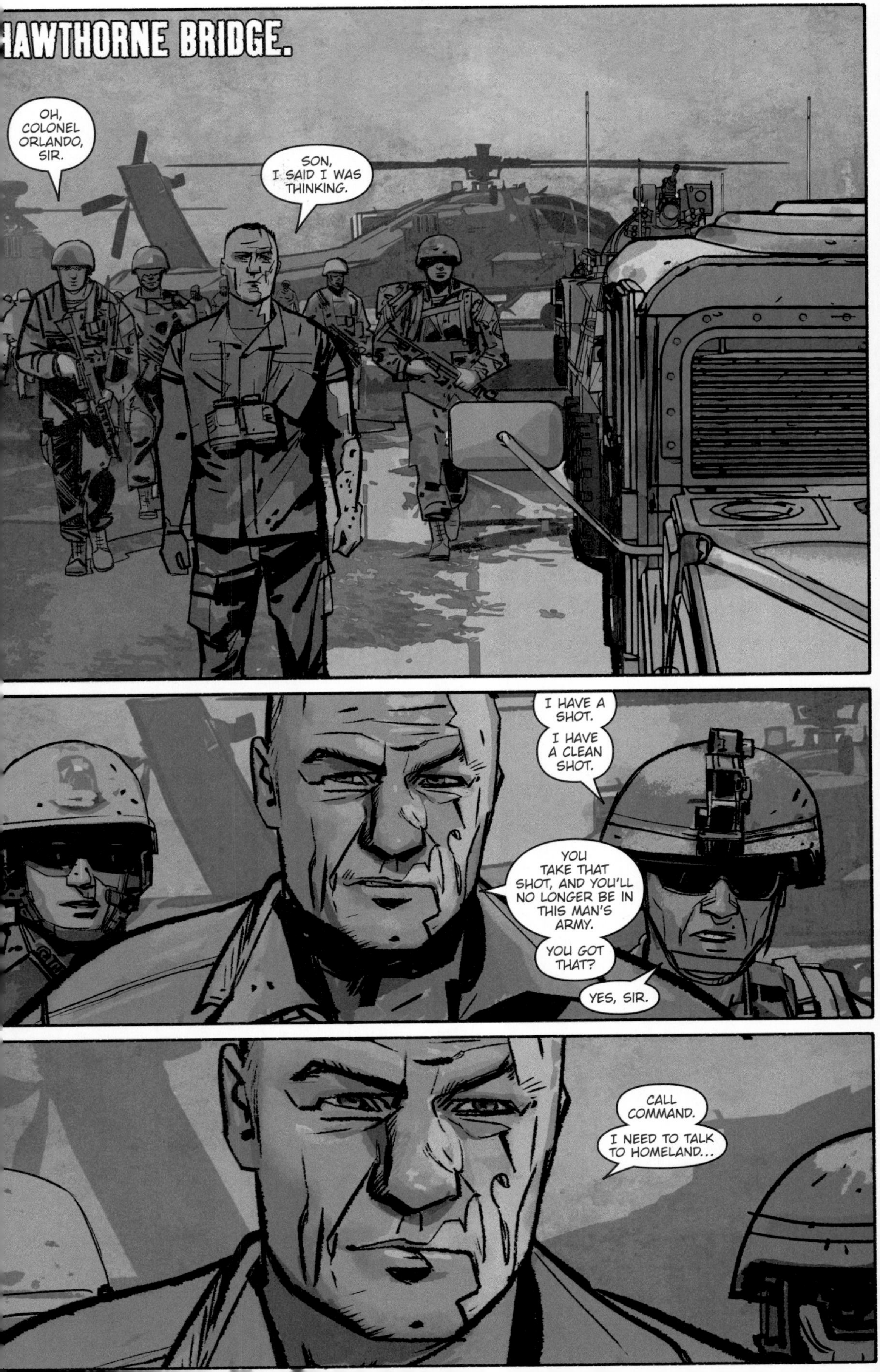
HAWTHORNE BRIDGE.
OH, COLONEL ORLANDO, SIR.
SON, I SAID I WAS THINKING.
I HAVE A SHOT.
I HAVE A CLEAN SHOT.
YOU TAKE THAT SHOT, AND YOU'LL NO LONGER BE IN THIS MAN'S ARMY.
YOU GOT THAT?
YES, SIR.
CALL COMMAND.
I NEED TO TALK TO HOMELAND...

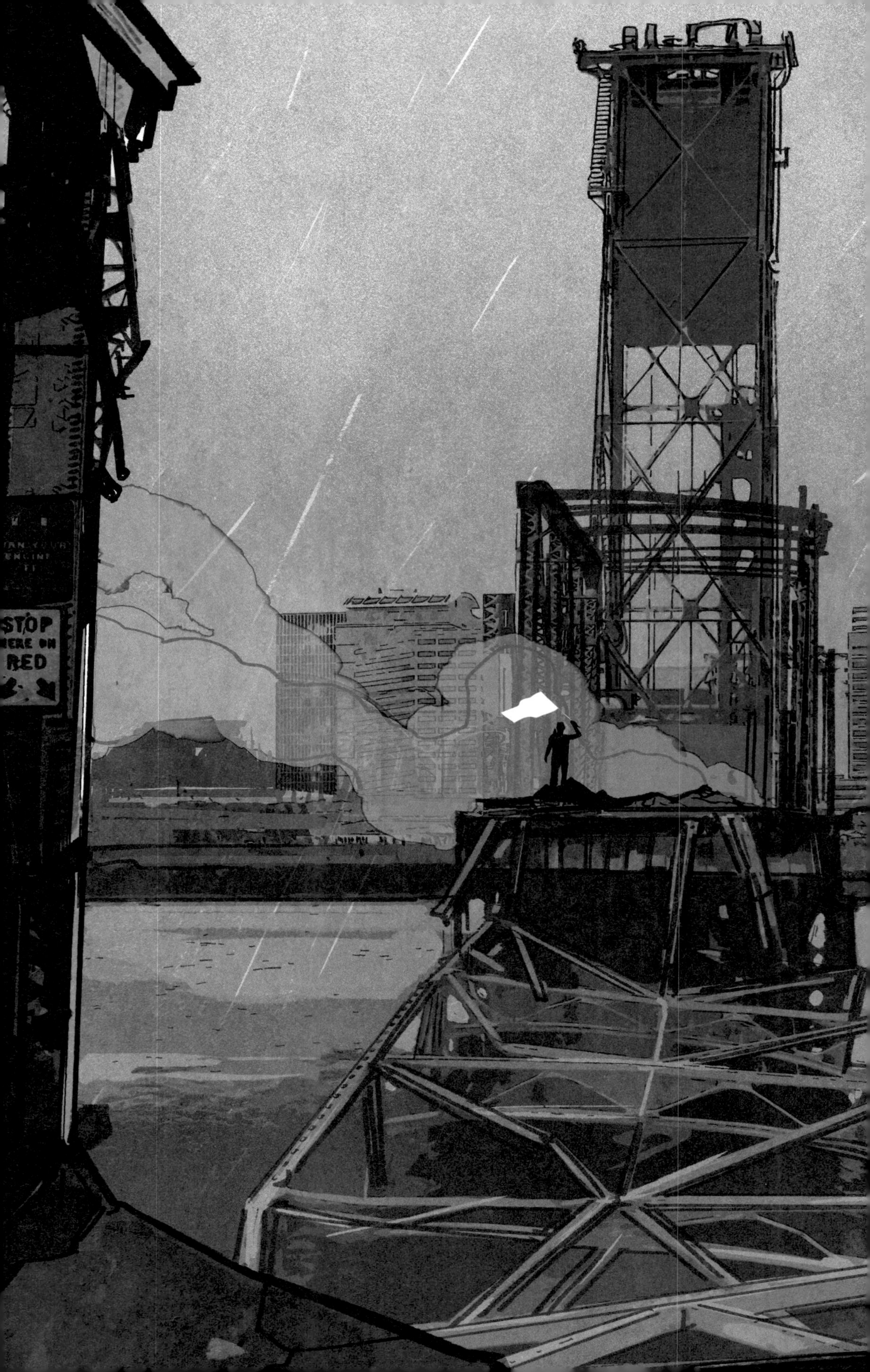
STOP
ERE ON
RED

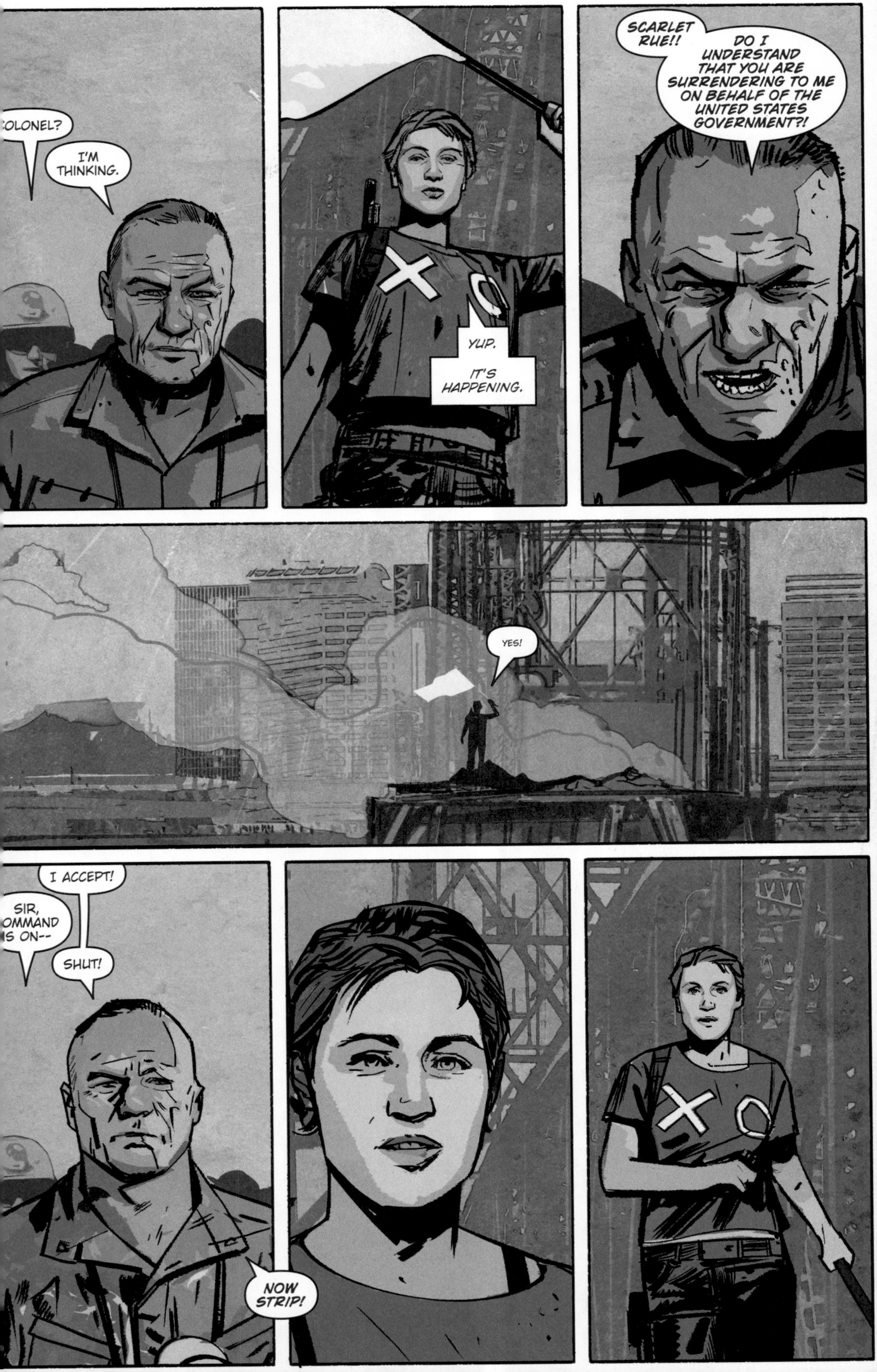
COLONEL?
I'M THINKING.
YUP.
IT'S HAPPENING.
SCARLET RUE!!
DO I UNDERSTAND THAT YOU ARE SURRENDERING TO ME ON BEHALF OF THE UNITED STATES GOVERNMENT?!
YES!
SIR, COMMAND IS ON--
I ACCEPT!
SHUT!
NOW STRIP!

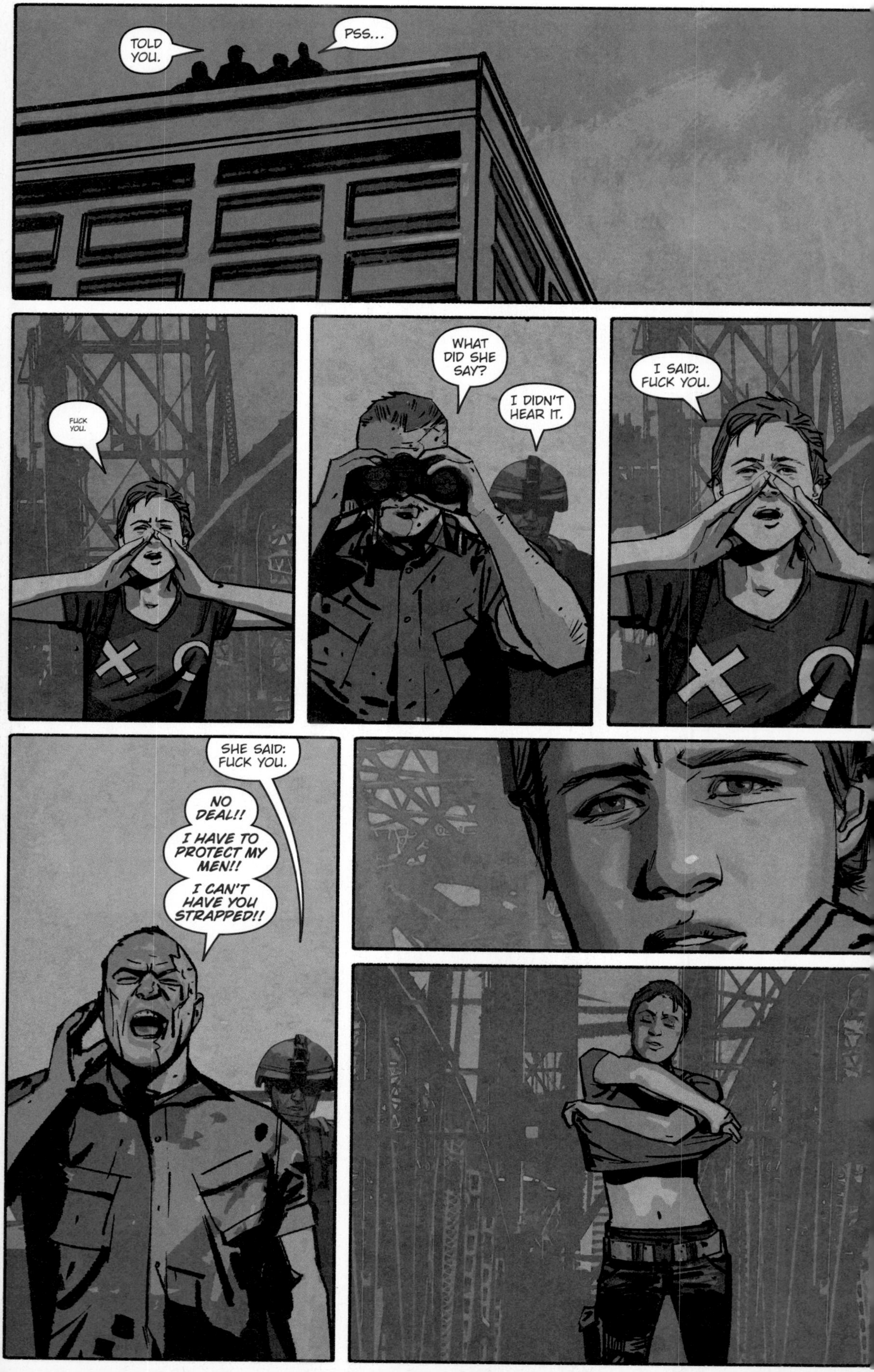
TOLD YOU.
PSS...
FUCK YOU.
WHAT DID SHE SAY?
I DIDN'T HEAR IT.
I SAID: FUCK YOU.
SHE SAID: FUCK YOU.
NO DEAL!!
I HAVE TO PROTECT MY MEN!!
I CAN'T HAVE YOU STRAPPED!!

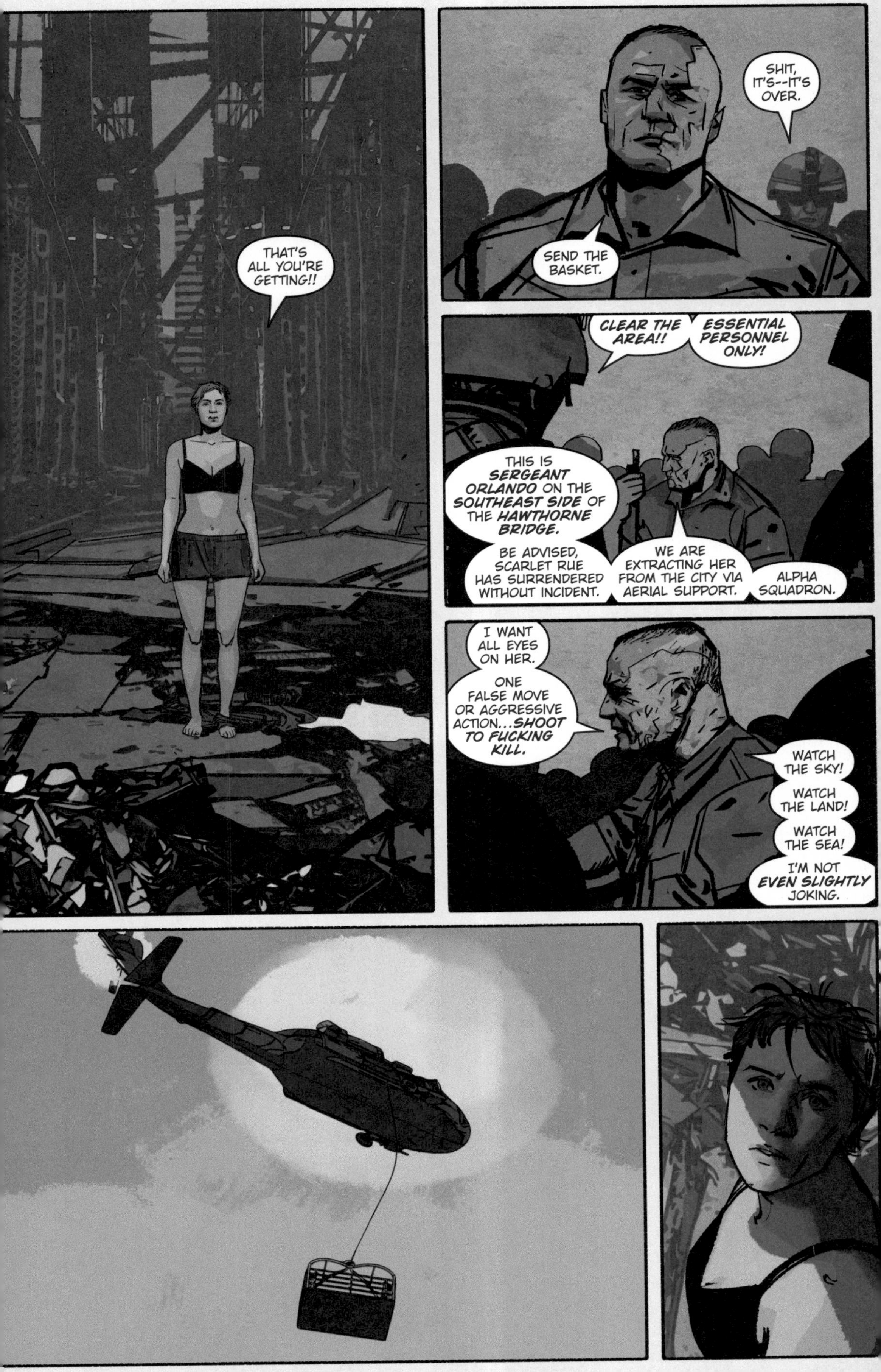
THAT'S ALL YOU'RE GETTING!!
SHIT, IT'S--IT'S OVER.
SEND THE BASKET.
CLEAR THE AREA!!
ESSENTIAL PERSONNEL ONLY!
THIS IS SERGEANT ORLANDO ON THE SOUTHEAST SIDE OF THE HAWTHORNE BRIDGE.
BE ADVISED, SCARLET RUE HAS SURRENDERED WITHOUT INCIDENT.
WE ARE EXTRACTING HER FROM THE CITY VIA AERIAL SUPPORT.
ALPHA SQUADRON.
I WANT ALL EYES ON HER.
ONE FALSE MOVE OR AGGRESSIVE ACTION...SHOOT TO FUCKING KILL.
WATCH THE SKY!
WATCH THE LAND!
WATCH THE SEA!
I'M NOT EVEN SLIGHTLY JOKING.

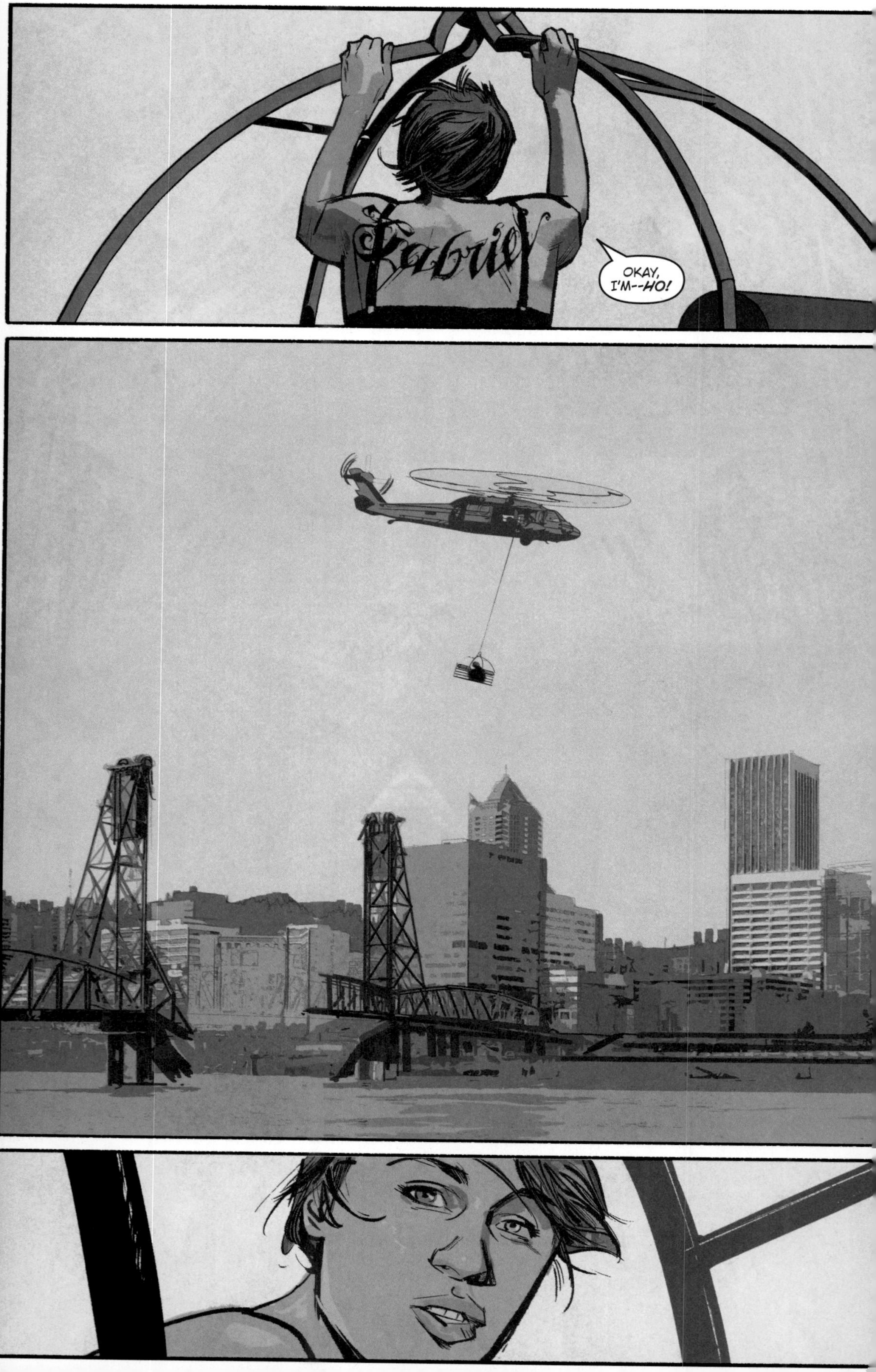
OKAY, I'M--*HO!*

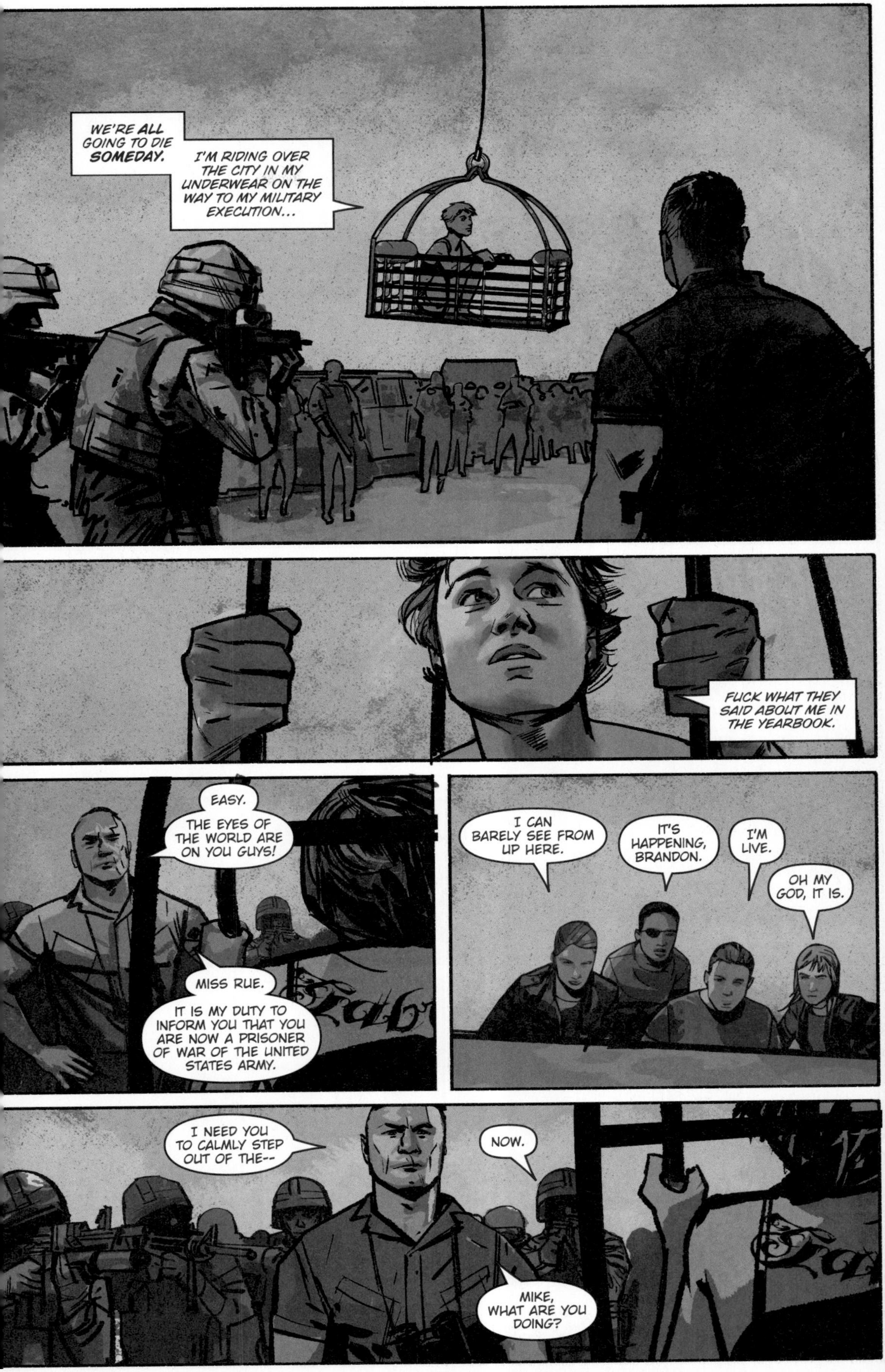
WE'RE ALL GOING TO DIE SOMEDAY.
I'M RIDING OVER THE CITY IN MY UNDERWEAR ON THE WAY TO MY MILITARY EXECUTION...
FUCK WHAT THEY SAID ABOUT ME IN THE YEARBOOK.
EASY.
THE EYES OF THE WORLD ARE ON YOU GUYS!
MISS RUE.
IT IS MY DUTY TO INFORM YOU THAT YOU ARE NOW A PRISONER OF WAR OF THE UNITED STATES ARMY.
I CAN BARELY SEE FROM UP HERE.
IT'S HAPPENING, BRANDON.
I'M LIVE.
OH MY GOD, IT IS.
I NEED YOU TO CALMLY STEP OUT OF THE--
NOW.
MIKE, WHAT ARE YOU DOING?

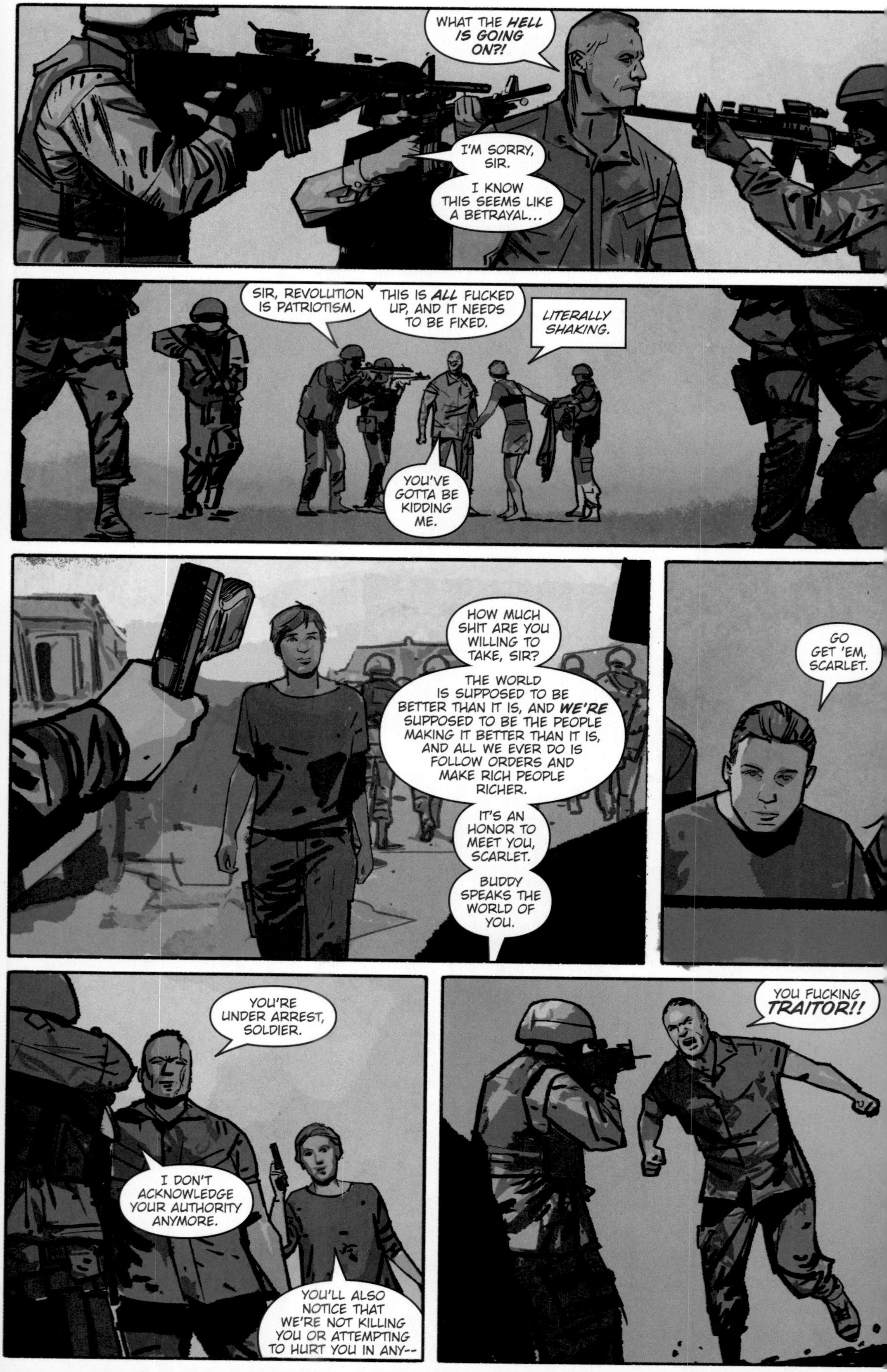
WHAT THE HELL IS GOING ON?!
I'M SORRY, SIR.
I KNOW THIS SEEMS LIKE A BETRAYAL...
SIR, REVOLUTION IS PATRIOTISM.
THIS IS ALL FUCKED UP, AND IT NEEDS TO BE FIXED.
LITERALLY SHAKING.
YOU'VE GOTTA BE KIDDING ME.
HOW MUCH SHIT ARE YOU WILLING TO TAKE, SIR?
THE WORLD IS SUPPOSED TO BE BETTER THAN IT IS, AND WE'RE SUPPOSED TO BE THE PEOPLE MAKING IT BETTER THAN IT IS, AND ALL WE EVER DO IS FOLLOW ORDERS AND MAKE RICH PEOPLE RICHER.
IT'S AN HONOR TO MEET YOU, SCARLET.
BUDDY SPEAKS THE WORLD OF YOU.
GO GET 'EM, SCARLET.
YOU'RE UNDER ARREST, SOLDIER.
I DON'T ACKNOWLEDGE YOUR AUTHORITY ANYMORE.
YOU'LL ALSO NOTICE THAT WE'RE NOT KILLING YOU OR ATTEMPTING TO HURT YOU IN ANY--
YOU FUCKING TRAITOR!!

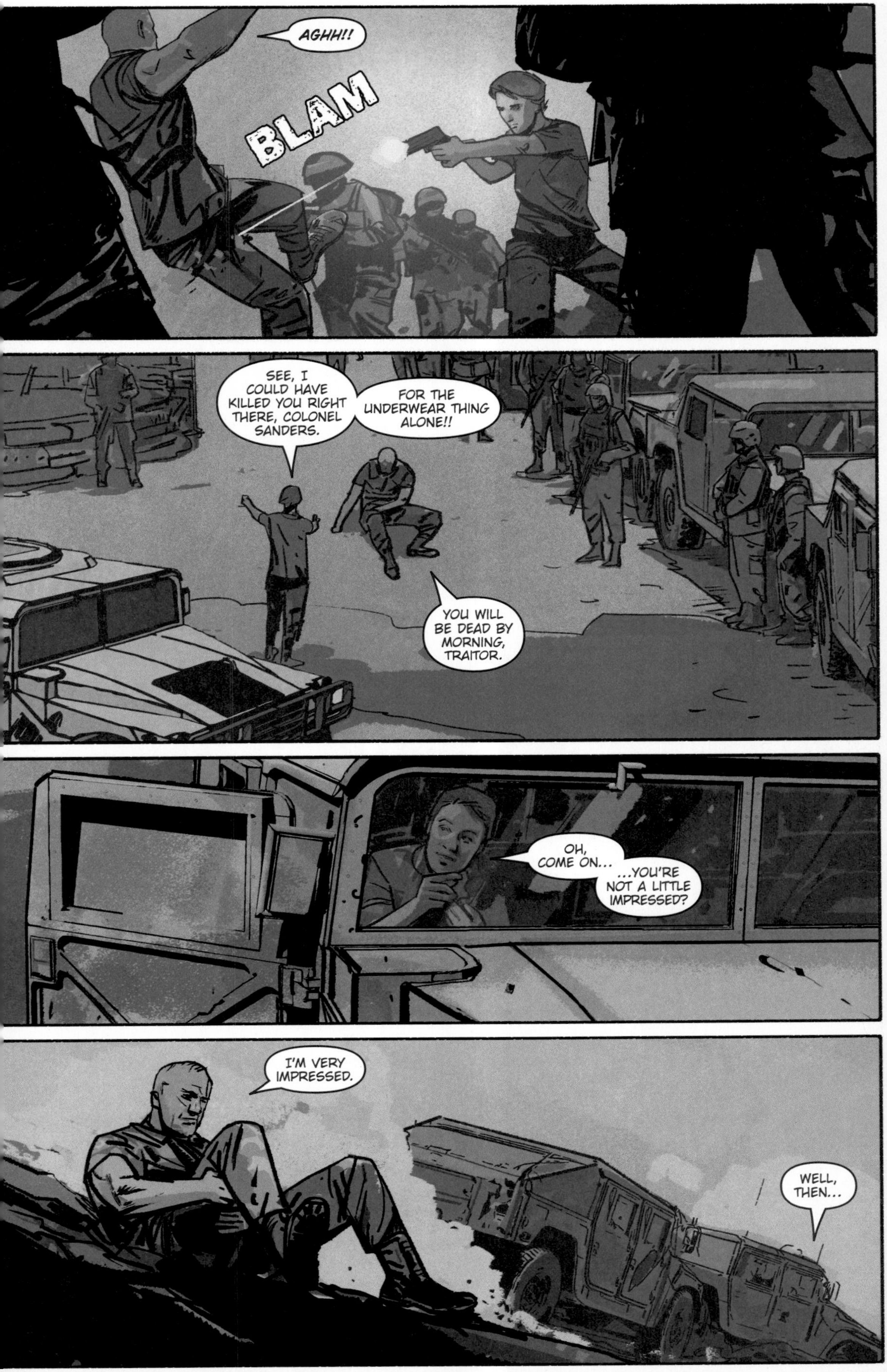
AGHH!!
BLAM
SEE, I COULD HAVE KILLED YOU RIGHT THERE, COLONEL SANDERS.
FOR THE UNDERWEAR THING ALONE!!
YOU WILL BE DEAD BY MORNING, TRAITOR.
OH, COME ON...
...YOU'RE NOT A LITTLE IMPRESSED?
I'M VERY IMPRESSED.
WELL, THEN...

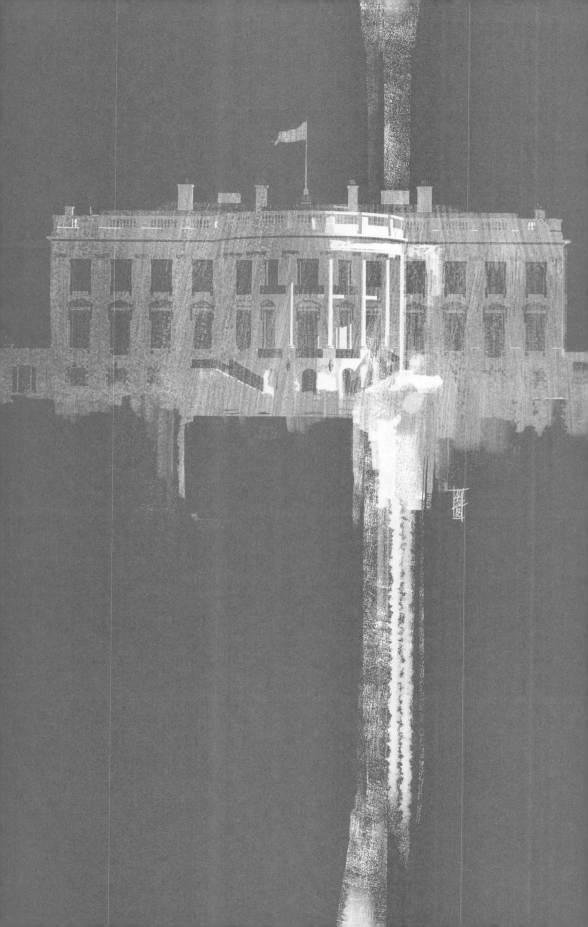

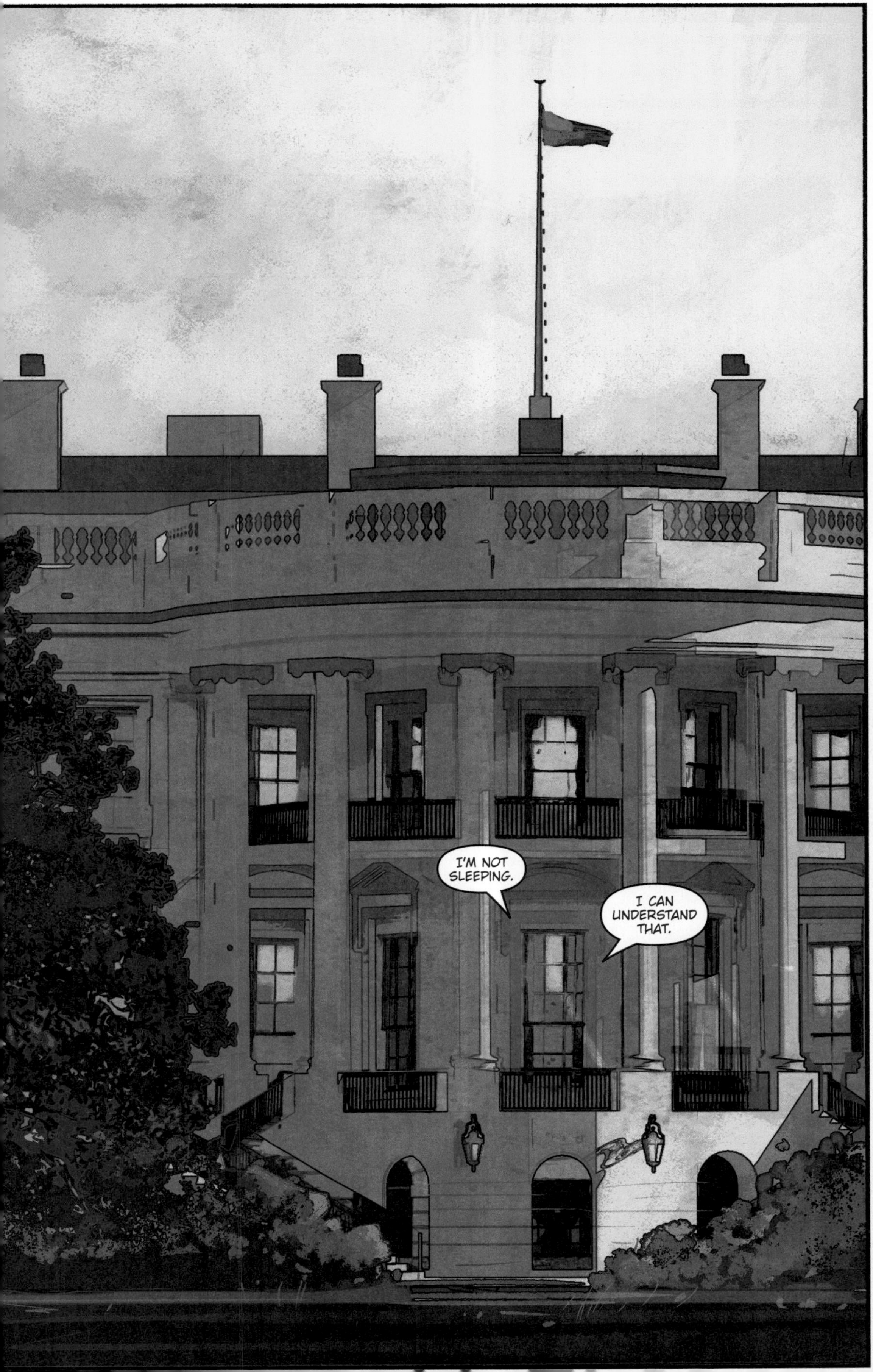
I'M NOT SLEEPING.
I CAN UNDERSTAND THAT.

PORTLAND.

WE HAVE FORTY SECONDS TOPS.

'KAY.

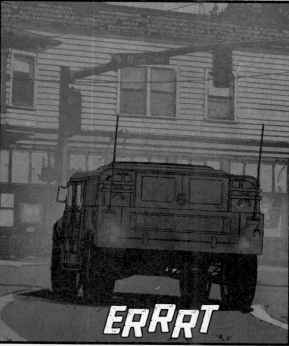

ErRRt

HAWTHORNE BOULEVARD.

SORRY.

NO WORRIES.

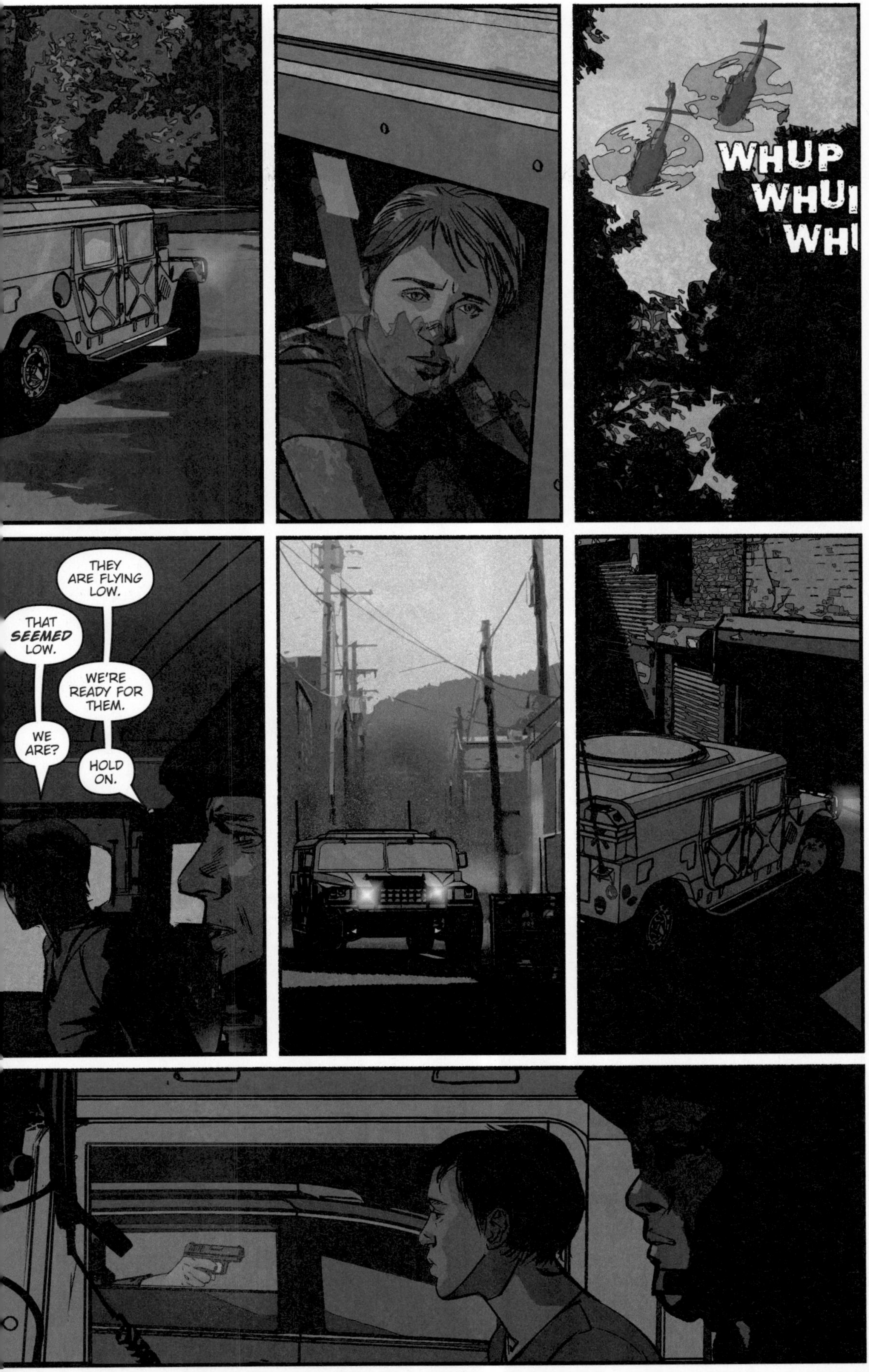
WHUP
WHU
WHU
THEY ARE FLYING LOW.
THAT SEEMED LOW.
WE'RE READY FOR THEM.
WE ARE?
HOLD ON.

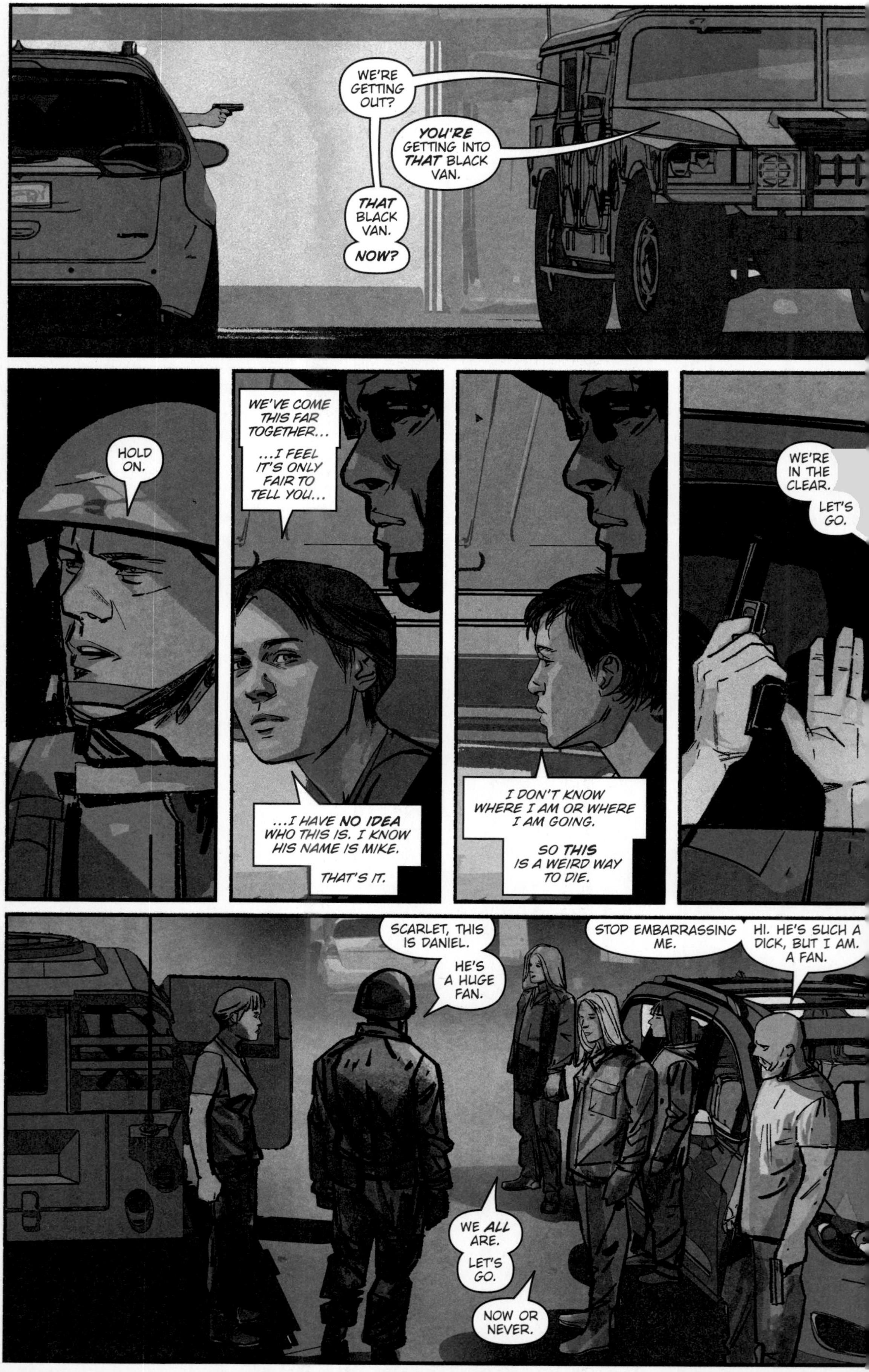
WE'RE GETTING OUT?
YOU'RE GETTING INTO THAT BLACK VAN.
THAT BLACK VAN.
NOW?
HOLD ON.
WE'VE COME THIS FAR TOGETHER...
...I FEEL IT'S ONLY FAIR TO TELL YOU...
...I HAVE NO IDEA WHO THIS IS. I KNOW HIS NAME IS MIKE.
THAT'S IT.
I DON'T KNOW WHERE I AM OR WHERE I AM GOING.
SO THIS IS A WEIRD WAY TO DIE.
WE'RE IN THE CLEAR.
LET'S GO.
SCARLET, THIS IS DANIEL.
HE'S A HUGE FAN.
STOP EMBARRASSING ME.
HI. HE'S SUCH A DICK, BUT I AM. A FAN.
WE ALL ARE.
LET'S GO.
NOW OR NEVER.

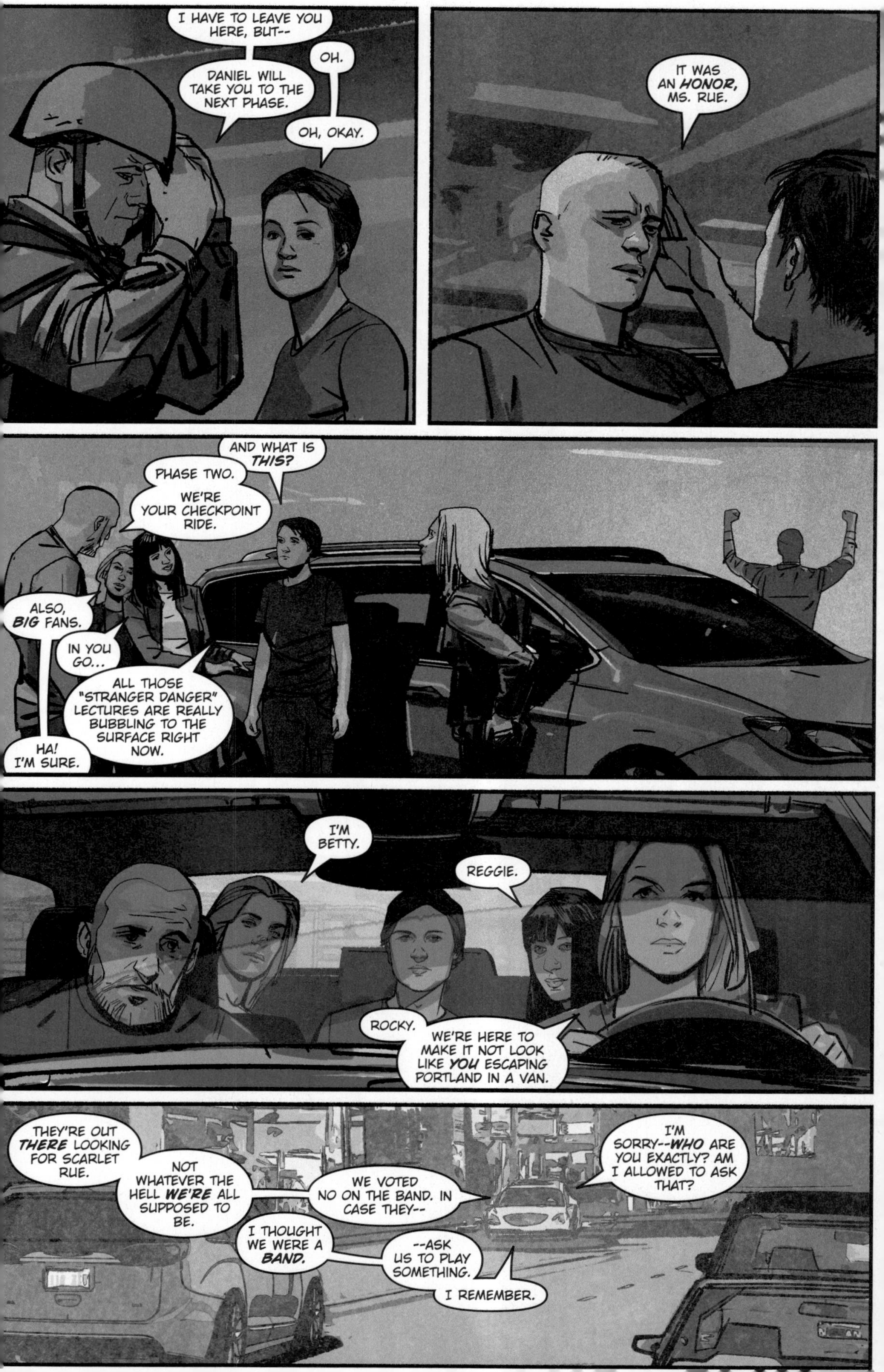
I HAVE TO LEAVE YOU HERE, BUT--
DANIEL WILL TAKE YOU TO THE NEXT PHASE.
OH.
OH, OKAY.
IT WAS AN HONOR, MS. RUE.
AND WHAT IS THIS?
PHASE TWO.
WE'RE YOUR CHECKPOINT RIDE.
ALSO, BIG FANS.
IN YOU GO...
ALL THOSE "STRANGER DANGER" LECTURES ARE REALLY BUBBLING TO THE SURFACE RIGHT NOW.
HA! I'M SURE.
I'M BETTY.
REGGIE.
ROCKY.
WE'RE HERE TO MAKE IT NOT LOOK LIKE YOU ESCAPING PORTLAND IN A VAN.
THEY'RE OUT THERE LOOKING FOR SCARLET RUE.
NOT WHATEVER THE HELL WE'RE ALL SUPPOSED TO BE.
I THOUGHT WE WERE A BAND.
WE VOTED NO ON THE BAND. IN CASE THEY--
--ASK US TO PLAY SOMETHING.
I REMEMBER.
I'M SORRY--WHO ARE YOU EXACTLY? AM I ALLOWED TO ASK THAT?

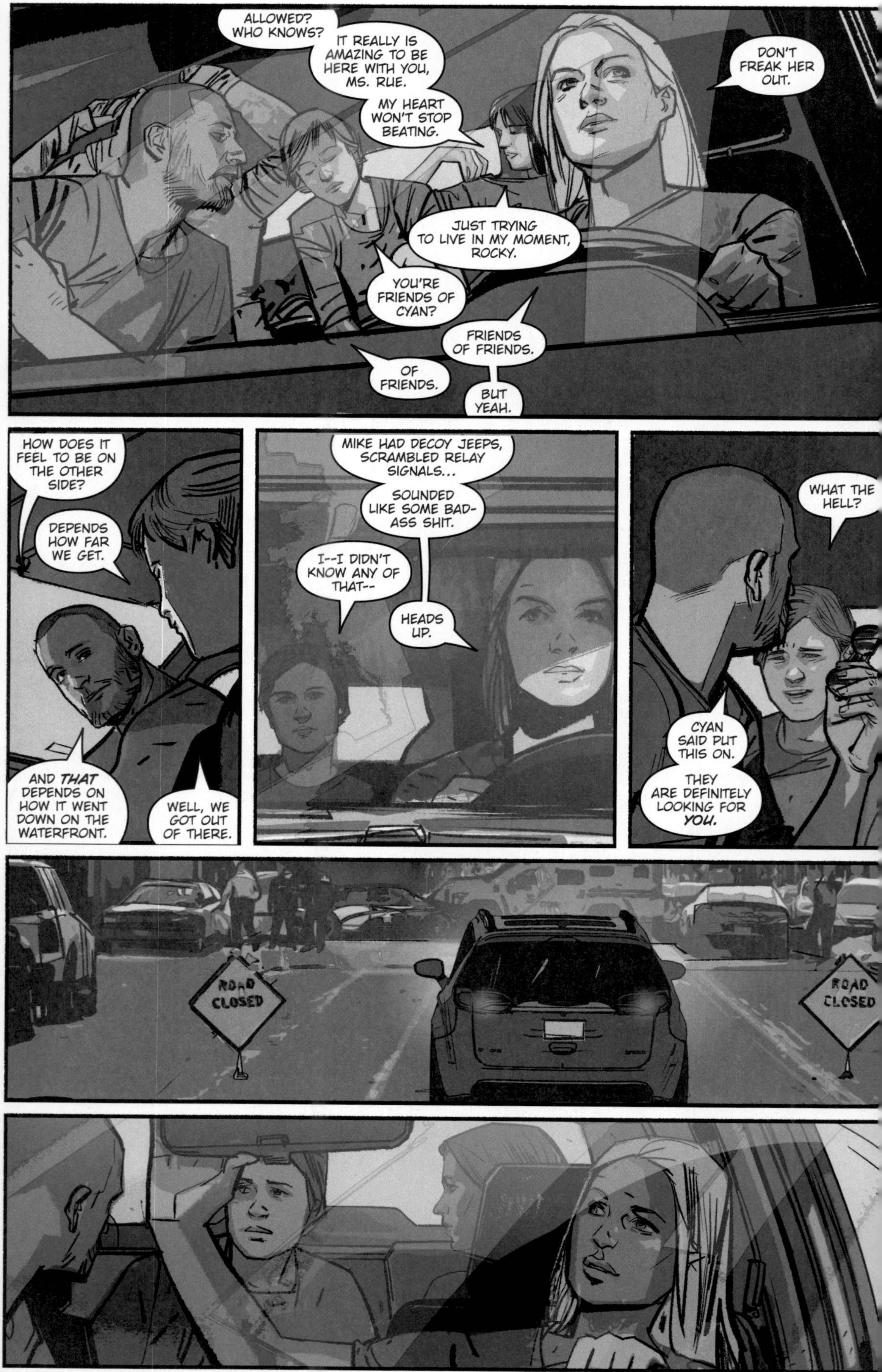
ALLOWED? WHO KNOWS?
IT REALLY IS AMAZING TO BE HERE WITH YOU, MS. RUE.
MY HEART WON'T STOP BEATING.
DON'T FREAK HER OUT.
JUST TRYING TO LIVE IN MY MOMENT, ROCKY.
YOU'RE FRIENDS OF CYAN?
FRIENDS OF FRIENDS.
OF FRIENDS.
BUT YEAH.
HOW DOES IT FEEL TO BE ON THE OTHER SIDE?
DEPENDS HOW FAR WE GET.
AND *THAT* DEPENDS ON HOW IT WENT DOWN ON THE WATERFRONT.
WELL, WE GOT OUT OF THERE.
MIKE HAD DECOY JEEPS, SCRAMBLED RELAY SIGNALS...
SOUNDED LIKE SOME BAD-ASS SHIT.
I--I DIDN'T KNOW ANY OF THAT--
HEADS UP.
WHAT THE HELL?
CYAN SAID PUT THIS ON.
THEY ARE DEFINITELY LOOKING FOR *YOU*.
ROAD CLOSED
ROAD CLOSED

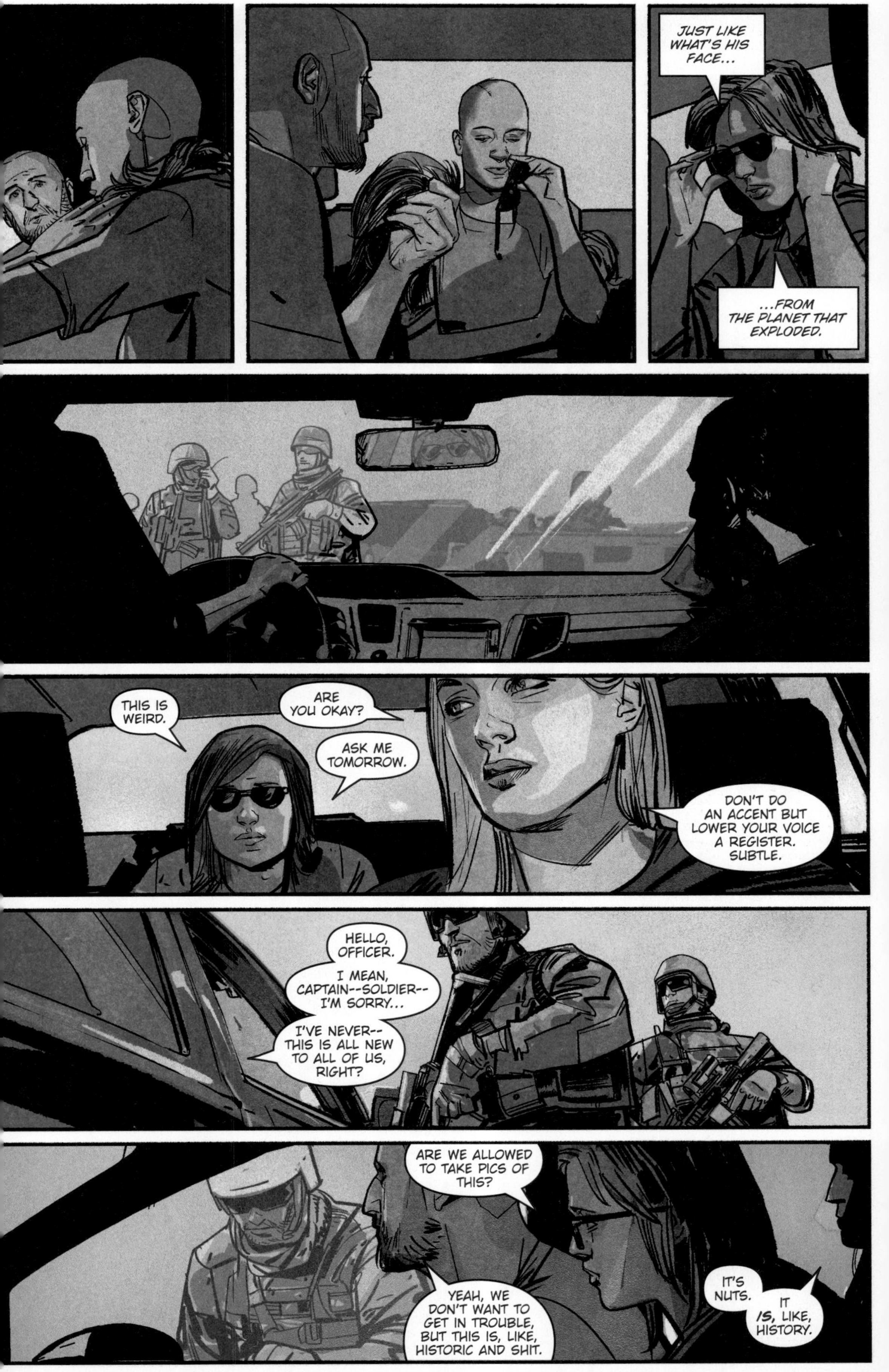
JUST LIKE WHAT'S HIS FACE...
...FROM THE PLANET THAT EXPLODED.
THIS IS WEIRD.
ARE YOU OKAY?
ASK ME TOMORROW.
DON'T DO AN ACCENT BUT LOWER YOUR VOICE A REGISTER. SUBTLE.
HELLO, OFFICER.
I MEAN, CAPTAIN--SOLDIER-- I'M SORRY...
I'VE NEVER-- THIS IS ALL NEW TO ALL OF US, RIGHT?
ARE WE ALLOWED TO TAKE PICS OF THIS?
YEAH, WE DON'T WANT TO GET IN TROUBLE, BUT THIS IS, LIKE, HISTORIC AND SHIT.
IT'S NUTS.
IT IS, LIKE, HISTORY.

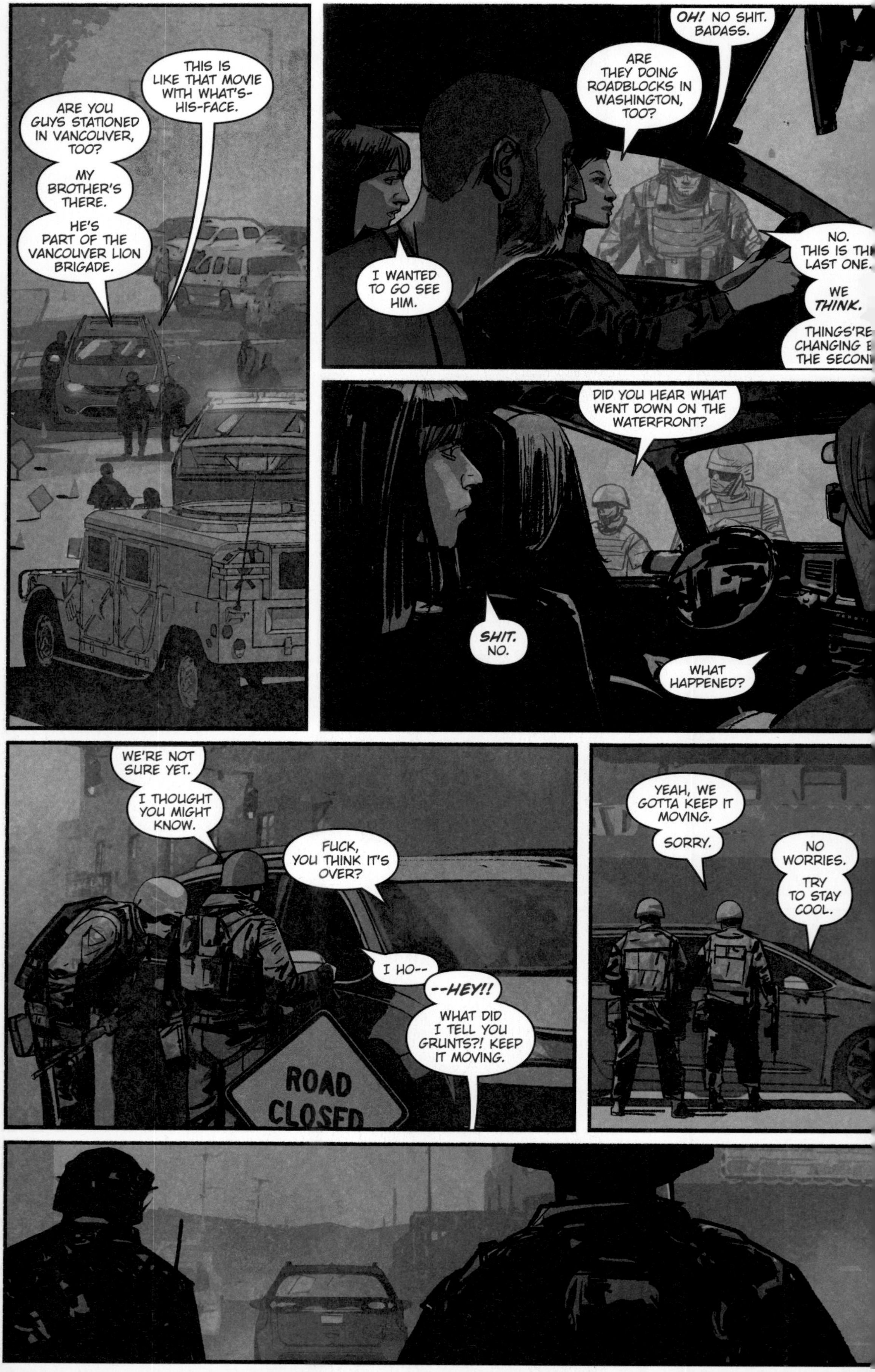
THIS IS LIKE THAT MOVIE WITH WHAT'S-HIS-FACE.
ARE YOU GUYS STATIONED IN VANCOUVER, TOO?
MY BROTHER'S THERE.
HE'S PART OF THE VANCOUVER LION BRIGADE.
OH! NO SHIT. BADASS.
ARE THEY DOING ROADBLOCKS IN WASHINGTON, TOO?
I WANTED TO GO SEE HIM.
NO. THIS IS TH LAST ONE.
WE THINK.
THINGS'RE CHANGING B THE SECON
DID YOU HEAR WHAT WENT DOWN ON THE WATERFRONT?
SHIT. NO.
WHAT HAPPENED?
WE'RE NOT SURE YET.
I THOUGHT YOU MIGHT KNOW.
FUCK, YOU THINK IT'S OVER?
I HO--
--HEY!!
WHAT DID I TELL YOU GRUNTS?! KEEP IT MOVING.
ROAD CLOSED
YEAH, WE GOTTA KEEP IT MOVING.
SORRY.
NO WORRIES.
TRY TO STAY COOL.

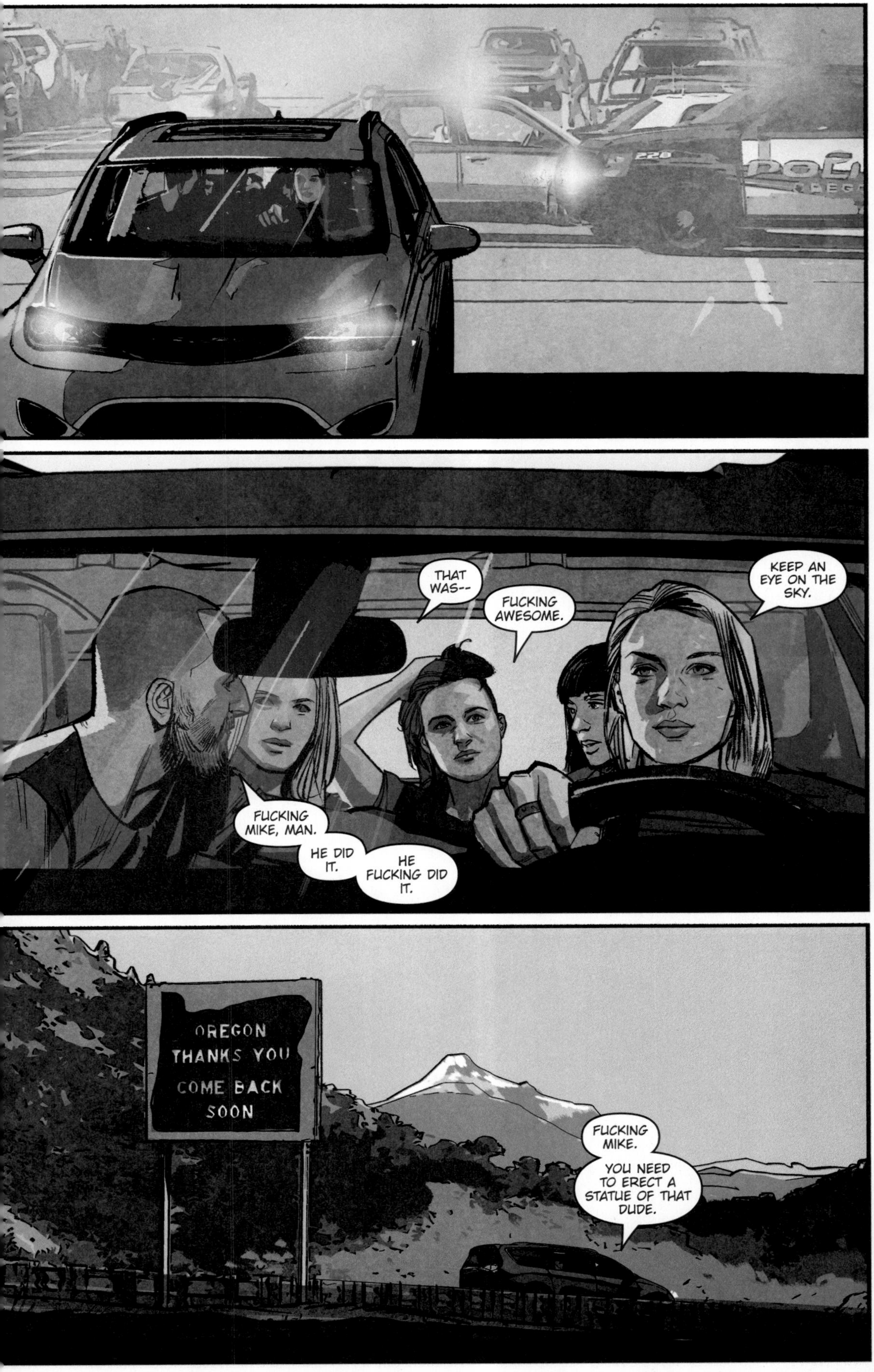
THAT WAS--
FUCKING AWESOME.
KEEP AN EYE ON THE SKY.
FUCKING MIKE, MAN.
HE DID IT.
HE FUCKING DID IT.
OREGON THANKS YOU COME BACK SOON
FUCKING MIKE.
YOU NEED TO ERECT A STATUE OF THAT DUDE.

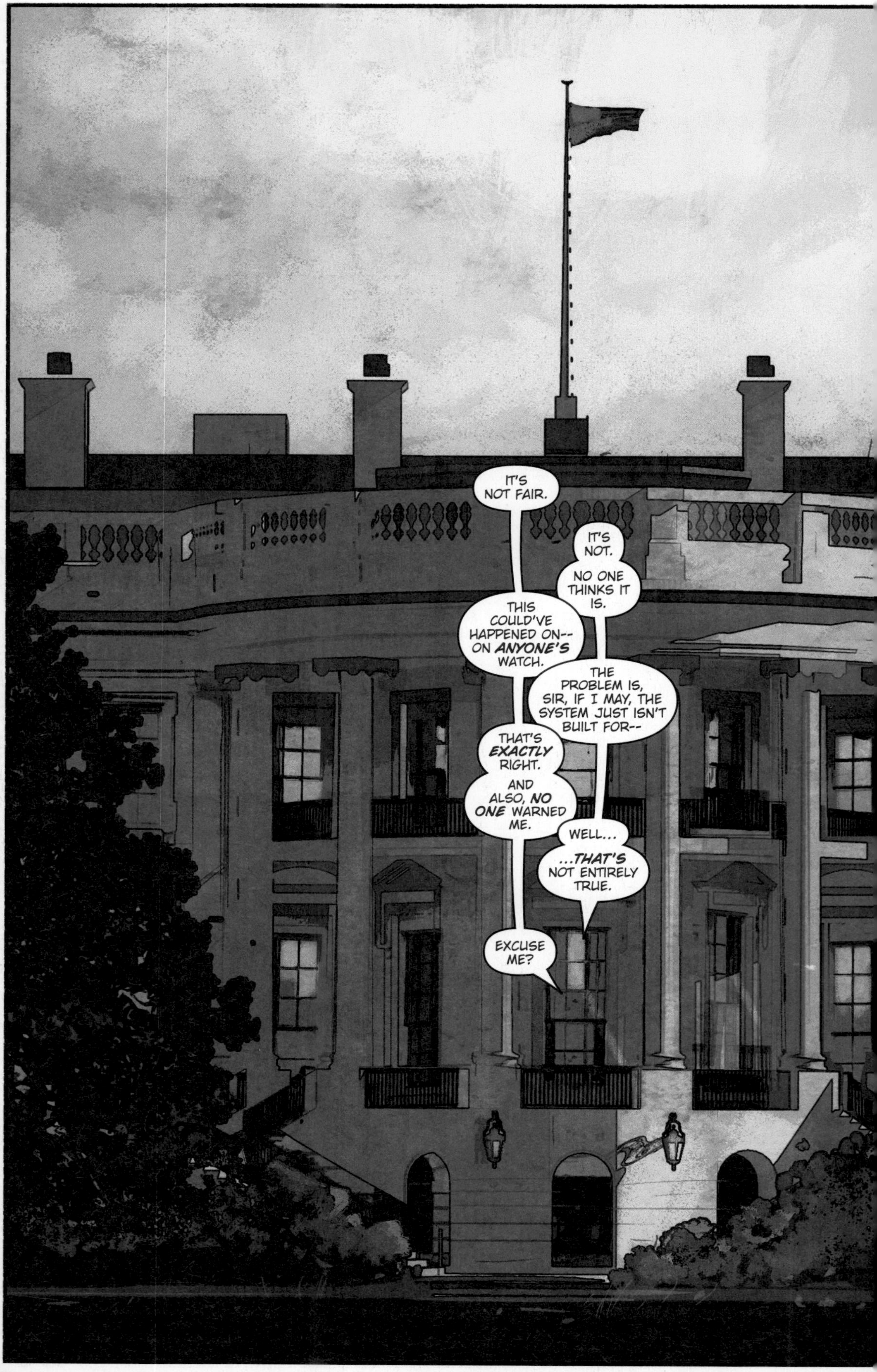
IT'S NOT FAIR.
IT'S NOT.
NO ONE THINKS IT IS.
THIS COULD'VE HAPPENED ON-- ON ANYONE'S WATCH.
THE PROBLEM IS, SIR, IF I MAY, THE SYSTEM JUST ISN'T BUILT FOR--
THAT'S EXACTLY RIGHT.
AND ALSO, NO ONE WARNED ME.
WELL...
...THAT'S NOT ENTIRELY TRUE.
EXCUSE ME?

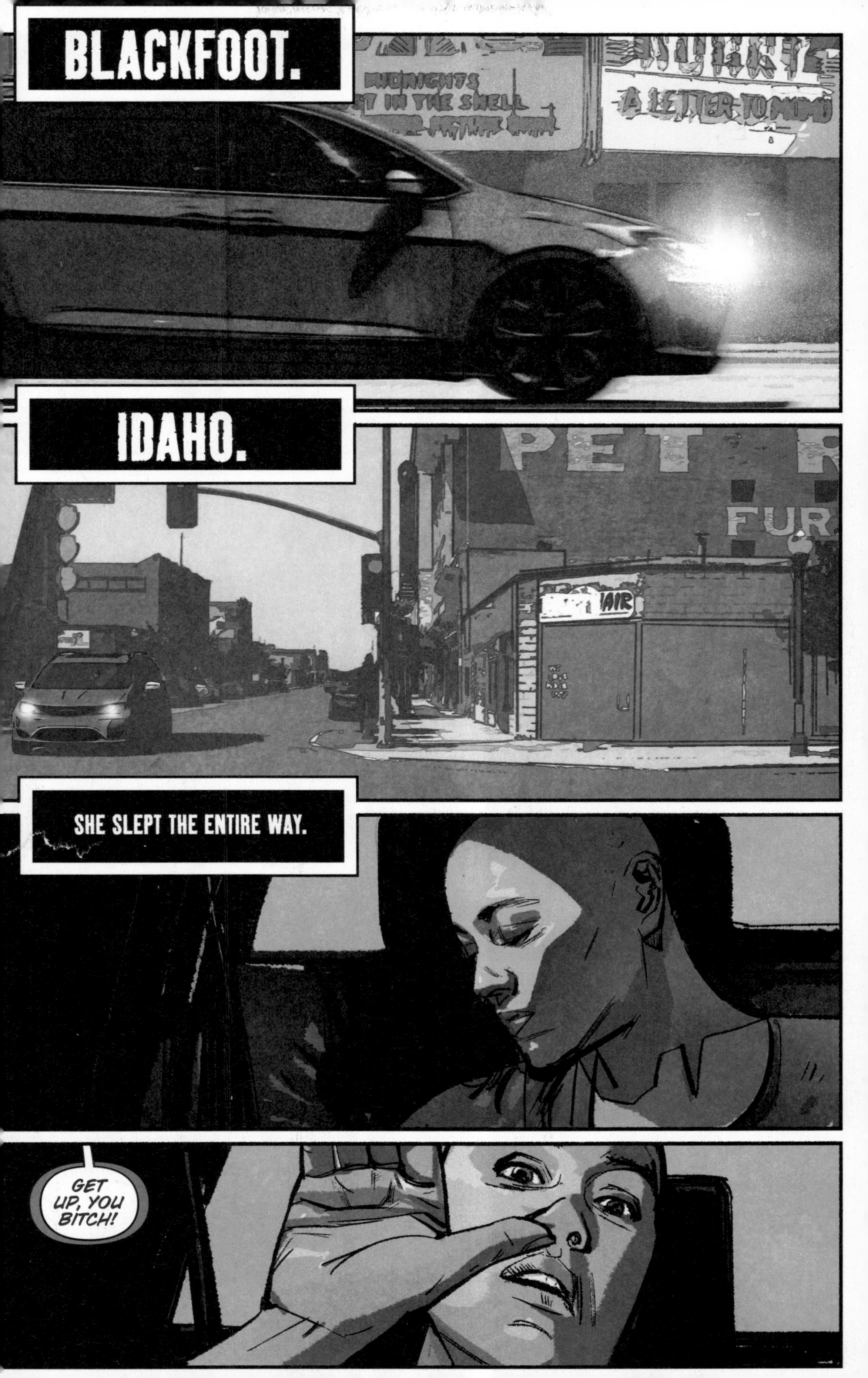
BLACKFOOT.
A LETTER TO MOMO
IDAHO.
AIR
SHE SLEPT THE ENTIRE WAY.
GET UP, YOU BITCH!

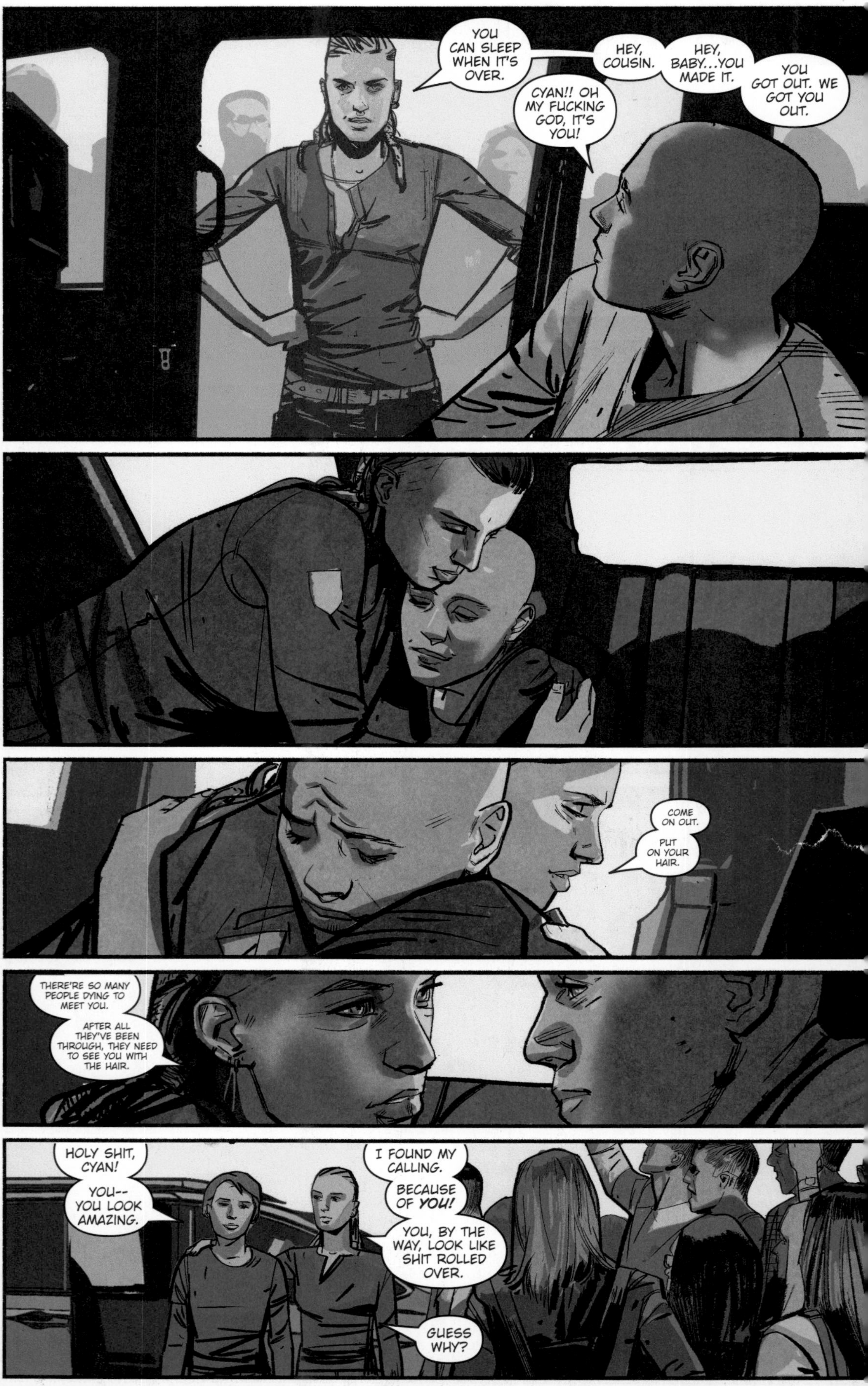
YOU CAN SLEEP WHEN IT'S OVER.
HEY, COUSIN.
CYAN!! OH MY FUCKING GOD, IT'S YOU!
HEY, BABY...YOU MADE IT.
YOU GOT OUT. WE GOT YOU OUT.
COME ON OUT.
PUT ON YOUR HAIR.
THERE'RE SO MANY PEOPLE DYING TO MEET YOU.
AFTER ALL THEY'VE BEEN THROUGH, THEY NEED TO SEE YOU WITH THE HAIR.
HOLY SHIT, CYAN!
YOU-- YOU LOOK AMAZING.
I FOUND MY CALLING.
BECAUSE OF YOU!
YOU, BY THE WAY, LOOK LIKE SHIT ROLLED OVER.
GUESS WHY?

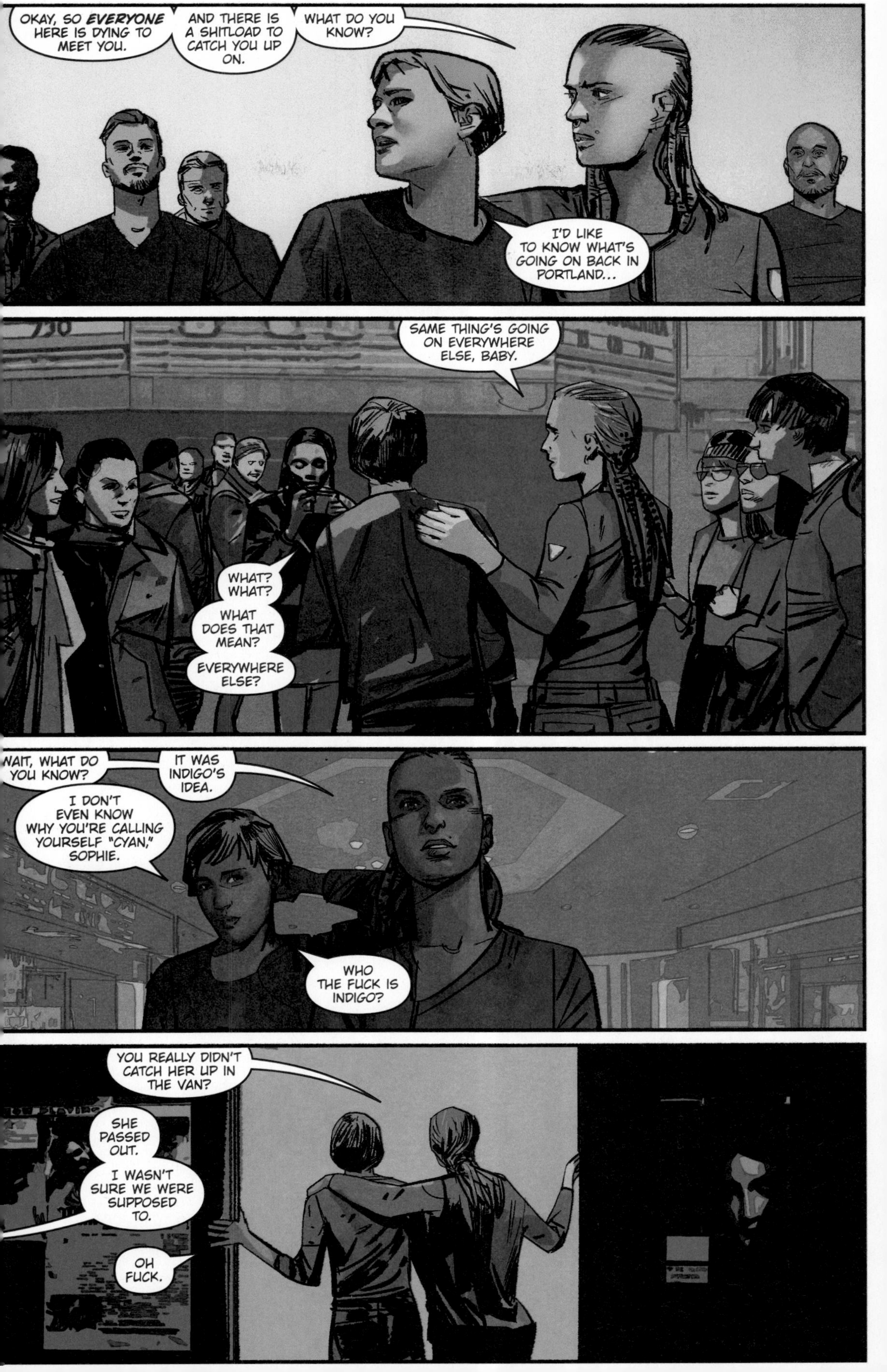
OKAY, SO EVERYONE HERE IS DYING TO MEET YOU.
AND THERE IS A SHITLOAD TO CATCH YOU UP ON.
WHAT DO YOU KNOW?
I'D LIKE TO KNOW WHAT'S GOING ON BACK IN PORTLAND...
SAME THING'S GOING ON EVERYWHERE ELSE, BABY.
WHAT? WHAT?
WHAT DOES THAT MEAN?
EVERYWHERE ELSE?
WAIT, WHAT DO YOU KNOW?
IT WAS INDIGO'S IDEA.
I DON'T EVEN KNOW WHY YOU'RE CALLING YOURSELF "CYAN," SOPHIE.
WHO THE FUCK IS INDIGO?
YOU REALLY DIDN'T CATCH HER UP IN THE VAN?
SHE PASSED OUT.
I WASN'T SURE WE WERE SUPPOSED TO.
OH FUCK.

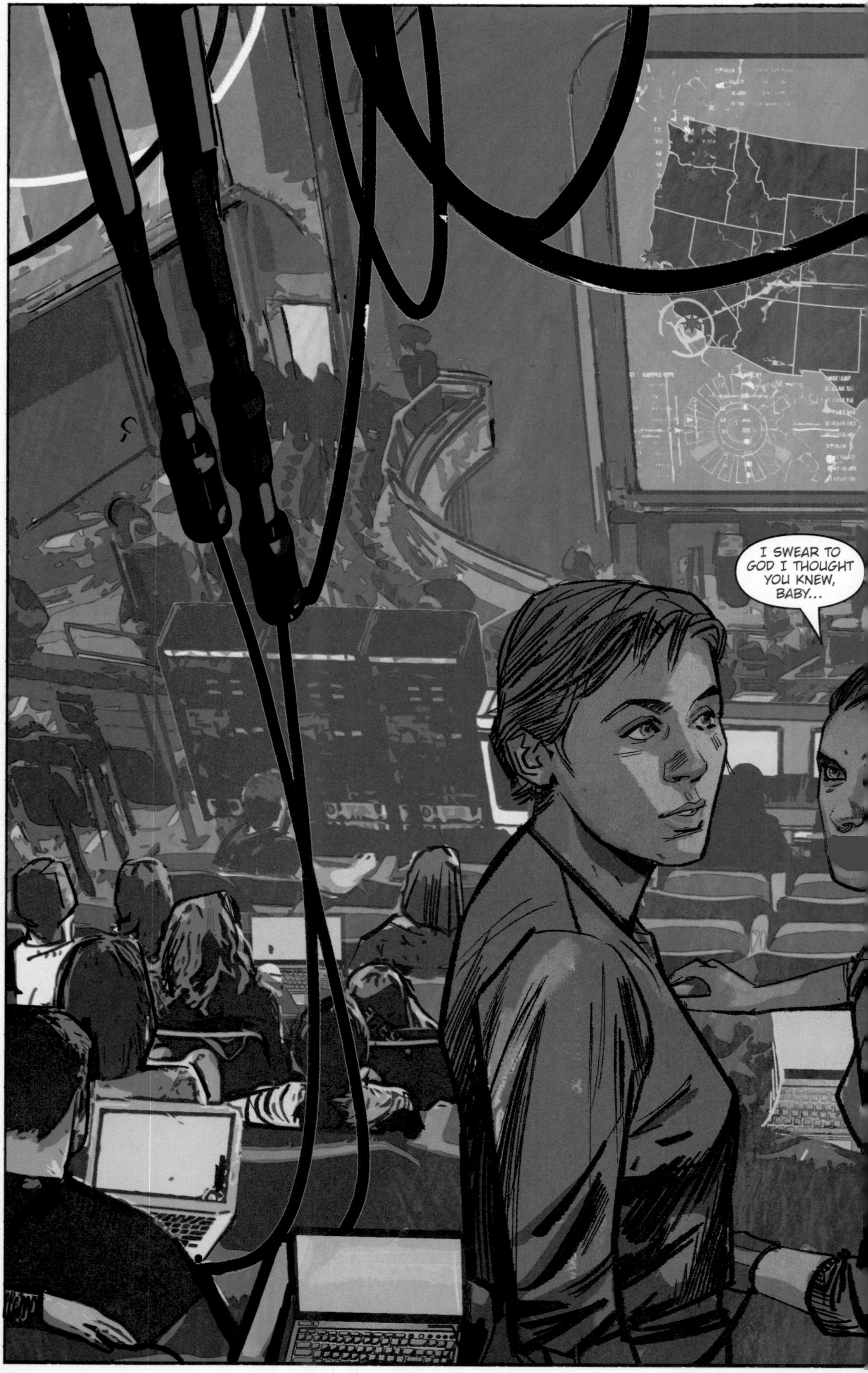
I SWEAR TO GOD I THOUGHT YOU KNEW, BABY...

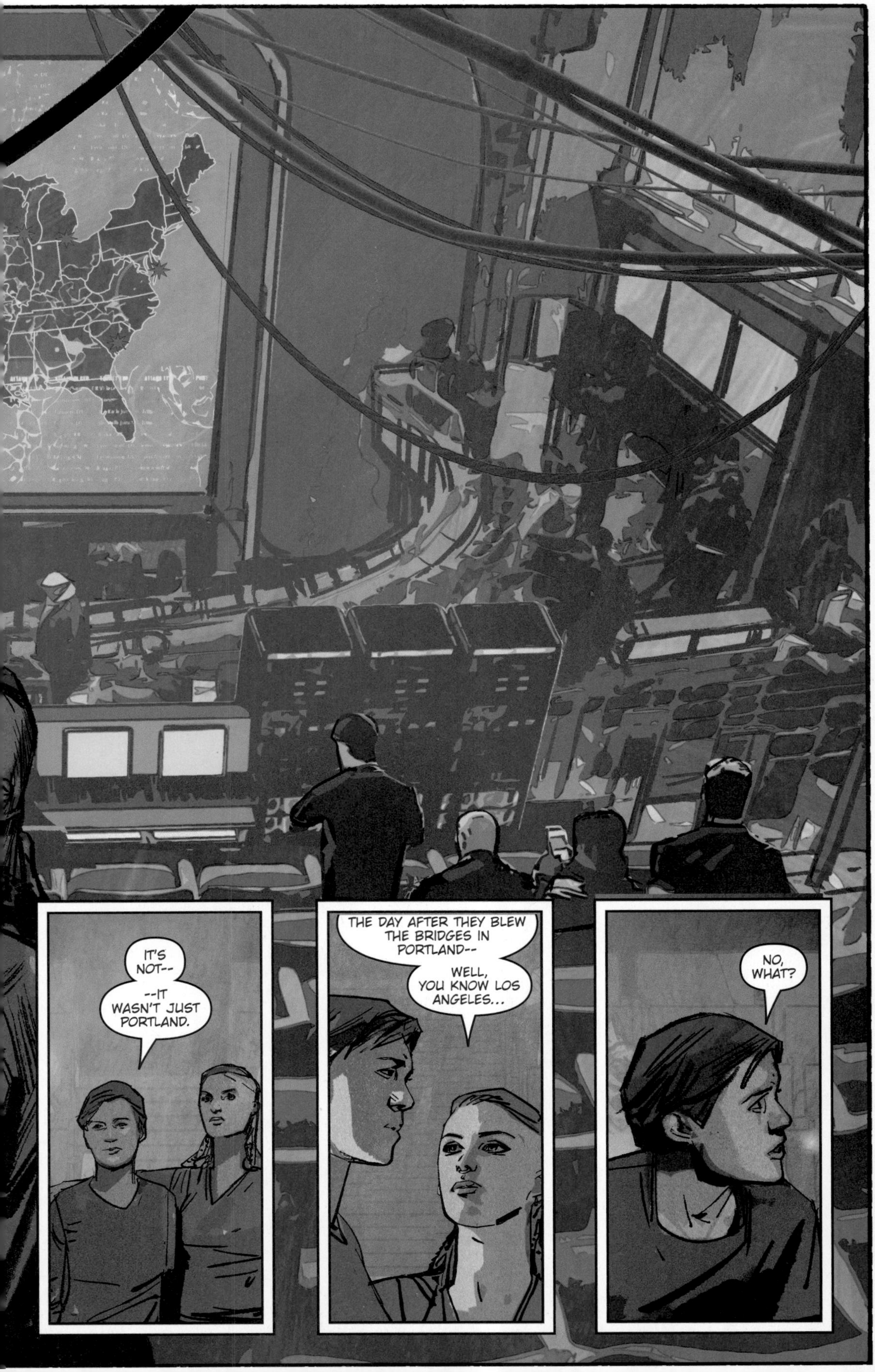
IT'S NOT--
--IT WASN'T JUST PORTLAND.
THE DAY AFTER THEY BLEW THE BRIDGES IN PORTLAND--
WELL, YOU KNOW LOS ANGELES...
NO, WHAT?

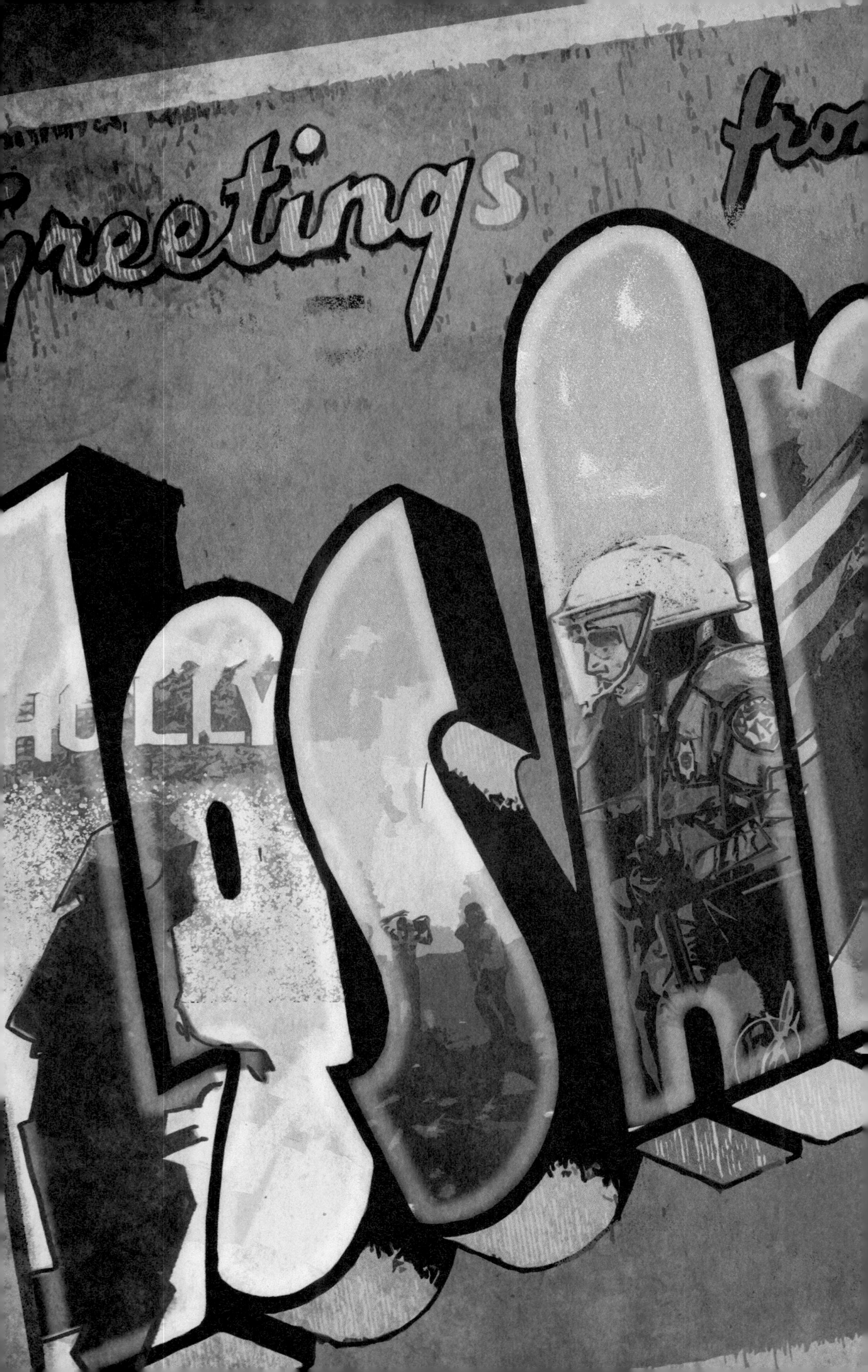

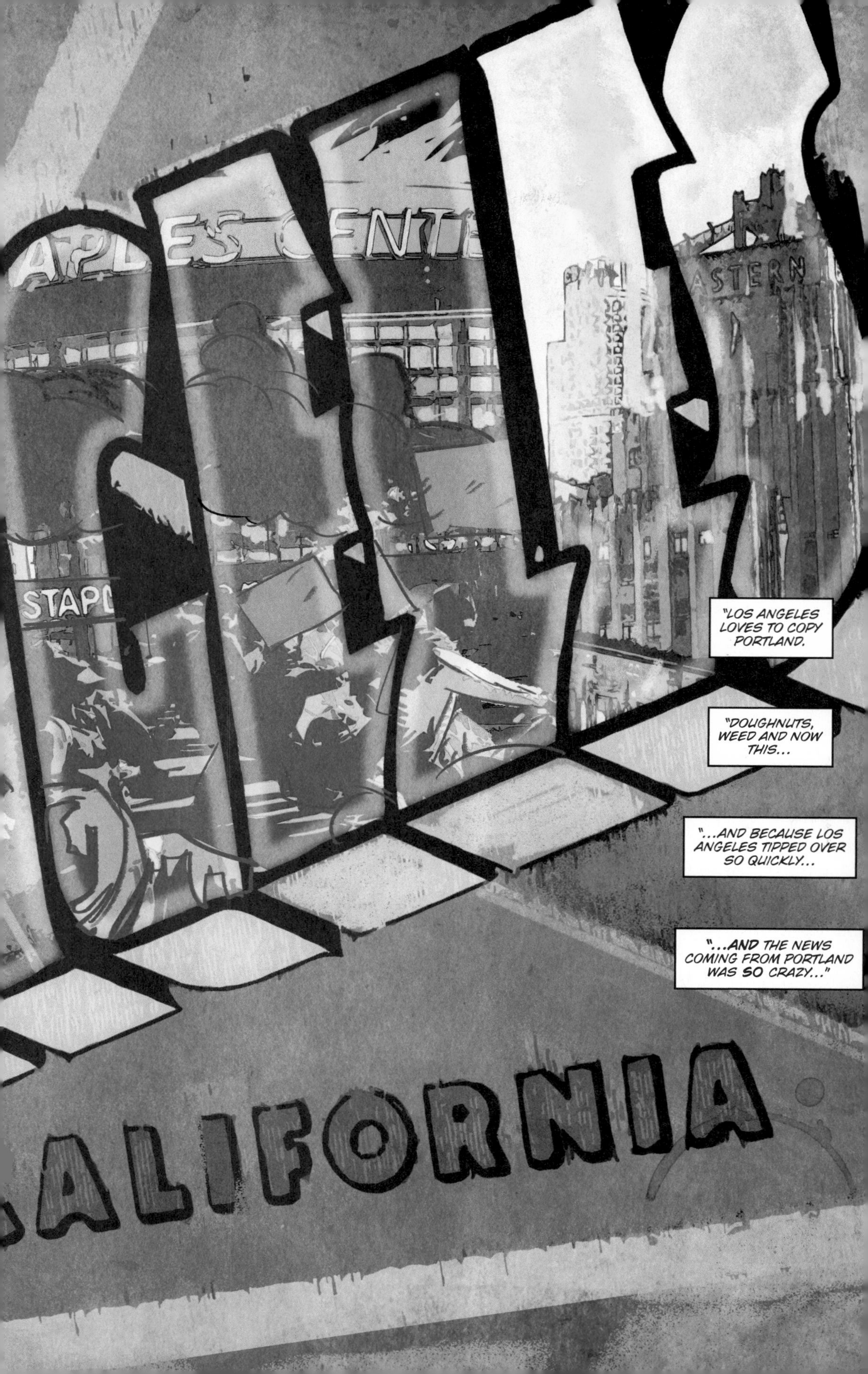

"LOS ANGELES LOVES TO COPY PORTLAND.
"DOUGHNUTS, WEED AND NOW THIS...
"...AND BECAUSE LOS ANGELES TIPPED OVER SO QUICKLY...
"...AND THE NEWS COMING FROM PORTLAND WAS SO CRAZY..."
CALIFORNIA

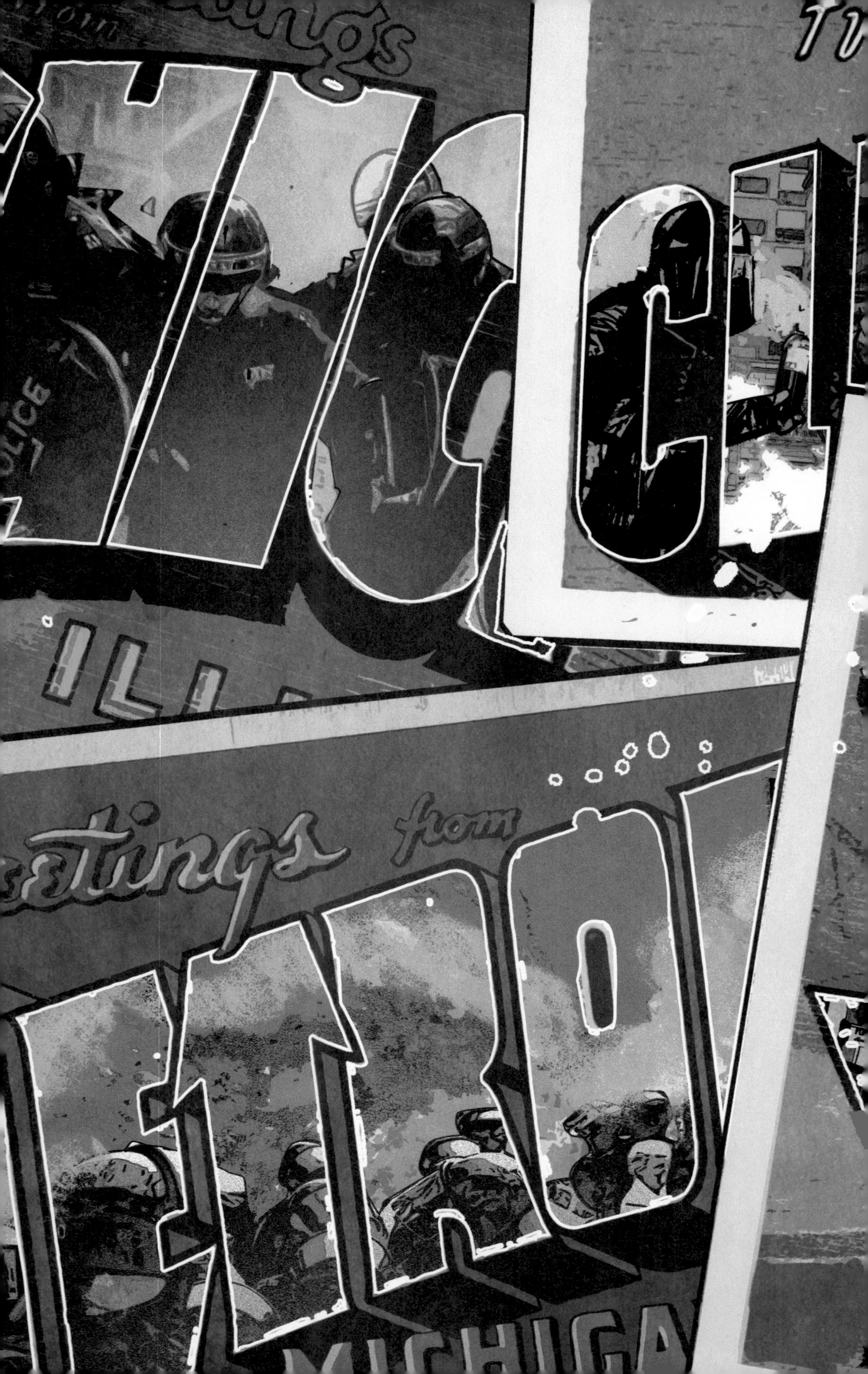
tings from
ICHIGA

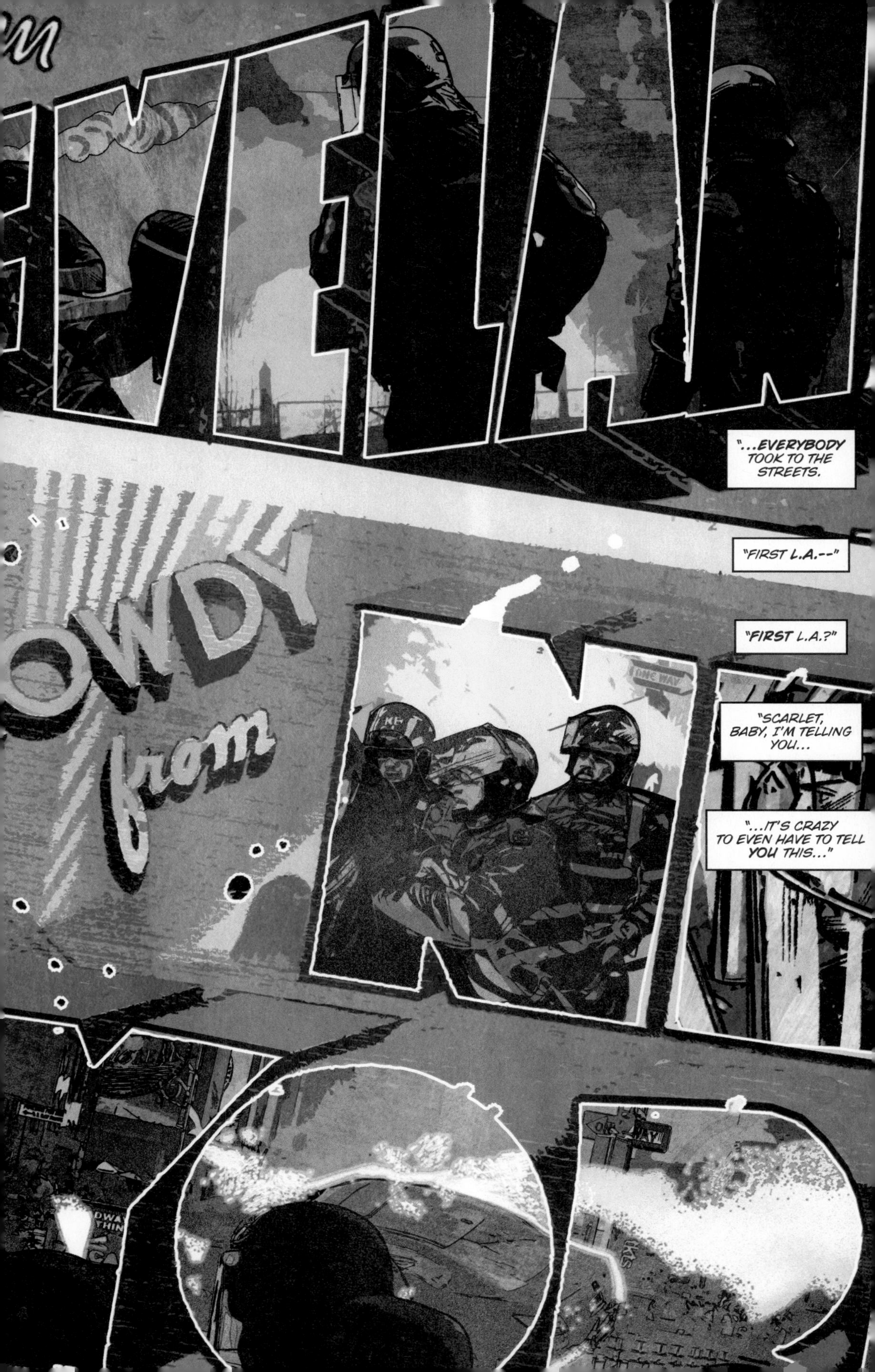

"...EVERYBODY TOOK TO THE STREETS.
"FIRST L.A.--"
"FIRST L.A.?"
"SCARLET, BABY, I'M TELLING YOU...
"...IT'S CRAZY TO EVEN HAVE TO TELL YOU THIS..."

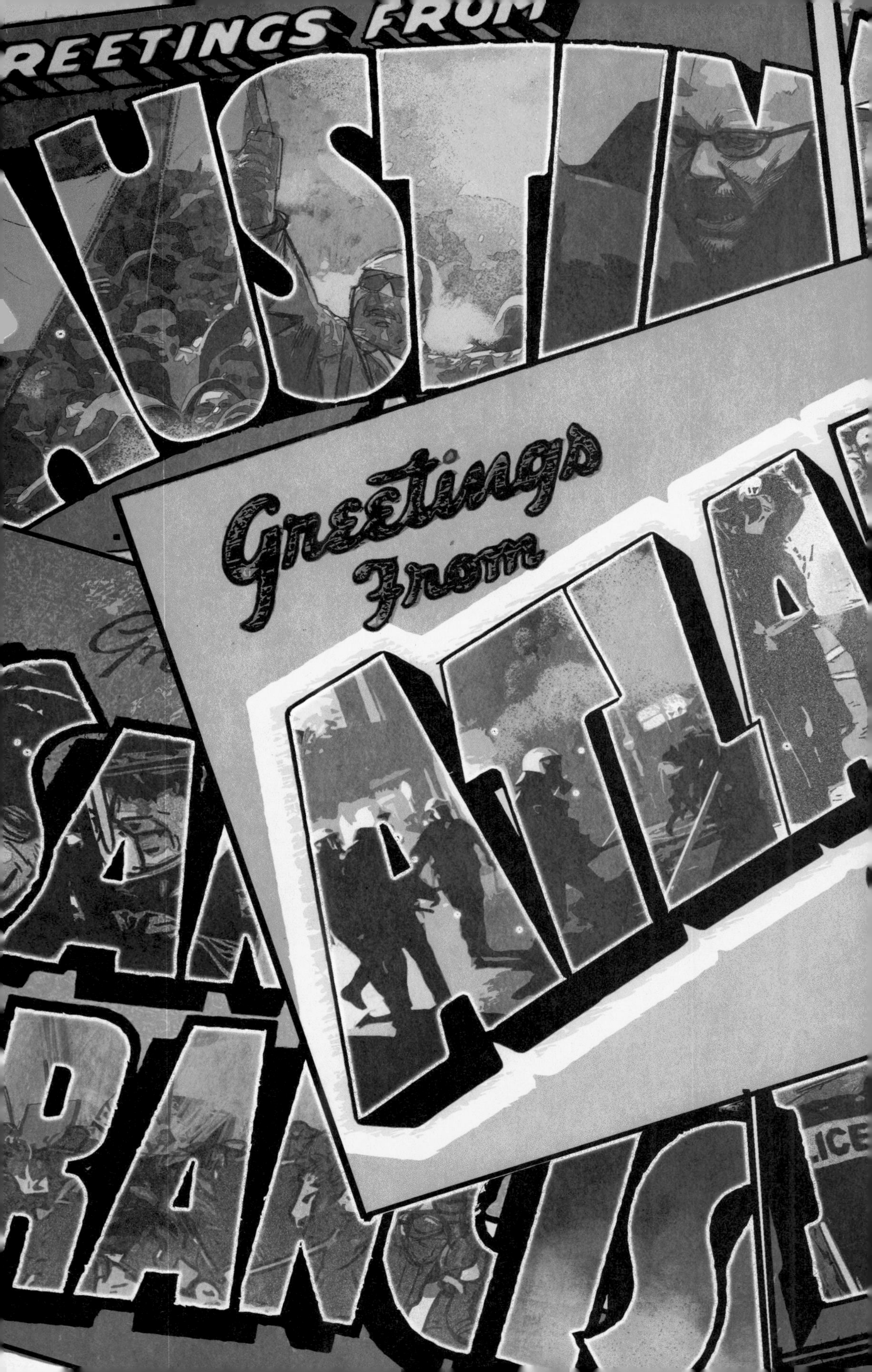
REETINGS FROM
Greetings From

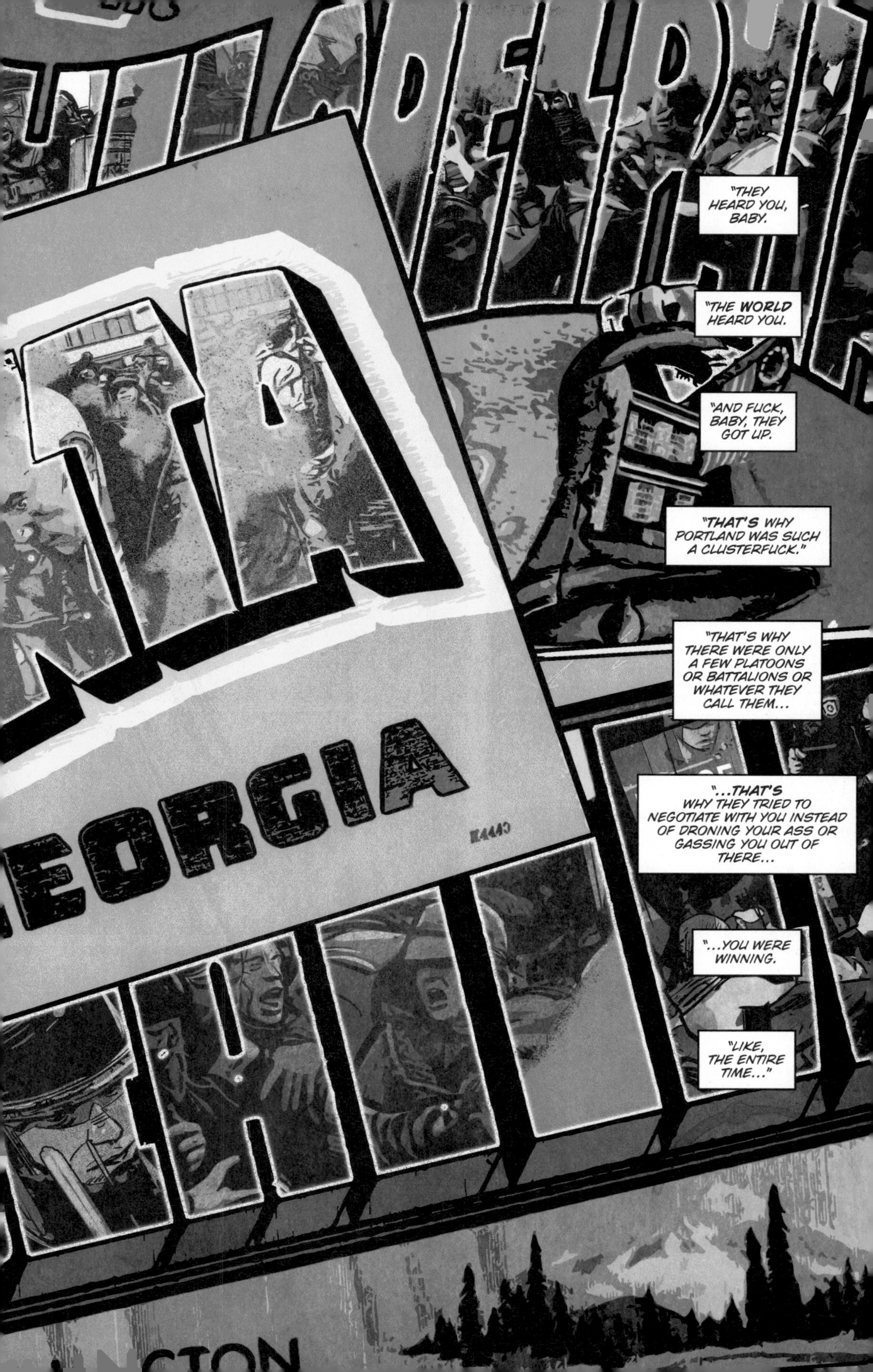
"THEY HEARD YOU, BABY.
"THE WORLD HEARD YOU.
"AND FUCK, BABY, THEY GOT UP.
"THAT'S WHY PORTLAND WAS SUCH A CLUSTERFUCK."
"THAT'S WHY THERE WERE ONLY A FEW PLATOONS OR BATTALIONS OR WHATEVER THEY CALL THEM...
"...THAT'S WHY THEY TRIED TO NEGOTIATE WITH YOU INSTEAD OF DRONING YOUR ASS OR GASSING YOU OUT OF THERE...
"...YOU WERE WINNING.
"LIKE, THE ENTIRE TIME..."
GEORGIA

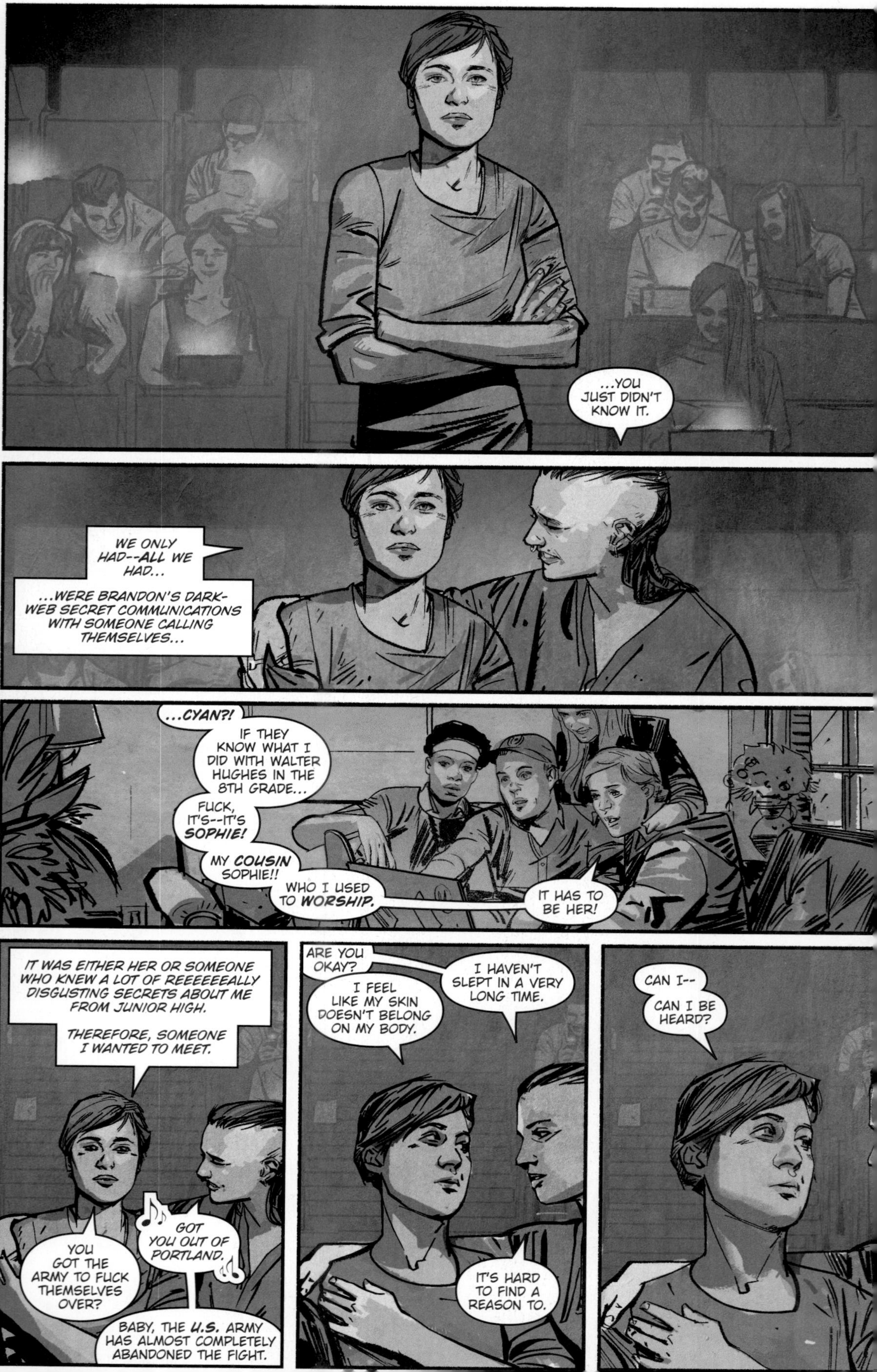

...YOU JUST DIDN'T KNOW IT.
WE ONLY HAD--ALL WE HAD...
...WERE BRANDON'S DARK-WEB SECRET COMMUNICATIONS WITH SOMEONE CALLING THEMSELVES...
...CYAN?!
IF THEY KNOW WHAT I DID WITH WALTER HUGHES IN THE 8TH GRADE...
FUCK, IT'S--IT'S SOPHIE!
MY COUSIN SOPHIE!!
WHO I USED TO WORSHIP.
IT HAS TO BE HER!
IT WAS EITHER HER OR SOMEONE WHO KNEW A LOT OF REEEEEEALLY DISGUSTING SECRETS ABOUT ME FROM JUNIOR HIGH.
THEREFORE, SOMEONE I WANTED TO MEET.
YOU GOT THE ARMY TO FUCK THEMSELVES OVER?
GOT YOU OUT OF PORTLAND.
BABY, THE U.S. ARMY HAS ALMOST COMPLETELY ABANDONED THE FIGHT.
ARE YOU OKAY?
I HAVEN'T SLEPT IN A VERY LONG TIME.
I FEEL LIKE MY SKIN DOESN'T BELONG ON MY BODY.
IT'S HARD TO FIND A REASON TO.
CAN I--
CAN I BE HEARD?

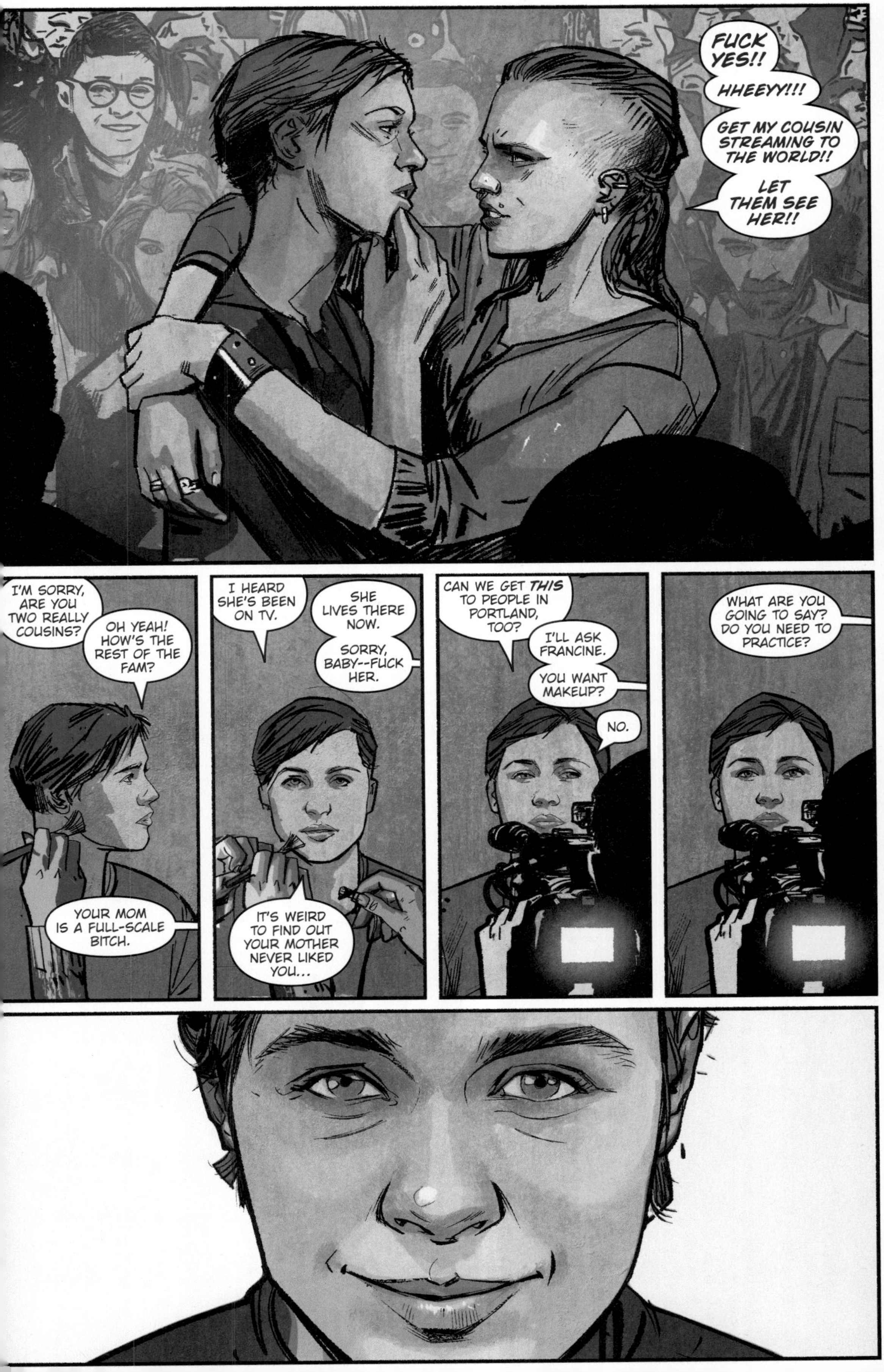
FUCK YES!!
HHEEYY!!!
GET MY COUSIN STREAMING TO THE WORLD!!
LET THEM SEE HER!!
I'M SORRY, ARE YOU TWO REALLY COUSINS?
OH YEAH! HOW'S THE REST OF THE FAM?
YOUR MOM IS A FULL-SCALE BITCH.
I HEARD SHE'S BEEN ON TV.
SHE LIVES THERE NOW.
SORRY, BABY--FUCK HER.
IT'S WEIRD TO FIND OUT YOUR MOTHER NEVER LIKED YOU...
CAN WE GET THIS TO PEOPLE IN PORTLAND, TOO?
I'LL ASK FRANCINE.
YOU WANT MAKEUP?
NO.
WHAT ARE YOU GOING TO SAY? DO YOU NEED TO PRACTICE?

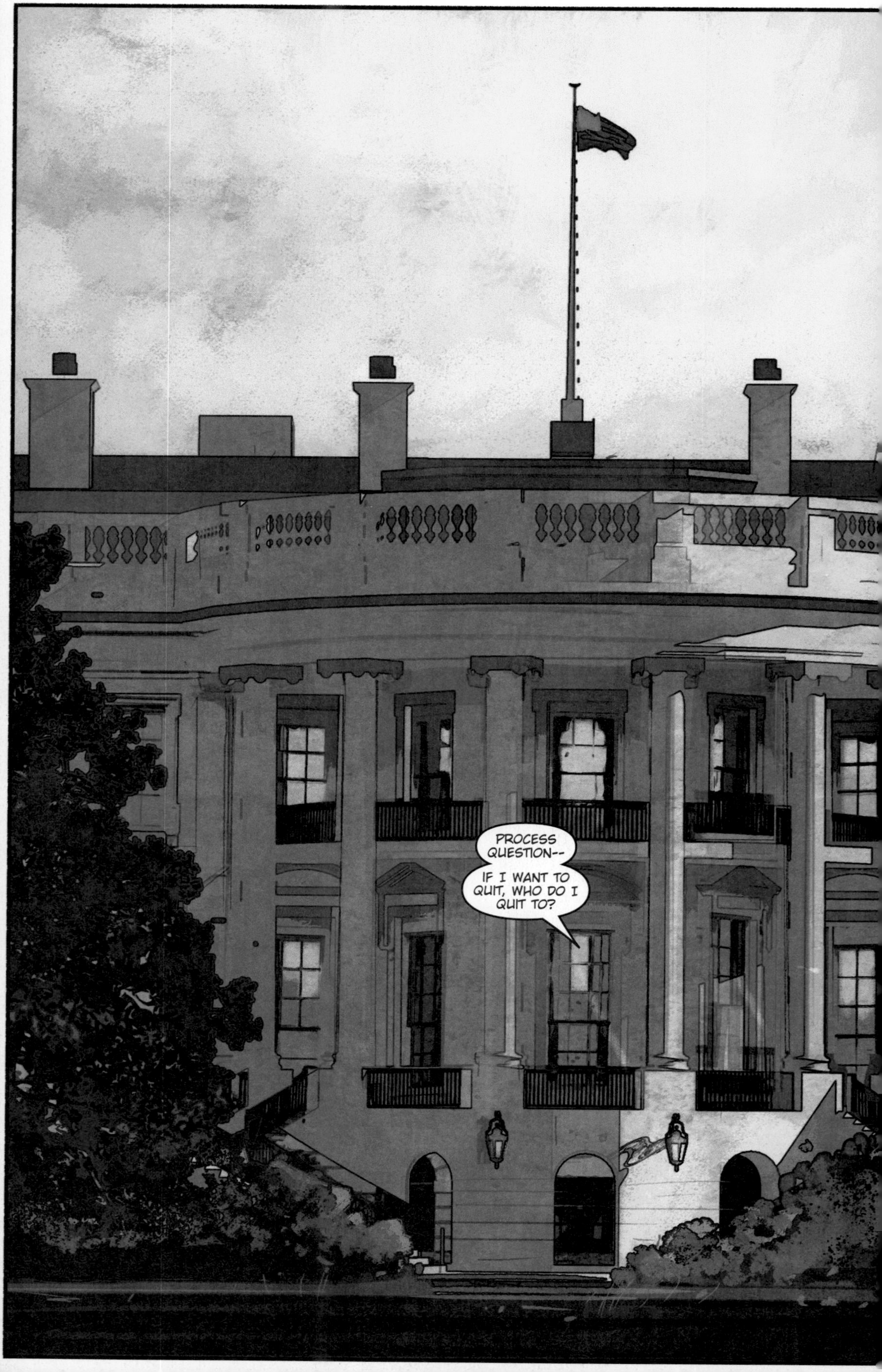
PROCESS QUESTION--
IF I WANT TO QUIT, WHO DO I QUIT TO?

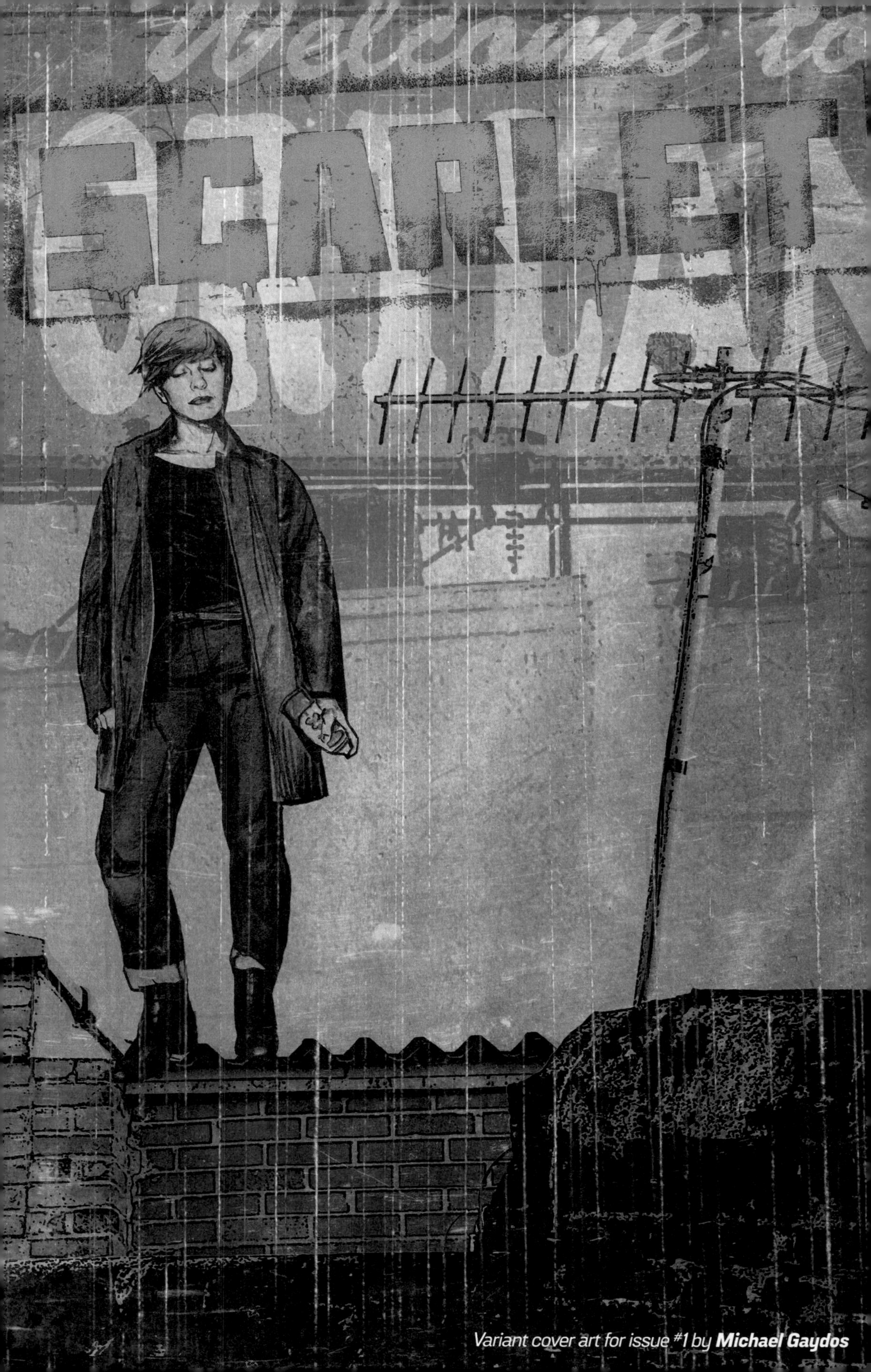
Welcome to
SCARLET

Variant cover art for issue #1 by **Michael Gaydos**

BENDIS & MALEEV Stage an Apolitical Revolution for the People in SCARLET

By Forrest Helvie, Newsarama Contributor

You say you want to start a revolution? Well, according to Scarlet, we all want to change the world... but perhaps she's the one to help make it happen? Brian Michael Bendis and Alex Maleev's SCARLET returned to comic shelves in August via DC Comics' new Jinxworld imprint, and the new limited series continues on with this week's #2.

Picking up shortly after Scarlet's successfully having coordinated multiple protests across Portland, which brought the city's corrupt officials to their knees, the young rebel finds herself at the head of a revolution that successfully took control of the city. Now, Scarlet and her band of rebels find themselves on the phone to talk terms with the President of the United States.

Newsarama took less drastic measures and talked about the terms of this first issue with Bendis, looking at what it was like picking up this series after a two-year hiatus along with how he sees this relaunch fitting into the cultural climate in which it now finds itself being published compared to its original releases in 2012 and 2016.

Newsarama: *Born out of the protests against the 1% in the wake of the "Great Recession" of the early 21st Century, you and Alex Maleev teamed up in 2012 to introduce readers to SCARLET, the story of a Portlander who sought revenge against the corrupt law enforcement* and elected officials of the town through killing those who served only themselves at the expense of others.

How well did the people of Portland receive this series when it first hit? Should I assume you're still waiting for your key to the city?

Brian Michael Bendis: *[Laughs]* Not likely to happen. I think I was happier that images presented weren't taken out of context. People can often take a panel—one out of dozens, mind you—and throw it up online and does it ever read differently! I was a little worried at the time about that happening because some of the panels in isolation could be read differently with a markedly different message than what we were telling in the story in a book like this.

Nrama: *In all seriousness though, your series dug deep into the anger and resentment that many Americans felt at the time and seems to do the same today. You've mentioned before that you don't set out to solve the world's problems when you tell a story, but it does seem the cultural influences around you at the time were bubbling more than a little close to the surface of this series, no?*

Bendis: The answer is "Yes!" Alex and I were seeking out what a creator-owned would look like between the two of us versus our previous work together. I guess that's sort of an easy problem to have, but when you're known for something, you have to put that into the mix of what you do next. Any filmmaker or musician does that. You make a heavy album and then you need to go make something lighter. And Alex and I were exploring the story behind SCARLET—what was the story and what was the truth that we wanted to dig into?

***Nrama:* Just looking at where you were coming from at the time, were any there specific incidents that set you and Alex off to say "That's it. There's our story" or was it something that just grew on its own between the two of you?**

Bendis: As I was doing research downtown, I saw a few cops come up to a young, red-headed girl and her friends in Pioneer Square in Portland, and it got hostile and rough. The cops grabbed and arrested her while she screamed "I didn't do anything!" My friends and I, along with hundreds of others, saw it all and were shocked. Keep in mind, none of us knows whether she did anything wrong or not. She could have been completely guilty for all we know. It was just this visceral experience that was shocking to see and it stayed with me. I sat down then and there to write it down when all of the sudden, a wedding pours out into the streets not long after, which I included in issue #3 of the original series.

It was fascinating. In the span of about 45 minutes, I see two women who looked almost identical have their lives either seemingly destroyed or brought to life on the very same street. It connected with me and ever since that happened, the story started coming together.

Of course, the other major influencer is the city of Portland itself. Ever since 2008 and especially throughout the Occupy Wall Street movement, there have been protests throughout the city. And it wasn't just Occupy. There were days when the whole city shut down. It became kind of normal. Even if the next American Revolution took place and started in Portland, my response would be "Eh, okay."

And that's what led me back to SCARLET. What would it take to start that revolution? What would take those protests to the next level? What would happen and it would be one person being pushed too far at the wrong time.

***Nrama:* So, you'd say it's between the protest movements of the 2000s and 2010s along with this one particular incident that gave rise to SCARLET?**

Bendis: Yes, but also...I go through the phases of watching the movie *Network* by Paddy Chayefsky, which at the time, it seemed like some sort of crazy depiction of our world. And of course, it's all come true! In one way or another, there's not one thing that hasn't already shown up as reality television we've all seen. So, what can we write today that would have that same sort of prescient nature. And that's where SCARLET gets some of its influence as well.

Nrama:* Of course, the politics of the nation have grown exponentially more divisive in just the six or so years since SCARLET first hit newsstands. In rereading the first two books alone, the 2014 conflict in Ferguson, Missouri stood readily to mind, despite being two years after your release of SCARLET. And as you point out with** **Network*, which came out in theaters decades before, there seems to be a confluence of fact and fiction here.

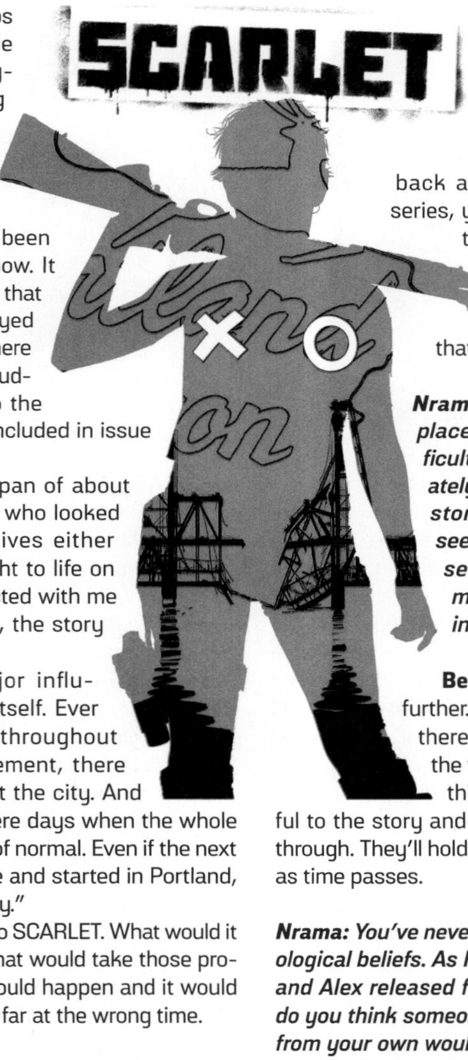
SCARLET

Bendis: I get a lot of tweets about this movie when they see me recommend it. But to rewind things a bit, what really rattled me is that I've never been on a book where the world has shifted so dramatically that the truth of the book still works so well. That was startling. Looking back at the older issues of some other series, you can see they're built on a world that could feel like a million years ago even though they're only two or three years aged. Not so with SCARLET. There's a truth to it that still rings loud and clear.

***Nrama:* With incidents like that taking place increasingly more often, how difficult do you find it now to avoid deliberately blending news headlines into your storylines when writing a story that seems to run a fairly close parallel—in sentiment if not in action—to what many of your readers are experiencing today?**

Bendis: It's very difficult and goes even further. It's true about anything you put out there. You hope it will translate well into the world it's being born into. You always think about this. If you're being truthful to the story and character though, that will get you through. They'll hold up to being true to the moment even as time passes.

***Nrama:* You've never been one to be shy about your ideological beliefs. As I was reading the first issue that you and Alex released from DC, one point struck me: How do you think someone of a political persuasion different from your own would respond to reading SCARLET #1? Is this a book you think all readers can get behind?**

Bendis: This is not a political book. This might surprise some people, but there are no politics in this book. Zero. And it wasn't even by design for this relaunch, but there is "no lecturing." Though we see Scarlet break the fourth wall in issue #1, and I get there can be a real temptation to roll up one's sleeves and lecture it up, there's no need to keep regurgitating that same point once she's gotten her message across. So, A. She's not lecturing anybody, and B. She's simply anti-corruption. She's anti people abusing the rules for their own benefit.

And you know what? I have yet to meet anyone who is for corruption and abuse of innocent people. Most people reading this book feel abused by those in power and marginalized by people in power. Wherever you are on the political spectrum, this is a problem we are dealing with and hasn't gone away. What's more? It seems to be getting worse.

Nrama: Okay, that's fair. But have you heard anything from people who fear you may be painting with a broad brushstroke?

Bendis: You may recall with the first series of books that I was getting some letters from readers who were police officers, and they did not like the way I was representing the police in this series. It was very interesting because one of the police departments I had been doing research about, where there were numerous instances of corrup-

tion and questionable behavior, ended up being where one of those writers came from! This was really interesting to see when one of the harshest complaints I was receiving was coming from one of the real-life places that helped inspire the story!

But overall, I've been really happy with how well I've been able to really adhere to the writing philosophies and theories that I've adopted for this story. I think this latest issue of SCARLET has proven successful because of its lack of politics, its lack of anchoring itself to real world incidents versus speaking to certain truisms. It's of itself while speaking to the real world. But talk to me in about five years and let's see where it falls.

Nrama: You bring up an interesting point—have you had many readers for this relaunch who never experienced the original two volumes of SCARLET? How does this first issue stand for them?

Bendis: It's like an entirely new book. I'm getting a lot of fascinating feedback. Everyone seems to be getting the fact it's a story we're telling because we don't want the world to be crazy, but SCARLET's Portland is what could happen if things keep going like they are. I want my kids to grow up and find happiness and many of us—creators and readers—aren't seeing that today.

Nrama: Taking one of the previous questions the next step further, I'd like to think we can all agree that killing people is bad, taking the law into our own hands is bad,

and that cops breaking the law for their own profit and at the detriment of others is also bad. But given the tenor of discourse here in the United States the past few years, is SCARLET doing something dangerous or risky in challenging its readers to be more critical of their elected officials and law enforcement officers and how close should comics get to the world in which their readers live?

Bendis: You're talking to me about what I literally just witnessed and that's Sen. Cory Booker doing what he thought was right before the senate committee and the American people. He was just saying what he thought was right, but that's also an incredible act of defiance and rebellion these days. I guess it made me feel like we live in a world where that kind of stuff needs to happen right now. Of course, we also live in a world where half of the people will say "That man is a hero!" while the other half will say "Wow, he's a villain!"

And keep in mind that we're not making a call for violence. We're not saying "Go and do this!" You're asking "How much farther can people be pushed?" It's every day that we see people doing things to others they shouldn't—people in power abusing those they should be looking out for.

That's what we're exploring and challenging people to ask of themselves and others.

Nrama: Scarlet clearly seems to think that challenging the status quo through revolution is what's required in her immediate world. Given the precipice upon which she and her revolutionaries stand in this latest issue, did you struggle at all with how to best catch readers up to the current moment—both in where the characters are in the story as well as the emotional and political movement built up over the previous two books?

Bendis: I looked to *The Shield* for inspiration in that regard. If you look at each season, they're like their own individual shows. Very, very solid crime fiction where you don't need to see each previous season, but if you do? Wow! It comes together amazingly.

What a grand opportunity with this relaunch then! We looked at where we wanted to take SCARLET and then simply had to determine where would be the best place to pick up with the revolution for old readers while simultaneously ensuring new readers would feel the excitement of this group's mission.

So, we see what happens when a protest goes too far and the protestors are prepared for that to happen.

Nrama: Shifting gears a bit, let's look a bit at the style of SCARLET, which is rather different from many of your other comic books. You break the fourth wall in this series frequently—and perhaps this upcoming issue most of all. What strengths do you find this has in terms of relating Scarlet's story? Are there any drawbacks to it?

Bendis: I think about this constantly. For years, I've been thinking about doing something like this, and I'm very inspired by the movie and book *High Fidelity* by Nick Hornsby. You get to see everything from the perspective of the main character, who lets you in on the first part of the movie only for the audience to discover by the end of the first half that he's the asshole of the story. He's not a nice person but the audience is so involved in his life that they almost feel guilty, too! And then the rest of the story has the main character slowly digging himself out of that hole for the audience to see why those mistakes were made and decide whether or not those problems can or should be fixed.

I was completely charmed by this, but the crime writer in me wanted to involve the reader in a crime. You start the narration off and bring the reader along, build some trust, and then you flip the script and introduce the crime leaving readers to say "Whoa! I didn't agree to that plan!"

Nrama: Where else did you look for how to handle this narrative approach apart from Hornsby's book and movie?

Bendis: Years ago, Matt Fraction and I saw a play by Aaron Sorkin called *The Farnsworth Experiment* and it's about the birth of television. You have two narrators who speak to the audience: One who invented television and one who was the president of RCA who stole the idea for television. Throughout the play, they tell their respective versions of the story about the rise of television and about halfway through, they begin fighting with each other very passionately. Matt and I looked at each other and asked "Who is stealing this idea first?!?" Of course, a brilliant narrative device like that needed the right kind of story to go along with it. I waited years and SCARLET was the right one.

The downside, of course, is if she starts lecturing about the obvious points readers are already seeing. How much is too much? How much is too little? You really need to balance it because a little bit will go a long way.

Nrama: You've also worked with Alex Maleev on a variety of other comic books in the past; however, I know you mentioned when we last spoke that you felt each one of your collaborators on the new Jinxworld relaunch was performing at their very best. How would you say that Alex is pushing himself beyond his past limits as a storyteller with the relaunch of SCARLET?

Bendis: I can tell you right away! The director of the SCARLET pilot just emailed me about Alex's color palette as being simply exquisite. It's hard to look that effortless. It's one of those things that other artists constantly complain to me about because they're just scaling that mountain that Alex has long since mastered. He has a number of years under his belt as an artist—not just as a comic artist but as a print maker and everything else he's brought into his work. If people find themselves captured by this story, it's because of Alex. He's the reason you want to spend more than one panel with her. She's done some terrible

things, but you still want to hang around with her and that feeling is real. That's Alex Maleev.

Nrama: The colors do tend to come out in certain elements of the panels more than others. This would be an example of where the artist uses color to help guide the reader's eye throughout, particularly during important moments, which seemed to occur pretty consistently throughout this first issue.

Bendis: That's exactly right. Every Jinxworld book has its own particular color palette and storytelling philosophy. Michael Gaydos is using color as a storytelling device in PEARL just as David Mack is in COVER and Mike Oeming and Taki Soma are in UNITED STATES VS. MURDER, INC. It's one of my personal joys seeing the use of bold coloring to help tell the storytelling clearly.

Sorry to be so braggy, but the point about coloring is something I'm immensely proud of. I've said it before, and I'll say it again: I really think these might be some of our very best books.

Nrama: And as a final question, where does Scarlet's revolution go? How far do you see her taking her quest for justice? Given how the first issue ends—which readers can check out this week—it seems her problems have leveled up exponentially.

Bendis: I make it very clear that they're in uncharted territory. There isn't a plan after the protests. She called for the revolution and it helped heal her, but once it was done, what next? I think we've all had some of those nervous breakdown moments, and the revolution she started was hers. And then we wake up the next morning and say "Whew!" But...she can't.

That is what we're writing and it's so interesting to write. It's like nothing I feel like I've done—no past reference point—and that's a great place to be when writing genre fiction. And based on the initial reactions to issue #1, it seems people are really responding to it. ●

ALEX MALEEV SKETCHBOOK

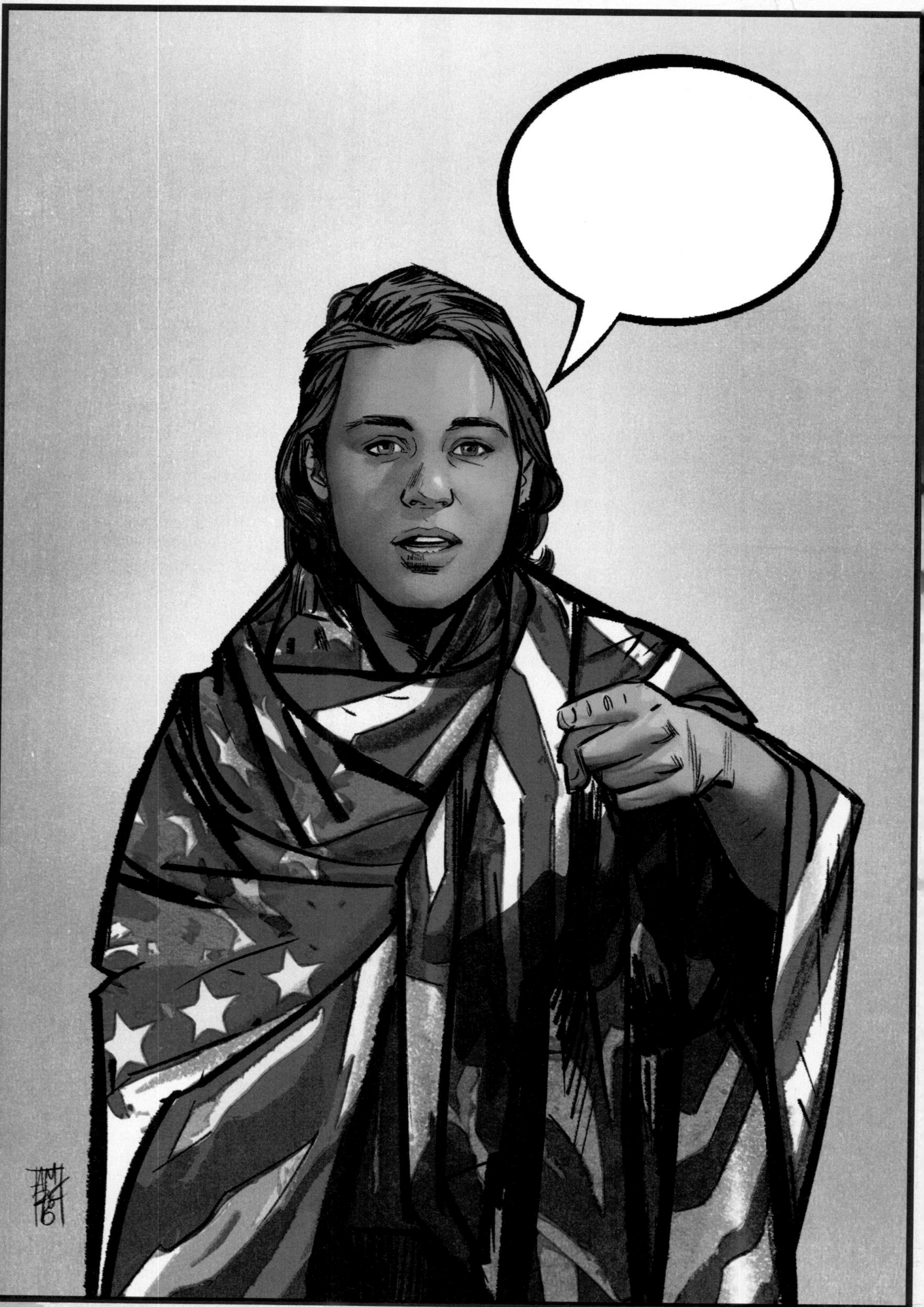

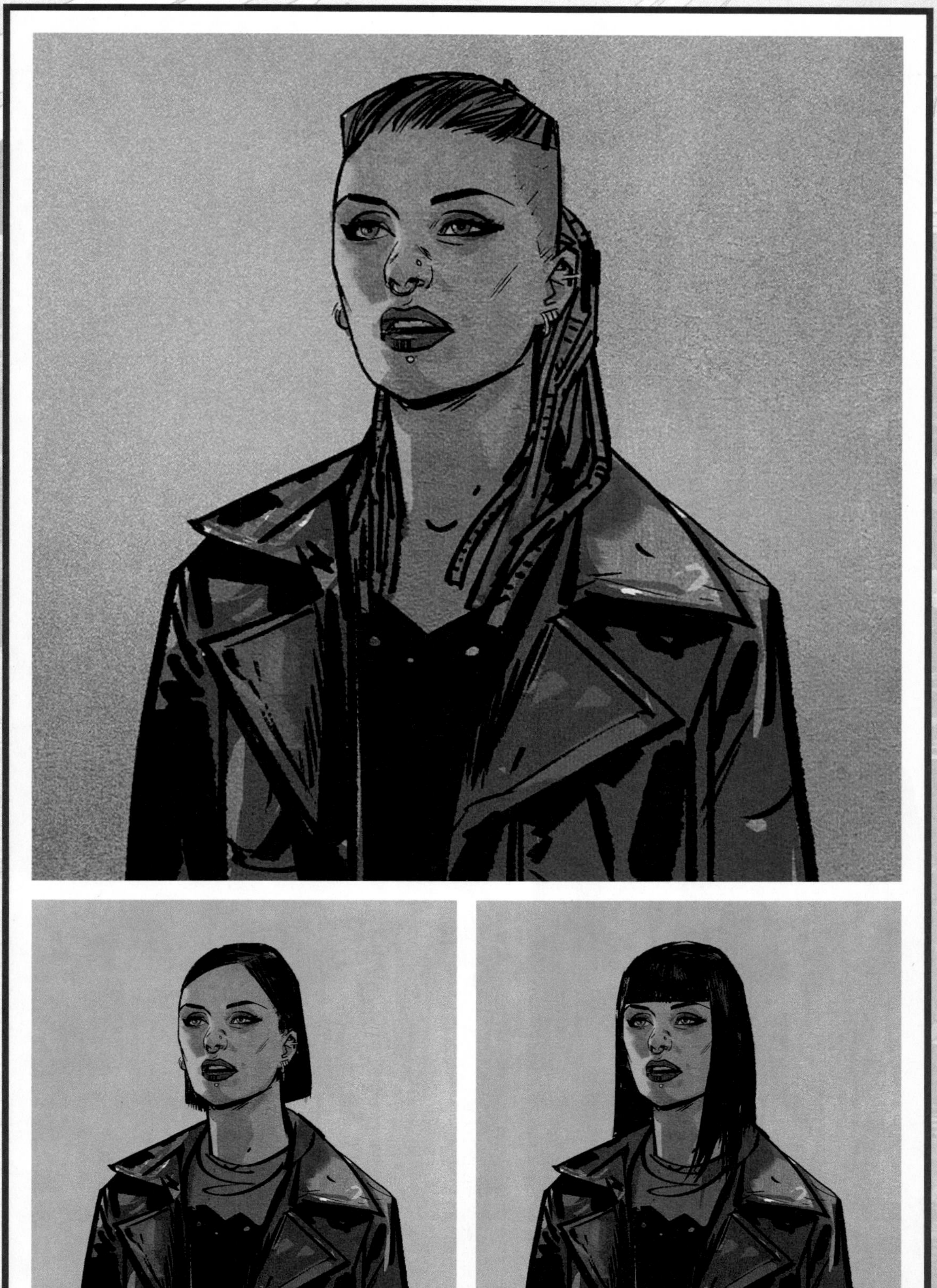

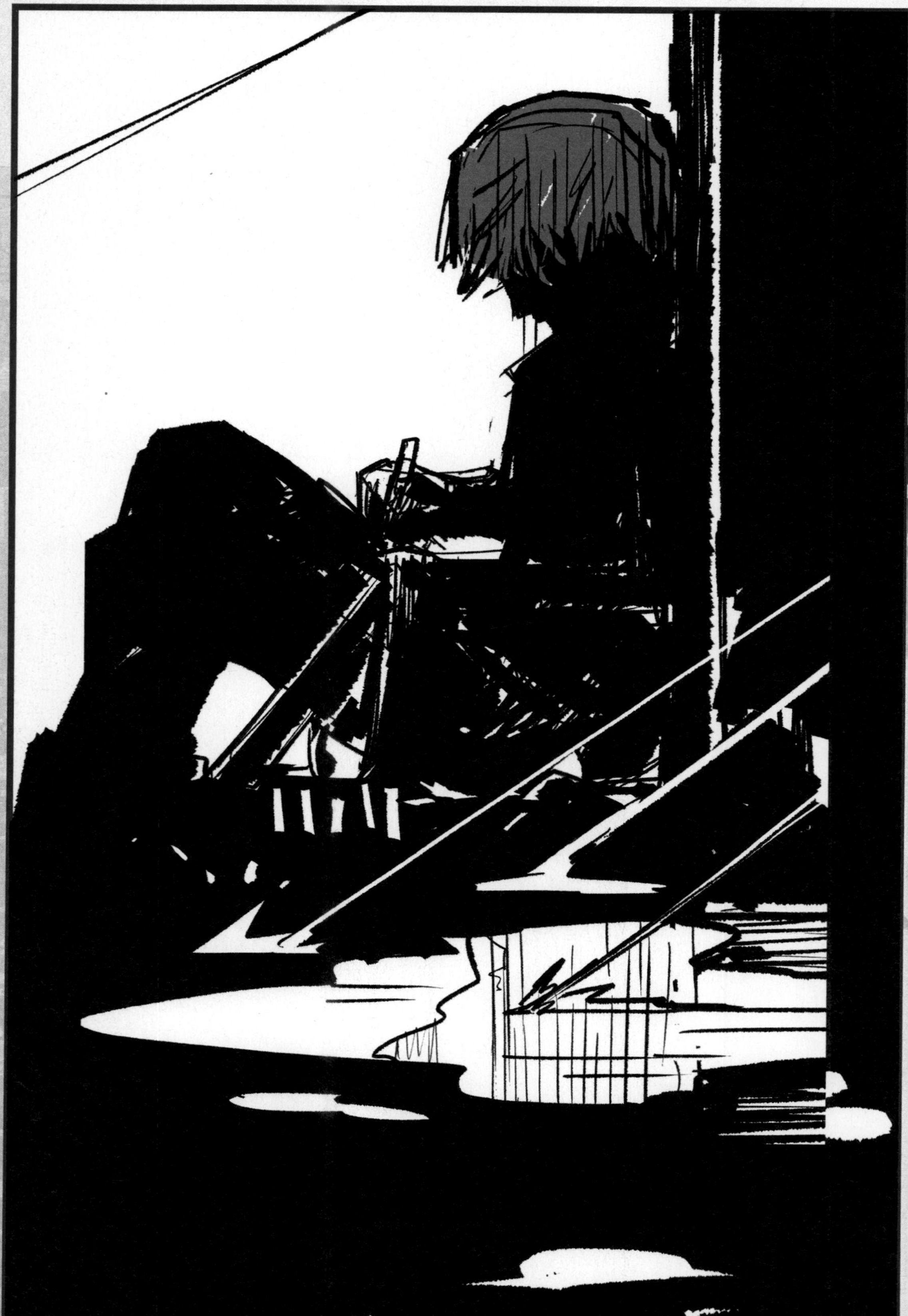

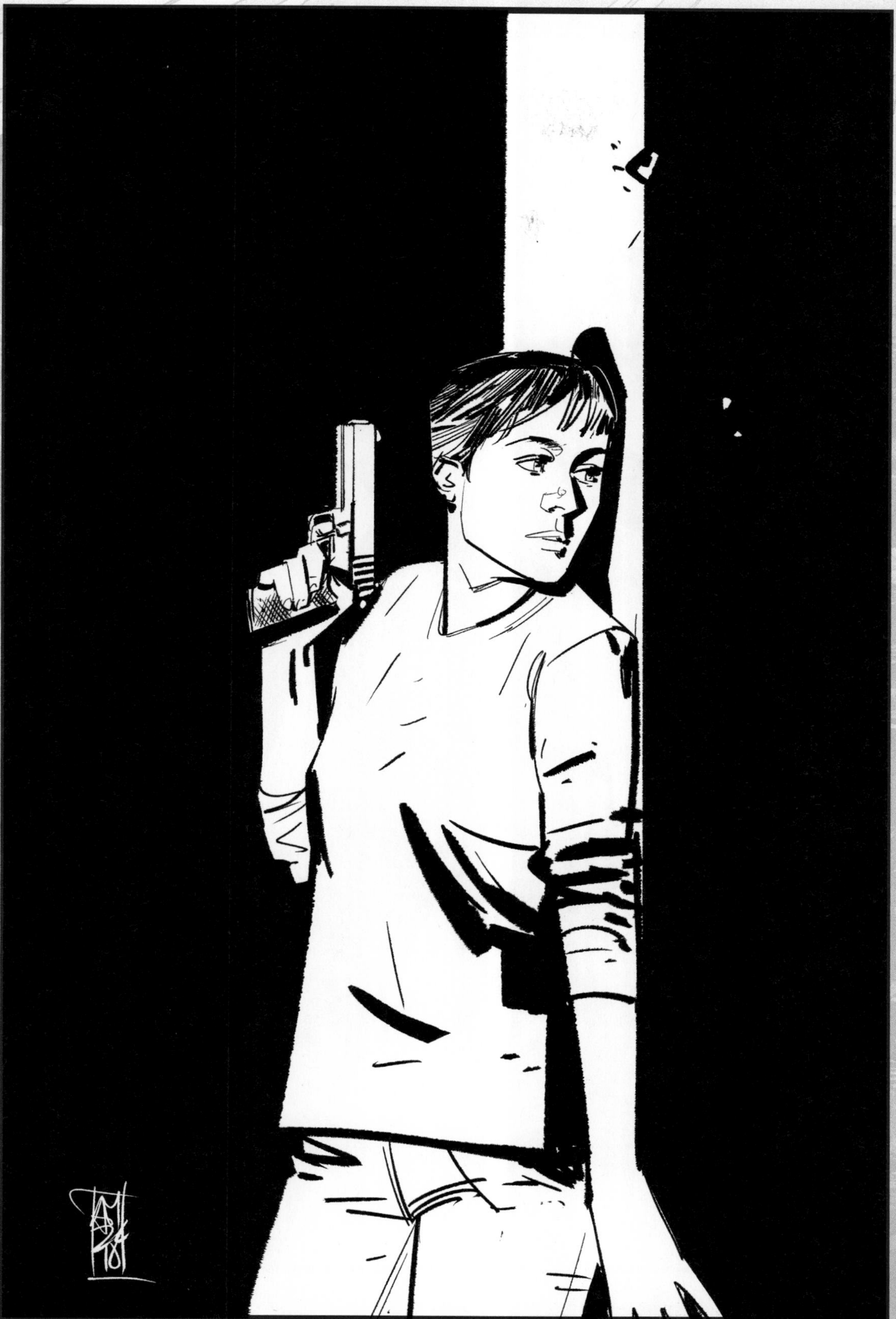

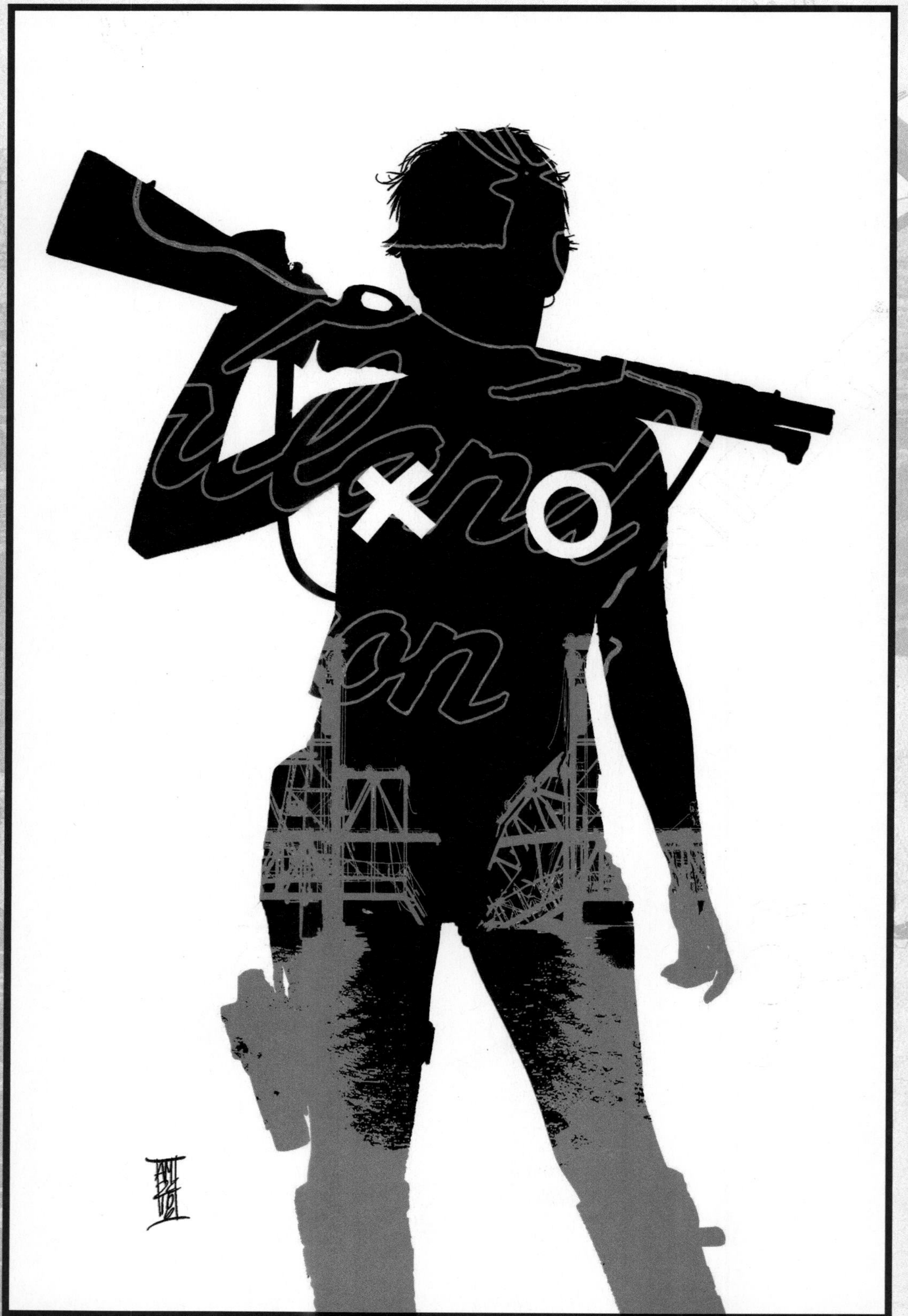

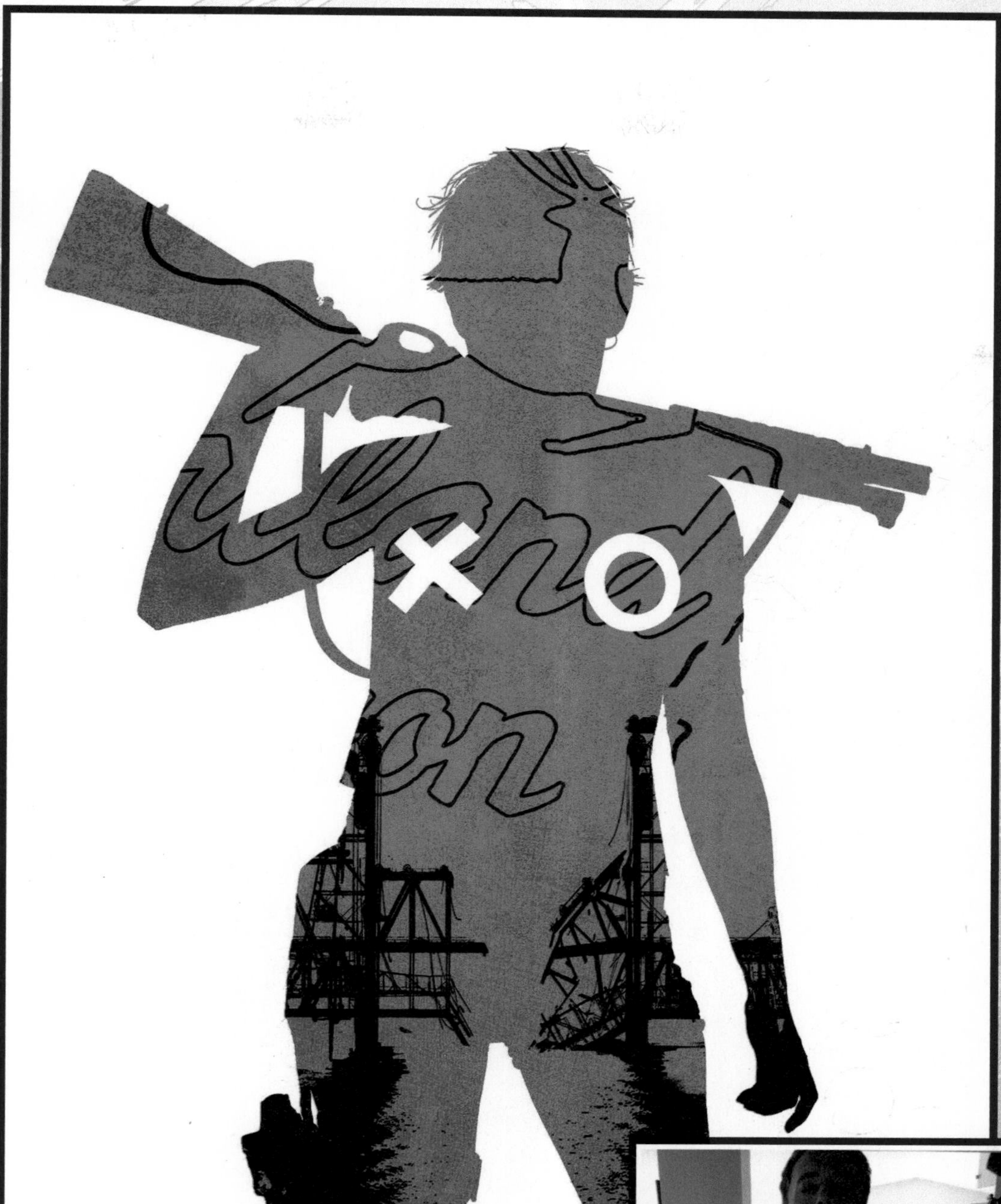

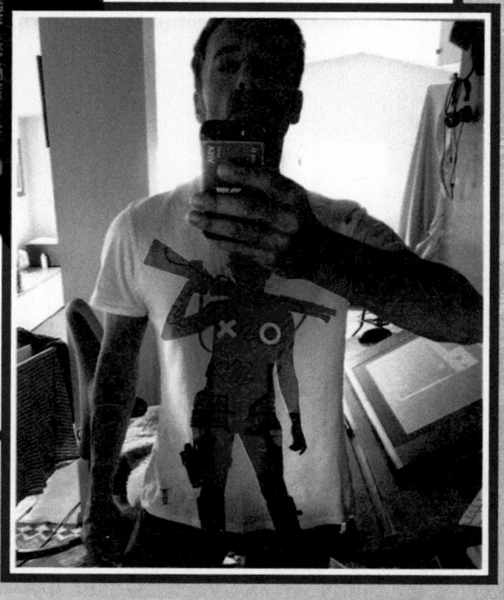

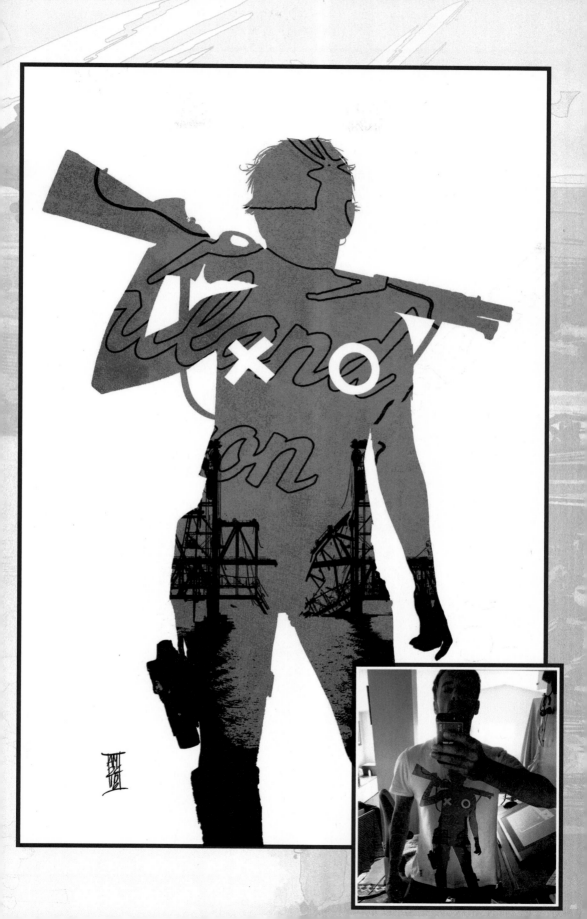

                    SCARLET
          That SEEMED low.

                    MIKE
          We're ready for them.

                    SCARLET
          We are?

                    MIKE
          Hold on.

5- Ext. Alley/ street

Mike turns the jeep down a very weird Portland street alley

https://dynamicmedia.zuza.com/zz/m/original_/5/d/5d65ed6f-
eaaf-4246-b8ff-
9170a543af1e/B823018574Z.1_20170127182524_000_GNT1Q9S3N.1_Gal
lery.jpg

6- Mike slowly pulls the jeep into a apartment building
garage on another alley.

http://www.northwestrents.com/wp-
content/uploads/2013/02/GarageView.jpg

https://dsdauphin.files.wordpress.com/2015/04/dsc_3737.jpg?w=
750&h=380&crop=1

7- Over Scarlet's shoulder, in the parking space a space away
is a black van opens the side door and a gun nozzle sticks
out of the shadows.

Is this the end of the road? Already?

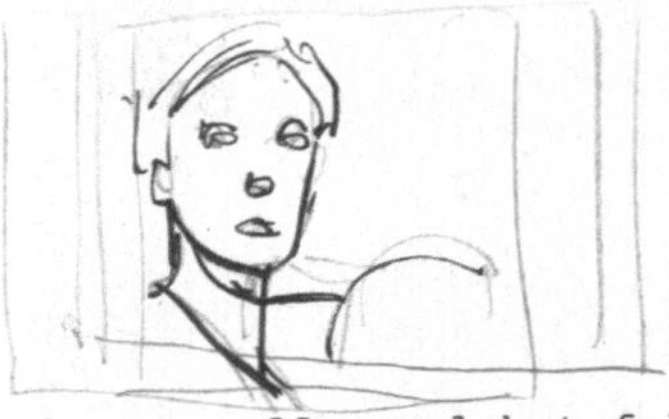

Page 4-

1- Int. Jeep

Scarlet can't take her eye off the gun off panel but follows private Mike's orders. She has no idea what is going on.

SCARLET
We're getting out?

MIKE
YOU'RE getting into THAT black van.

SCARLET
THAT black van.

NOW?

2- Private Mike watches past her and waits for it. She waits for him. He listens for copters and other following noises.

MIKE
Hold on.

3- Same. Scarlet looks at us.

SCARLET NARRATION
You know, we've come this far together I feel it's only fair to tell you...

I have NO IDEA who this is.

I know his name is Mike.

That's it.

4- Scarlet looks to see what he is looking at.

SCARLET NARRATION
I don't know where I am or where I am going.

So THIS is a weird way to die.

5- Scarlet's pov. The van door is open and the gun sticks out but is now pointed up and a man's hand gives a high five signal. The 'coast is clear.'

MIKE
We're in the clear.

Let's go.

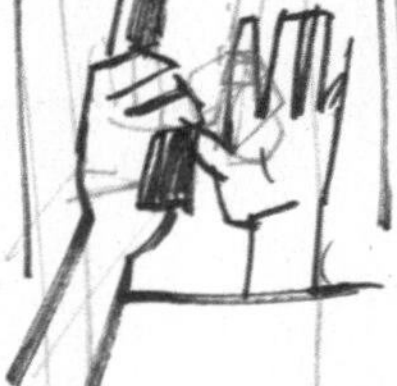

Page 6-1

1- Int. Van

Everyone is putting on new clothes and handing Scarlet new clothes to wear. She is changing as they ride. They all are.

Scarlet watches intently. Her new friends. They revere her and its weird.

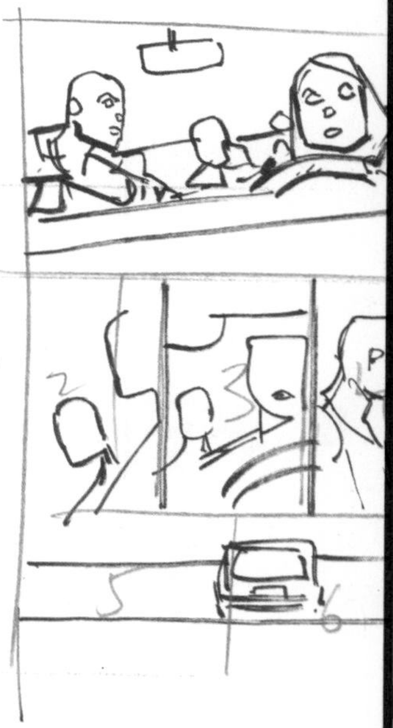

REGGIE
Allowed? Who knows?

It really is amazing to be here with you, ms. Rue.

My heart won't stop beating.

VERONICA
Don't freak her out.

REGGIE
Just trying to live in my moment, V.

SCARLET
You're friends of Cyan?

REGGIE
Friends of friends.

DANIENL
Of friends.

VERONICA
But yeah.

2- Daniel looks at Scarlet. She has no idea what to make of this guy

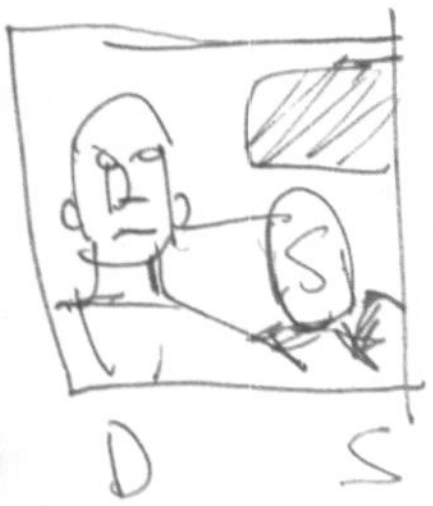
D
S

DANIEL
How does it feel to be on the other side?

SCARLET
Depends how far we get.

DANIEL
And THAT depends on how it went down on the waterfront.

Page 22-

1- Int. Movie theater/ command center

Almost half a page. Scarlet looks right past us at the screens all around her. She is absolutely stunned. Happy but stunned. Her cousin and everyone is right behind her.

A moment of complete euphoria as Scarlet's eyes filled with tears of joy.

2- Cyan comes around and puts her arms around her like a family member. For all of us. You did it scarletQ! Scarlet looks right at us.

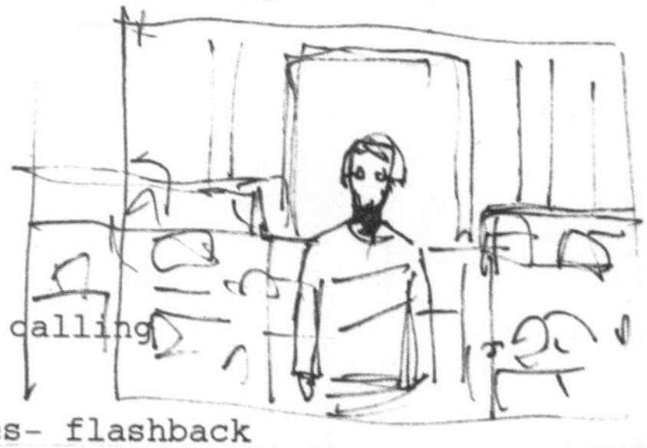

CYAN
You just didn't know it.

SCARLET NARRATION
We only had- ALL we had...

Brandon's dark web secret communications with someone calling themselves...

3- Int. Portland / hotel room the nines- flashback

The old gang in Portland. Brandon and Scarlet are reading his screen. Isis is clapping. Its a life line. The entire gang is there. Kit.

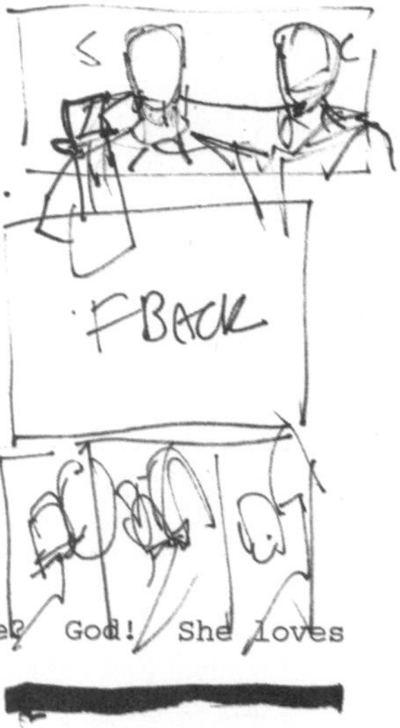
S
C
FBACK

SCARLET
Cyan!?

If they know what I did with Walter Hughes in the 8th grade...

Fuck, it's- it's SOPHIE!

SCARLET NARRATION
My COUSIN Sophie!!

Who I used to WORSHIP.

SCARLET
It has to be her!

4- Int. Movie theatre- today

Scarlet holds her cousin's arm. Is it true? God! She loves Cyan so fucking much. She loves her

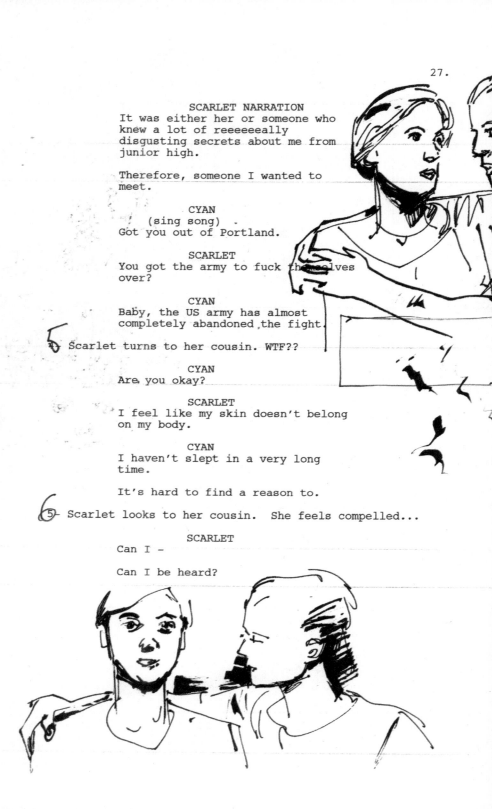

                    SCARLET NARRATION
          It was either her or someone who
          knew a lot of reeeeeeally
          disgusting secrets about me from
          junior high.

          Therefore, someone I wanted to
          meet.

                    CYAN
               (sing song)
          Got you out of Portland.

                    SCARLET
          You got the army to fuck themselves
          over?

                    CYAN
          Baby, the US army has almost
          completely abandoned the fight.

     Scarlet turns to her cousin. WTF??

                    CYAN
          Are you okay?

                    SCARLET
          I feel like my skin doesn't belong
          on my body.

                    CYAN
          I haven't slept in a very long
          time.

          It's hard to find a reason to.

     Scarlet looks to her cousin. She feels compelled...

                    SCARLET
          Can I -

          Can I be heard?

Page 23-

1- Cyan smiles wide and folds her arms. Everyone around her hops too. Cyan is so happy to see Scarlet that its all she cares about.

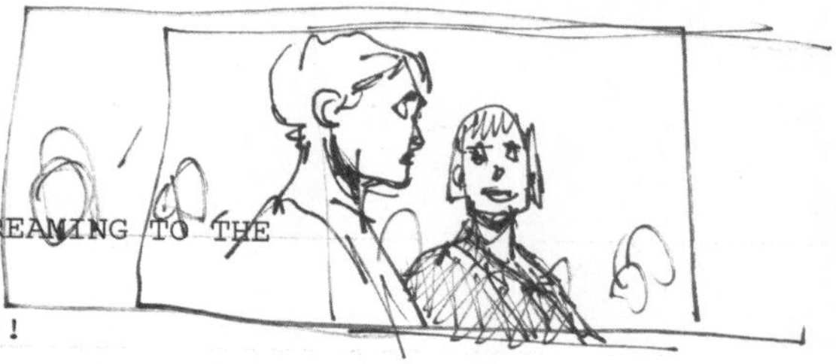

CYAN
Fuck YES!!

HHEEYY!!!

GET MY COUSIN STREAMING TO THE WORLD!!

LET THEM SEE HER!!

2- Scarlet is being cleaned up for cameras and lights and a camera and being put in position. Daniel has the mic.

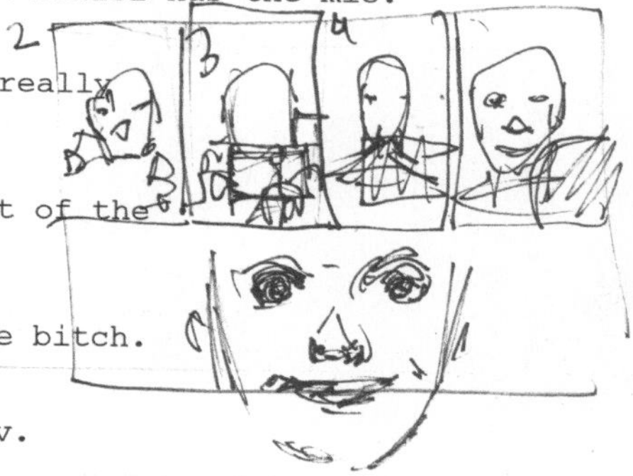

DANIEL
I'm sorry, are you two really cousins?

SCARLET
Oh yeah! How's the rest of the fam?

CYAN
Your mom is a full scale bitch.

SCARLET
I heard she's been on tv.

CYAN
She lives there now.

Sorry baby, Fuck her.

3- From behind the digital camera that's going to broadcaster alive, Scarlet is getting ready to be broadcast all over the world.

SCARLET
It's weird to find out your mother never liked you...

Can we get THIS to people in Portland too?

CYAN
I'll ask Francine.

You want makeup?

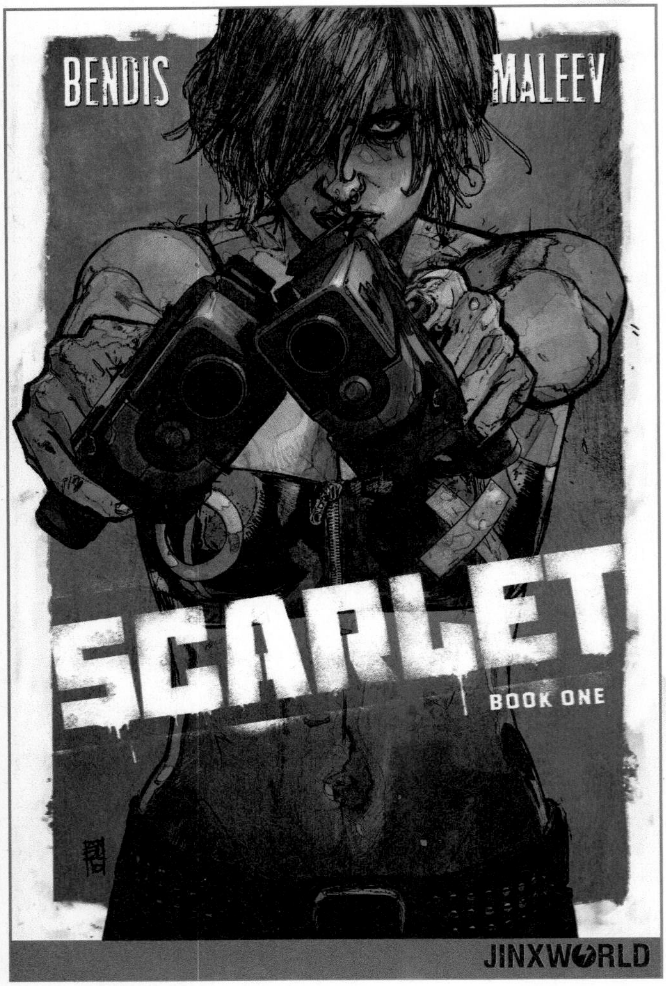
BENDIS
MALEEV
SCARLET
BOOK ONE
JINXWORLD

"Bendis is the funny pages descendant of Sam Fuller, Martin Scorsese and Quentin Tarantino."
–ENTERTAINMENT WEEKLY

"The best work from Bendis in years, and maybe the best work from Maleev ever."
–CBR

SCARLET

BOOK ONE

BRIAN MICHAEL BENDIS
ALEX MALEEV

ALSO BY BRIAN MICHAEL BENDIS:

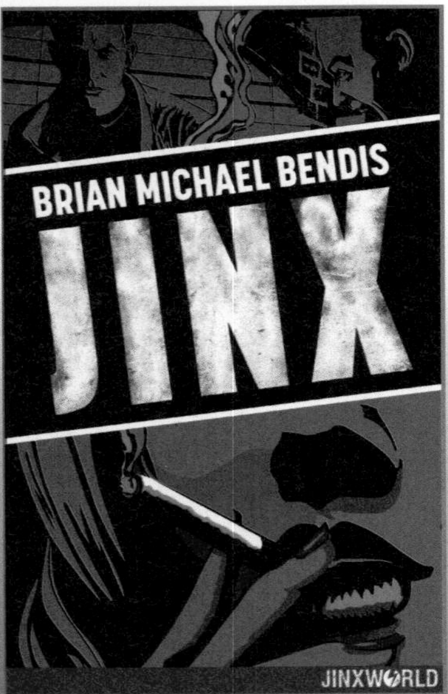
BRIAN MICHAEL BENDIS
JINX
JINXWORLD

JINX

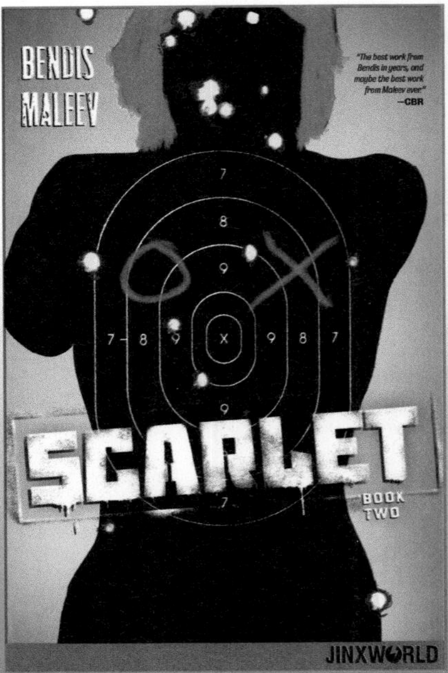
BENDIS
MALEEV
"The best work from Bendis in years, and maybe the best work from Maleev ever." –CBR
SCARLET
BOOK TWO
JINXWORLD

SCARLET BOOK TWO

Get more Jinxworld graphic novels wherever comics and books are sold! JINXWORLD